THE HOLLOW CROWN

TRANSFORMING GOVERNMENT

This important and authoritative new series arises out of the seminal ESRC Whitehall Programme and seeks to fill the enormous gaps in our knowledge of the key actors and institutions of British government. It examines the many large changes during the postwar period and puts these into comparative context by analysing the experience of the advanced industrial democracies of Europe and the nations of the Commonwealth. The series reports the results of the Whitehall Programme, a four-year project into change in British government in the postwar period, mounted by the Economic and Social Research Council. *The Hollow Crown* is the first title in the series.

The Hollow Crown

Countervailing Trends in Core Executives

Edited by

Patrick Weller
Director
Centre for Australian Public Sector Management
Griffith University
Queensland

Herman Bakvis
Professor of Political Science and Public Administration
Dalhousie University
Nova Scotia

and

R. A. W. Rhodes
Professor of Politics
University of Newcastle

First published in Great Britain 1997 by
MACMILLAN PRESS LTD
Houndmills, Basingstoke, Hampshire RG21 6XS and London
Companies and representatives throughout the world

A catalogue record for this book is available from the British Library.

ISBN 0–333–68194–0 hardcover
ISBN 0–333–68195–9 paperback

First published in the United States of America 1997 by
ST. MARTIN'S PRESS, INC.,
Scholarly and Reference Division,
175 Fifth Avenue, New York, N.Y. 10010

ISBN 0–312–17702–X

Library of Congress Cataloging-in-Publication Data
The hollow crown : countervailing trends in core executives / edited
by Patrick Weller, Herman Bakvis, R.A.W. Rhodes.
p.   cm. — (Transforming government series)
Includes bibliographical references and index.
ISBN 0–312–17702–X (cloth)
1. Cabinet system.   2. Prime ministers.   3. Comparative
government.   I. Weller, Patrick Moray.   II. Bakvis, Herman, 1948–
.   III. Rhodes, R. A. W.   IV. Series.
JF331.H65 1997
321.8'043—dc21   97–18985
                                                                  CIP

This book is printed on paper suitable for recycling and made from fully managed and
sustained forest sources.

10   9   8   7   6   5   4   3   2   1
06   05   04   03   02   01   00   99   98   97

Printed and bound in Great Britain by
The Ipswich Book Company, Suffolk.

For God's sake let us sit upon the ground
And tell sad stories of the death of kings:
How some have been deposed, some slain in war,
Some haunted by the ghosts they have deposed;
Some poisoned by their wives, some sleeping killed;
All murdered: for within the hollow crown
That rounds the mortal temples of a king
Keeps Death his court, and there the antick sits,
Scoffing his state and grinning at his pomp;
Allowing him a breath, a little scene.
To monarchize, be feared, and killed with looks,
Infusing him with self and vain conceit
As if this flesh which walls about our life
Were brass impregnable; and humoured thus
Comes at the last, and with a little pin
Bores through his castle-wall, and farewell king!
(Richard II. III. ii. 155)

Contents

List of Figures and Tables

Preface

There are enormous gaps in our knowledge of the key actors and institutions in British government. We cannot do simple things like describing the work of ministers of state, permanent secretaries, and their departments. Also, there have been large changes in British government during the postwar period, such as: the growth of the welfare state; the professionalization of government; the consequences of recession; the effects of New Right ideology; the impact of the European Union; the effects of new technology; the hollowing out of the state; and the New Public Management with its separation of policy and administration. We do not know how these changes affected British government. And we cannot understand the effects of these changes by focusing only on Britain. We must also analyse the experience of the advanced industrial democracies of Europe and the Commonwealth.

To repair these gaps in our knowledge and to explain how and why British government changed in the postwar period, the Economic and Social Research Council (ESRC) mounted the Whitehall Programme entitled, 'The Changing Nature of Central Government in Britain'. This series, on 'Transforming Government', reports the results of that four-year research programme. The series has five objectives.

1. Develop theory — to develop new theoretical perspectives to explain why British government changed and why it differs from other countries.
2. Understand change — to describe and explain what has changed in British government since 1945.
3. Compare — to compare these changes with those in other European Union member states and other states with a 'Westminster' system of government.
4. Build bridges — to create a common understanding between academics and practitioners.
5. Dissemination — to make academic research accessible to a varied audience covering sixthformers and senior policy makers.

The books cover six broad themes:

1. developing theory about the new forms of governance;
2. the hollowing out of the state in Britain, Europe and the Commonwealth;
3. the fragmenting government framework;
4. the changing roles of ministers and the senior civil service;

5. constitutional change;
6. new ways of delivering services.

Understanding change in British government in the postwar period is a demanding task and one which can only be tackled by placing Britain in a broader context. Membership of the European Union is a key aspect of that context. However, lessons can be learnt not only from our European partners but also from the ways in which other versions of the Westminster model have evolved. There is no comparative study which traces the developing characteristics of the Westminster model and explains how a changing world changed the institutions; how political traditions shaped and were shaped by institutions; and how traditions and institutions shaped policy. This book begins that exploration.

It is the first volume in a set of comparative studies within the ESRC's Whitehall Programme and it focuses on core executives in five parliamentary democracies. It compares the core executives of three Westminster systems of parliamentary democracy (Australia, Canada and Britain) and two continental parliamentary democracies (Germany and the Netherlands). It explores whether governments can provide coherent policy, examining: political parties and the processes of building and maintaining political support; the practices of collective government; policy advice; resource allocation; coordination; and the New Public Management and decentralization. It tries to answer the question 'What is the impact on political leadership in the core executive of: complexity and interdependence, caused by both external and internal forces, and of internal fragmentation and rationalization?' It adopts an institutional approach, arguing that institutional differentiation and pluralization, coupled with globalization, shackle political leadership in both Westminster and Continental systems of parliamentary democracy. The heroic model of a decisive political leadership solving society's problems is less persuasive than a humdrum model which recognizes the vast array of constraints on core executives.

R. A. W. Rhodes
Director, ESRC Whitehall Programme and
Professor of Politics, University of Newcastle

Acknowledgements

This book is, more than most, a cooperative venture. The editors invited contributors from a number of countries to work on a project that compared the central capacity of five countries. It sought to tackle executive studies in a way that was indeed comparative.

The papers that emerged were discussed in two seminars. The first was held at the OECD in Paris, the second at the University of Newcastle. We appreciate the hospitality of Pierre Rostaing and his colleagues at the OECD for providing the venue, participating in the discussions and providing assistance to the contributors. The second meeting was co-funded by the Economic and Social Research Council's Whitehall Programme and we are grateful for that support. Charlotte Dargie and Susan Latiff provided invaluable assistance in organizing the workshop.

Several people attended the seminars and gave us the benefit of their insights. Hans-Ulrich Derlien and Colin Campbell attended both meetings. Pierre Rostaing, David Shand, Philip Selth and Bidya Bowornwathana joined us in Paris. Vincent Wright, Jack Hayward and Ed Page from the ESRC's Whitehall Programme were incisive critics in Newcastle. Charlotte Dargie took careful notes of our Newcastle discussions in a way that assisted the final working of the drafts.

The chapters were regularly circulated to other contributors for comment and our debts are therefore mutual. In addition to those, Herman Bakvis would like to thank Martin Thunert and Steven Wolinetz for providing detailed information on persona and organizations in Germany and the Netherlands, and Donna Brothers for her careful research assistance. Financial support from the Social Sciences and Humanities Research Council of Canada is gratefully acknowledged. Rod Rhodes is grateful to Charlotte Dargie for her comments and Michael Saward wishes to thank John Edwards. John Wanna would also like to thank Bob Jackson, Maurice Wright, Gerry Kreffer and Ton Bestebreur.

The production of the book was completed at Griffith University's Centre for Australia Public Sector Management, where Patricia Gauvin patiently corrected and set the many drafts. Sue Eggins, Emma Craswell, Robyn Davies and Melissa O'Rourke all acted as research assistants for the authors based there. To them all our thanks.

Above all, we as editors would like to thank the contributors for participating in this process of cooperative writing spread around the world.

P. M. W.
H. B.
R. A. W. R.

Contributors

Rudy Andeweg is professor of Political Science at Leyden University. In 1982 and 1983 he was an assistant to the Netherlands government's Commission for Administrative Reform. He has been a visiting fellow at Oxford University and the University of Michigan. He has published extensively on voting behaviour, cabinet government and legislatives and is co-author of *Dutch Government and Politics* (1993) and editor of *Ministers en Ministerraad* (1990).

Peter Aucoin is McCulloch Professor in Political Science and Professor of Public Administration at Dalhousie University, Halifax, Canada. He is currently a senior fellow of the Canadian Centre for Management Development (Government of Canada) and a Fellow of the Institute for Research on Public Policy. He has served as a research coordinator for the federal Royal Commission on the Economic Union and Development Prospects for Canada and as research director for the federal Royal Commission on Electoral Reform and Party Financing. He has served as Director of the School of Public Administration and Chair of the Department of Political Science at Dalhousie University. In 1995–96 he was President of the Canadian Political Science Association.

He has authored and edited ten books and authored over forty articles and book chapters on Canadian government and comparative public administration. His most recent book, *The New Public Management: Canada in Comparative Perspective*, is published by the Institute for Research on Public Policy (1995).

Herman Bakvis is Professor of Political Science and Public Administration at Dalhousie University, Nova Scotia, Canada. He has also held visiting appointments and fellowships at the Australian National University, Queen's University, the University of Saskatchewan and the University of Toronto. From 1990 to 1992 he was Research Co-ordinator with the Royal Commission on Electoral Reform and Party Financing.

He has authored, co-authored or edited eight books, including: *Catholic Power in the Netherlands* (McGill–Queen's University Press, 1981); (with William Chandler) *Federalism and the Role of the State* (University of Toronto Press, 1987); (with Peter Aucoin) *The Centralization–Decentralization Conundrum* (Institute for Research on Public Policy, 1988); and *Regional Ministers: Power and Influence in the Canadian Cabinet* (University of Toronto Press, 1991). He has published approximately 35 articles and book chapters, including articles in journals such as the *Australian Journal of Political Science*, *Canadian Journal of Political Science*, *Canadian Public Administration*, *Canadian Public Policy*, *Comparative Political Studies*, *Comparative Politics* and *Publius*.

His current research interests are focused on the role of think tanks and management consultants in the policy process, party finance and electoral reform, and intergovernmental relations and alternative service delivery models. At present he is a core member of the Working Group on Alternative Delivery Systems in Canadian Public Services, sponsored by the Institute of Public Administration of Canada and the KPMG Centre for Government Foundation.

Glyn Davis is Associate Professor in Politics and Public Administration at Griffith University. He is also co-editor of the *Australian Journal of Public Administration*, a QE II Research Fellow and Principal Researcher at the Centre for Australian Public Sector Management.

Dr Davis previously held a range of senior posts with the Queensland state government, most recently as Director-General of the Office of the Cabinet, a post he resigned in February 1996. From 1990 he was Commissioner for Public Sector Equity with the Public Sector Management Commission, and subsequently Executive Director in the Office of the Cabinet.

Dr Davis holds a doctorate in political science from the Australian National University, and was a 1987–88 Harkness Fellow in the United States, working at the University of California, Berkeley, the Brookings Institution in Washington and the Kennedy School of Government at Harvard University.

His most recent book is *A Government of Routines: Executive Coordination in an Australian State* (Macmillan, 1996), and his most recent report is a study of consultation mechanisms in policy formulation for the OECD.

Rod Rhodes is Professor of Politics (Research) at the University of Newcastle-upon-Tyne. Between 1989 and 1995, he was Professor of Politics and Head of Department at the University of York. Between 1987 and 1989, he was Reader in Government and Chair of Department at the University of Essex. He also held permanent appointments at the University of Birmingham and the University of Strathclyde, and visiting appointments at the Australian National University (Canberra), European Institute of Public Administration (Maastricht), European University Institute (Florence), and the University of the West Indies (Jamaica).

He is the author or editor of 15 books including: *Public Administration and Policy Analysis* (Saxon House, 1979); *Control and Power in Central–*

Local Relations (Gower, 1981); *The National World of Local Government* (Allen & Unwin, 1986); *Beyond Westminster and Whitehall* (Routledge, 1988); (with D. Marsh, eds) *Policy Networks in British Government* (Clarendon Press, 1992). He has also published more than 60 articles in such major journals as *Political Studies, British Journal of Political Science, Public Administration, Parliamentary Affairs, West European Politics* and *Public Administration Review*. Recently he published four edited collections including (with David Marsh) *Policy Networks in British Government* (Clarendon Press, 1992), (with Patrick Dunleavy) *Prime Minister, Cabinet and Core Executive* (Macmillan, 1995) and *Understanding Governance* (Open University Press, 1996).

Currently, he is Director of the Economic and Social Research Council's Whitehall research programme; chair of the ESRC's research programme, 'Local Governance'; chair of the Public Administration Committee of the Joint University Council for Social and Public Administration; and chair of the Political Studies Association of the United Kingdom's Specialist Group in Public Administration. He has been editor of *Public Administration* since 1986.

Michael Saward is Lecturer in Politics at Royal Holloway, University of London. He is the author of *Co-optive Politics and State Legitimacy* (1992) and various recent articles and chapters covering issues in democratic theory, green political thought, political legitimacy and policy networks. He was British Consulting Editor for the *Encyclopedia of Democracy* (Congressional Quarterly and Routledge, 1995). His latest book, *The Terms of Democracy,* will be published in 1997.

John Wanna is Associate Professor in Politics and Public Policy and Principal Researcher, Centre for Australian Public Sector Management, Griffith University, Australia. He has taught at Adelaide University, Flinders University and Canterbury University, NZ, and been a visiting scholar at York University, UK. He is currently co-editor of the *Australian Journal of Public Administration*, and was previously an editoral board member on the *Australian Journal of Political Science*.

He has written or edited nine books on politics and public sector managment including: *Budgetary Management and Control* (with J. Forster); *Public Policy in Australia* (with G. Davis, P. Weller and J. Warhurst); *Public Sector Management in Australia* (with P. Weller and C. O'Faircheallaigh), *Government–Business Relations in Australia* (with S. Bell); *Power and Politics in the City* (with J. Caulfield) and *Entrepreneurial Management in the Public Sector* (with J. Forster and P. Graham). His research interests include government budgeting and the management of public expenditure, government–business relations and public sector management. He is currently engaged on a research project funded by the Australian Research Council on expenditure management in Australia and Canada.

Patrick Weller is Director of the Centre for Australian Public Sector Management and Professor of Politics and Public Policy at Griffith University.

He is the (co-)author of several books including *Treasury Control in Australia* (Novak, 1976), *Politics and Policy in Australia* (UQP, 1978); *Can Ministers Cope?* (Hutchinson, 1981); *First Among Equals: Prime Ministers in Westminster Systems* (Allen & Unwin, 1985); *Public Policy in Australia* (Allen & Unwin, 1988); *Malcolm Fraser PM* (Penguin, 1989); *Public Sector Management in Australia* (Macmillan, 1992); and editor or co-editor of, *inter alia*, *Caucus Minutes 1901–1949* (Melbourne University Press, 1975), *Reforming the Public Service* (Macmillan, 1993); *Royal Commissions and the Making of Public Policy* (Macmillan, 1994); *Menzies to Keating* (Christopher Hurst, 1992); *New Ideas, Better Government* (Allen & Unwin, 1996).

He was editor of *Politics*, the journal of the Australasian Political Studies Association, from 1984 to 1987 and president of the association in 1990–91. He was chair of the Queensland Corrective Services Commission from 1994 to 1996. He has acted as a consultant for federal and state governments, the Commonwealth parliament, the Commonwealth Secretariat, the UNDP and a number of private companies.

1 The Hollow Crown: Coherence and Capacity in Central Government

Patrick Weller and Herman Bakvis

Can governments provide coherent policy or follow consistent processes? Does the centre of government have the capacity to direct or control the branches? Modern governments are frequently described as incoherent. As leaders become more exposed to analysis and criticism, as the media provides instant criticism, as the expectations of government become more jaundiced, so the demands for better government grow. In hard economic times, there is greater intolerance of alleged 'inefficiency' or duplication of functions. Unsuccessful administration may receive a vote of no confidence at the next election; a government that does not know what it wants may not survive.

That situation probably always existed to some extent. Governmental consistency has never been complete; the complexity of competing organizations and unanticipated consequences always made it difficult to achieve harmony among government programmes.

But the argument has now gone further. The state, it is suggested, has been 'hollowed out' by a range of factors that limit its capacity. Rhodes has identified for Britain the new limitations on the scope of government, the loss of functions to the alternative delivery systems and to the European Union, and the new emphasis on political controls and managerial accountability. He concludes:

> This combination of fragmentation and accountability points to another meaning for the phrase 'hollowing out' of the state: it can also refer to a decline in central capability. Fragmentation constrains the centre's administrative ability to coordinate and plan. Diminished accountability constrains the centre's ability to exercise political control. In sum, current trends erode the centre's capacity to steer the system — its capacity for governance (Rhodes, 1994: 149).

Rhodes cites Sir Robin Butler's (1994: 404) concern 'to maintain a degree of cohesion across the service as a whole' and his warning that 'it is essential that it does not reach the point where individual Departments and

1

their Agencies become simply different unconnected elements in an overall public sector, with little in the way of staff transferability and no real working mechanisms for policy coordination'. Rhodes's is a striking conclusion. But it is one which needs to be tested empirically and then evaluated normatively.

What led to this problem becoming more acute — or perhaps more noticeable? The change can be traced to a range of factors, part governmental practice, part theory. In the former category is the economic crisis that has undermined confidence in many Western governments; the belief in the capacity of governments to solve problems has been reduced, and scepticism about their efficiency and effectiveness has grown. Even the new trends in administrative reform are treated with suspicion, encapsulated in President Reagan's quip that 'governments are not the solution, they are the problem'. The electorate has become more impatient and volatile, as the 1993 Canadian and 1996 Australian electoral routs of incumbent governments so dramatically illustrated. Interest groups use the media to create a 'new politics'.

Partly as a consequence, the last decade saw a divestment of governmental capacity to control a range of activities. Privatization, corporatization, contracting out, the floating of currencies, the internationalization of business through GATT and other initiatives all reduced the mechanisms by which governments directed their affairs. Market forces may determine conditions over which governments formerly had authority. International demands may influence sectoral policy areas. Globalization may not only reduce the capacity of the state because the key decisions are increasingly being made by the market or outside the boundaries of the nation state, but also, at the same time, making lower levels (states/provinces/*Länder*, even municipalities) more relevant as economic actors. In other words the central core faces pressure from both sides — externally and locally. The consequence is that many of the levers or instruments of authority are no longer in the hands of governments. Governments are either experimenting with new procedures or still searching for ways of controlling the environments. In these countries what then is the remaining capacity to ensure coherence?

In theoretical terms, some explanatory theories have diverted attention to factors that lead to a disaggregation of decision making. First, the long-recognized influence of institutions, now reinvigorated by the ideas of the 'new institutionalism', emphasizes the independent capacity of governmental institutions to shape outcomes. Policy is negotiated between interests and determined by the impact of processes. Organizations create expectations, demands and clientele. The machinery of government is thus crucial in determining the nature of outcomes. Institutional design has been recognized as significant. Success is not dependent exclusively on the influence of good people, but on the way that influence is structured and procedures determined. Structures and routines turn ideas into action; they coordinate, facilitate and settle compromises in the search for government coherence (Davis, 1996). Yet, despite this influence, do these institutions have the capacity to steer the system, to develop policies and make them stick? Recognition of influence may be different from an appreciation of impact.

Second, the development of the concepts of policy communities identifies the existence of subgovernments; government is divided into sectors, each dominated by policy communities that may be entirely discrete. The autonomous state may have given way to the interdependent state. Expertise in policy communities has not only become more specific, but the interests of bureaucracies have become more interwoven with client groups, reducing the capacity of the government at large to move forward and make decisions. To understand government it is necessary to identify and understand these discrete parts. There is therefore a distinction between the individual interests of the policy communities and the whole-of-government view of the centre. As governments become more complex, and expertise in policy communities becomes more specific, so the difficulties at the centre become more marked. Indeed, it may be necessary to run all the harder, just to stay in the same place. The constant pressure to improve the advisory support for leaders may be as much a sign of recognized weakness at the centre as it is a desire for increased controls. The push for coherence, for leadership and for direction may not always be equalled by capacity.

Governments struggle at two levels. They need to ensure that the different sections of the governmental machinery work in harmony — or at least appear to. The arguments in favour of government coherence may seem obvious. Overlapping programmes may be expensive. Gaps between programmes leave recipients without assistance they need. Governments look foolish and appear unable to manage their own affairs. Government officials argue in public about the programme they sponsor. There would appear to be few good reasons to accept incoherence and inconsistency in government policy. Yet, obvious though such an ambition may appear, there are often other interests at stake. Within the structures of government are a range of interests, representing divergent opinions and clients, protecting their careers and pursuing strategies that suit their staff and their ministers. Incoherence indicates far more than a mere lack of agreement.

That is not always a matter of institutional shortcomings alone. Coherence reflects a set of values that give a high significance to a united image and that emphasize the importance of efficiency, consistency and a lack of unnecessary duplication. But coherence may not be the only value built into the institutional structures. Demands for greater accountability may require frameworks that put a higher value on political responsiveness or parliamentary controls than on administrative efficiency. Beliefs in the importance of markets may deliberately allow divergent policies in order to maximize competition. Professional values among medical or legal practitioners may demand that coherence be subordinated to those professional ethics that require independence of action. There is also a belief that overlapping jurisdictions and internal policy competition may lead to *better* policy. Coherence is therefore always a contested objective, even if given rhetorical support as a national necessity.

Even within governments, there is considerable ambivalence. There is at the same time a push for cohesion and demands for decentralized managerial autonomy. Governments talk of strategy, while their managerial units want administrative systems that are close to, and responsive to, their clients. Governments wish to speak internationally with one voice; local authorities want managerial discretion. Public servants espouse the principles of neutrality, political leaders demand responsiveness. If the pendulum used to swing from the extremes of local managerial autonomy and detailed central controls, now it seems to be swinging both ways at once: greater political control and greater managerial autonomy (Aucoin, 1990). In other words, the commitment to a single government view may be rhetorical; the pressures of office often run against coherence.

The need for coherence is a particular problem for collective governments. Where one person has sole authority, it may be (theoretically) easier to ensure consistency. Cabinet government presupposes the need to convince others to take collective action. It assumes the notion of participation in decision making and then of joint action. In such a debate, it is often difficult to determine who is important, whether indeed a cabinet makes the crucial decisions or rather endorses decisions effectively made elsewhere. The problem is not only to explore the balance between leaders and ministers — although that remains a significant issue — but also to determine the boundaries and capacity of the collective group to identify and solve the substantial problems. The issue is further complicated by the constitutional assumptions of ministerial responsibility. Ministers in parliamentary systems have executive authority, and in some countries that authority is jealously protected against central authority, either by tradition or basic political necessity. Cabinet government may be collective, but not necessarily coherent. Aucoin (1991a) has suggested that more is at stake than merely a division between collective and individual aspects of political leadership. In Figure 1.1 he identifies four modes of leadership — command, collegial, corporate and conglomerate — which may be appropriate for leaders in changing circumstances. In command mode, prime ministers may act in an essentially unilateral way. In corporate mode, the prime ministers work across a range of portfolios, sharing responsibilities with several different ministers. In collegial government cabinet may predominate. In conglomerate government, policy is managed by specialized departments (Aucoin, 1994a: 110–14).

	Integrated	**Differentiated**
Centralized	Command	Corporate
Decentralized	Collegial	Conglomerate

Figure 1.1 *Models of cabinet government decision making*

This model can be further differentiated in another way, devised by Andeweg (and utilized in Chapter 4). He proposes that an 'ideal' cabinet is both collegial (treating ministers as equal) and collective (with decisions made in cabinet). As decision making moves away from that ideal towards individualized decisions made by prime ministers and ministers, so it becomes first segmented, then fragmented. Both models direct attention to the fact that decision making may not only vary between nations or governments of different parties; a single government may change over time, or even from one policy area to another. We cannot assume that coherence is always the primary objective.

At a second level, governments struggle to have an impact on their communities. Their actions may be judged not only by what they seek to do — government intentions — but also by what their policies achieve — their outcomes. Of course these impacts are harder to analyse because outcomes are so often dependent on forces outside the control of governments. It would be possible for a government to be consistent and coherent, and yet ineffective.

Analysis of the search for coherence therefore creates some interesting theoretical challenges that lie at the heart of an understanding of how government works. The first question is the conceptualization of coherence. As suggested above, the explorations may be sociocentric or statecentric. The former will explore the influence of government on society and the ability of governments to shape it. The latter is more limited: it requires only that the government is able to control its own instrumentalities and ensure consistency among its *intentions* for policy implementation.

A second issue relates to the determination of who can or should be involved as part of the centre. Power is clearly dispersed; no analysis of parliamentary systems proposes that power is entirely centralized. There is a need to consider the contributions made by the different actors. There may be a constitutional view that authority should reside with elected officials, but the reality is always more complex. Hence the usefulness of a broader concept that includes those at the centre who have an interest in developing a coherent strategy for governments.

In every government there is a range of actors at the centre who have the responsibility for ensuring, to a greater or lesser extent, that their government's policies are consistent. Their titles may change. Some may be elected, others appointed. Some are party partisans, others selected for their neutrality and competence. What they share is the challenge, and the constant search for capability that will allow them to achieve their objectives. Rhodes and Dunleavy (1995) have proposed the notion of a core executive that includes not only prime ministers or chancellors and their ministerial colleagues and advisers, but also those central agencies responsible for policy advice, budgeting and policy coordination. There may be a mix of partisan and professional appointees, but this group will be responsible for maintaining the all-of-government view that underlies the concept of policy coherence. If it exists, the core executive will regard policy coherence as an essential objective. There is thus a recognition of the inevitable mixing of policy and administration, of official and political factors, despite institutional arrangements which assume they are separate. The institutional arrangements may vary; the task remains common.

Any analysis must accept that there is a constant search for better procedures and different structures. It needs to determine not only what happens in one year, but how those procedures have changed and whether those changes have increased the government's capacity. Analysis needs to identify the impact of change. But there is of course a problem of determining what is or is not significant. When is a change in the activities of the core executive or in the apparent capacity to coordinate merely a minor variation or when does it have an extensive impact? In a single-country study, the boundaries of political action are often so well established by historical or ideological forces that it becomes difficult to imagine alternative arrangements. Small changes within those boundaries may be seen as important constitutional changes when they are in practice far less influential in shaping political practice than institutional arrangements taken for granted by observers and practitioners alike. These arrangements may refer not only to the formal or legal parts of the political system such as the electoral system, but also to the informal arrangements. Thus Rose (1980a: 45) is able to say that the advent of an advisory staff in No. 10 is the most substantial constitutional change in Britain since 1945; a brief survey of other similar parliamentary democracies would have shown that similar bodies have existed for some time without having the significant implications for cabinet government that Rose implies. In Canada party leaders are elected by convention. The process is accepted as democratic and normal, but its implications as an influence on the decision-making processes only becomes significant when compared to the leaders elected by parliamentary parties in Britain and Canada, by the exigencies of coalition in Dutch politics or by a Chancellor sitting at the head of a party ticket. Comparisons can provide insights that single-country studies may fail to provide.

Comparative Studies of Executives

These issues are obvious. Governance is the most significant of activities and the analysis of power the subject of political science for decades. Analyses of national or subnational governments are among the most frequent of subjects. Yet they are usually single-country studies. If comparative studies of executives are to be pursued, what is available as a model for research? The answer is very little. Perhaps there was no reason to expect much. As Hague and Harrop (1987: 238) commented, 'There are many works of distinction on the political executive, yet few are genuinely comparative'. Page (1995) notes the limited number of thematic comparisons.

All the recent surveys of political science literature illustrate that little has been done comparatively on the role of executives. Page's (1990) review of comparative politics suggested that between 1981 and 1989 *Political Studies, APSR*, the *British Journal of Political Science* and the *European Journal of Political Research* included only three comparative articles on executives and reviews of 24 books. Rhodes's (1991) review of the 197 articles in *Public Administration* from 1980 to 1989 noted that only 11 per cent were comparative at all (how many of that 11 per cent examined executive government is not recorded) and 4 per cent were concerned with British central government. Dunleavy and Rhodes (1990) list only four comparative studies of executives: Headey (1974); Campbell (1983); Mackie and Hogwood (1985); Rose and Suleiman (1980). Even though the list is by no means exhaustive, the lack of comparative references in the special issue on core executives is notable.

Several areas contingent to studies of executives are often explicitly comparative, but do not provide readily accessible benefits for the study of executives.

1. The social and career data for executives have been collected for several nations, providing patterns of background or prospects (Dogan, 1989; Blondel, 1991). But neither study appears to take the next step and ask how these different careers have influenced their behaviour in office.
2. Studies of leadership are often not clearly related to how leaders act in particular structural contexts. Burns's (1978) distinctions between transactional and transformational leadership may seem useful in

general but there is still a need to see how organization and situation have an impact on the strategies available to leaders.
3. Organizational studies of institutions and bureaucracies, perhaps best reflected in March and Olsen's *Rediscovering Institutions* (1989) or James G. Wilson's *Bureaucracy* (1989), do not translate directly into easy comparison of executive behaviour. They explain how organizations work, and take illustrations from a range of countries, but it is less clear that their insights can be readily applied to explaining the differences between two countries.
4. There are a number of comparative studies that illustrate the problems of government capability and executive behaviour without focusing on the specific roles of executives. Thus the contributors to Weaver and Rockman (1993) explore industrial, energy and pension policy and questions of cleavage management in the USA, Canada, Japan and France, though Weaver and Rockman are decidedly cautious in attaching much causal significance to either institutional or leadership factors. There is much useful comparative analysis, but little that explains the specific role of executives.

Multi-authored books on executives provide some insights, but fewer than they should. The principal problem is that the literature is usually multinational, rather than comparative. The inclusion of introductory or concluding chapters that draw together the lessons or intentions is often an inadequate procedure for proper analysis, unless particularly thoughtful or well done. Studies of comparative executives need to be better integrated if they are to work adequately. There are a few partial exceptions. Rose and Suleiman's (1980) review of presidents and prime ministers is assisted by a substantial comparative conclusion on governments and subgovernments. Mackie and Hogwood's (1985) collection of studies of cabinet committees is put into some perspective by an introductory section that considers many of the issues and findings. Plowden's *Advising the Rulers* (1987) included both national chapters, brief cross-cutting analyses that referred back to the particular chapters and to the discussion at the conference and a substantial conclusion by Yehezkel Dror (1987).

More typical of the genre is *Executive Leadership in Anglo-American Systems* (1991), edited by Colin Campbell and Margaret Wyszomirski. It was the outcome of a conference held at Georgetown University and attended by many experts on executive government from both sides of the Atlantic and the Pacific. Yet most of the chapters limit their analysis to the executive process in one country; only the two final chapters draw explicit comparisons and only the last actually looks at Anglo-American systems. Any comparative lessons, such as they may be, have to be drawn by the reader.

In Blondel and Müller-Rommel's (1988) edited collection of cabinet government in Western Europe, each author kept to the pre-set structure, but the book still concludes with tentative generalizations and proposals for research. Müller-Rommel acknowledges the difficulty of determining the proper unit of analysis — when any particular cabinet begins or ends has often been a vexed question (Dodd, 1984; Lijphart, 1984; Strom, 1988). He argues that if the definition of a cabinet is one with the same prime minister, with the same supporting party or parties, and in the same legislative period, then between 1965 and 1987 there are around 160 cabinets in Western Europe to study. He argues for the value of a substantial number of examples for analysis. Müller-Rommel finally proposes six dimensions of comparative research: the historical dimension, the institutional dimension, the political dimension, the ministerial background, the ministers' role perceptions and prime ministerial leadership. Yet, by this stage, it might be asked when comparative volumes on executives are going to contain some genuinely comparative conclusions, rather than setting out yet again a future research agenda.

Laver and Shepsle (1994a) take different models of cabinet decision-making — bureaucratic government, legislative government, party government, prime ministerial government and cabinet government — and ask to what extent government policy is affected by the partisan composition of cabinet, and by the allocation of portfolios between parties and within parties. Separate authors then examine a number of countries, applying the model with varying degrees of seriousness. In the conclusion the authors make some interesting comments on the comparative method; they make some generalizations on the capacity of individual ministers to defy cabinet, on ministerial discretion and on the strength of the departmental structure and the party system in parliamentary governments. They minimize the ability of the executive to import a sense of direction to policy making. But, while they go further than most works in pursuing a number of questions across a number of countries, they still deal with each country individually.

If the search then is limited to comparative studies on executives, the pickings are scarce. Where they do exist, they often tend to be Anglo-American, following Neustadt's (1969) efforts to find functional equivalents. One attempt to translate comparison into lessons is Walter Williams's *Washington, Westminster and Whitehall* (1988). Williams set out to use his Washington experience to bring recommendations for change to Britain that will 'modernize' the British parliament and government. His cures may not be persuasive, but the effort should be applauded for asking some fairly fundamental questions. Even if many of his solutions might be regarded as too unsympathetic to be adopted by the British political culture, finding a logical reason why the changes should *not* be adopted might itself be instructive.   Alternatively the executive's authority is one part of a broader comparative discussion.   Lijphart's (1984) discussion of democracies or Mény's (1993) comparative analysis of government in Britain, France, Italy and Germany considers the similarities and differences of those nations across all parts of the political system.   The emphasis is deliberately wide ranging.

Williams's study illustrates the problems of drawing comparisons between two different political systems.   There is a need to find functional equivalents (to use Neustadt's (1969) term) and then to explain the different impacts of institutions by reference as much to the broad political systems as to the institutional consequences.   The UK–USA comparisons provide a useful study in contrasts.

Any comparative study, designed to illustrate the impact of different institutional arrangements on policy outcomes, has to find a balance in the choice of systems it chooses to compare.   Too many cases may mean that the subtle nuances are lost in the analysis.   If we are to ask why practices differ in limited areas, we need to be able to understand what is to be explained in each case, without being overwhelmed by a kaleidoscope of variables.   Blondel's (1982, 1985, 1987) capacity to assimilate data from massively divergent countries in his studies of ministers or government organizations is impressive, but the discussion then has to be carried out at an inevitably high level of generality — too broad to be of any specific use for the experiences of a single government, even if usefully related to more general problems of governance.   Using too few countries, particularly when they have similar institutional arrangements, may not bring out the diversity that the study is seeking to explain.

What has been achieved so far?   In his comparative review of central agencies Colin Campbell (1983) analysed the role of senior officials in Washington, Ottawa and London and then proposed some principles that might be significant for the structure of central agencies, and some particular prescriptions for change in each country.   For instance, Campbell emphasizes the benefits that can be gained from a 'priorities-and-planning' style in good times, and a broker-politics style in bad times.   He recommends the use of policy secretariats that balance the public service, partisan and professional interests in the selection of staff.   In *First Among Equals* (1985a), a comparative study of the position of prime ministers across four parliamentary systems, Weller sought to identify what factors strengthened or weakened the position of prime ministers.   They included vulnerability to removal, control over parties, influence in cabinet committees, the ability to hire or fire ministers, the range of patronage, the level of policy advice and the control over parliament.   Basing conclusions on the analysis of these factors, it is possible to show which countries vest the greatest independence and power in their prime ministers.   That exercise was useful because some changes regarded as substantial in one political system were regarded as routine in others.

The obvious result of this brief survey is that there is little comparative work available to act as a model for the study of executive coherence. Why is there so little? Two explanations spring to mind:

1. The concepts are inadequate, so every study proposes an agenda for research but makes few advances itself. The field remains open for conceptual and empirical breakthrough that will assist better understanding of executive problems. Even after the decades of study, the challenge remains.

2. The belief that executives are too complex and unique to learn from experiences elsewhere: what Rose called 'uniqueness by false particularisation' (1991b: 450). The greater the appreciation of the complexities, the less value in simplifying to allow comparisons to be meaningful.

However much the lack of comparative models to follow may have limited or restrained academic research, it never restricted practitioners. They have always been prepared to examine alternative models. Visits to analyse the performance of other countries are common; and comparative lessons are drawn. As communications have improved, so practitioners have sought to benefit from experience elsewhere. There is plenty of adaptation and borrowing across nations.

The Challenges

There are two principal challenges facing the authors of this book: to assess the institutional influences that shape the core executive's capacity to develop strategic coherence, and to do so in a comparative format that draws distinctive lessons from one country to another, a format that is, to use Hans-Ulrich Derlien's (1992) phrase, comparative rather than merely comparable.

To take the second problem first: how many countries should there be compared — and which should they be? The first choice is between similar or dissimilar countries. We sought to tie the choices to the questions we wanted to answer. The study of central capability in governments is essentially about the management of systems, institutions and routines — the micro-management of the political centre. To put that activity into context we need to hold as much constant as we can. There is a strong argument for comparing systems of sufficient similarity so we can take as given some frameworks for the exercise of power. Therefore, we selected countries which had parliamentary systems of government. Their governments depend for their maintenance of power on continued party support within the parliament. Their cabinets are collective in their responsibility for broad policy, with the government expected to be consistent. The public services are primarily non-partisan, able to serve the elected government by providing advice and implementing its policy. The leaders are, at least notionally, *primus inter pares*; they do not have unlimited authority and must work with or through their ministerial colleagues. They face regular elections which can remove the government from office, either as a direct consequence of the electoral results or by a negotiation of coalition arrangements.

Each of these statements may be amended in part by local conditions. But, in comparison with other systems of government, they are broadly true. None the less, although our countries have parliamentary systems in common, there are also significant differences in the following areas:

- Federal (Australia, Canada, Germany) and unitary (the Netherlands, Britain).
- Parties in parliament (from 4 in Australia to 12 in the Netherlands).
- Coalition governments (Germany, Netherlands) and single-party governments (Britain, Canada).
- Stability (3 changes of government since 1950 in Australia and Germany, to 7 in Canada and 19 in the Netherlands).
- Electoral systems (proportional representation in Germany and the Netherlands; first past the post in Britain and Canada).
- Ministers (from 15 in the Netherlands to around 90 in Britain).
- Size of parliaments (147 in Australia to 662 in Germany).
- Upper houses (elected by popular vote in Australia to nominated by governments in Canada and Britain).

Of course the choice of countries can always be debated. Other countries may have been selected in lieu of any of the five here. New Zealand or any of the Scandinavian countries would have provided alternative views and perspectives. But the *number* had to remain limited to make it possible to consider any nuances of institutional impact.

Once the countries have been selected, the method of comparing them becomes an issue. The most common approach is to agree on a list of questions or issues to be discussed, and then to consider the questions in the context of each nation. The concepts become the variable, the method multinational rather than comparative. Such a process then requires either the reader or the editor to draw the lessons. As the review of existing work suggests, that process has not always been fruitful.

We chose to reverse the process, to use the countries as variables and ask how they undertook the functions selected for analysis. Comparisons are therefore made *within* each chapter of the impact of the function on the capacity to provide coherence. Inevitably this approach means that some countries received greater attention than others, in those places where their unique characteristics deserve comment. There has been no effort to determine mechanistically exactly how much attention each country should receive, but rather to ask how best the concepts can be explored.

What exactly is being compared? Executive coherence may be described broadly as the capacity of the core executive to ensure that the component parts of government, and the policies they seek to implement, are consistent and not contradictory. The notion of coherence is not necessarily a requirement for rationally derived policy. Indeed, policy is always bound to be negotiated through institutions, interest groups and established procedures. But is it thereafter consistent? Coherence is thus concerned with values, procedures and institutions, some of which will assist, others diminish, that capacity.

Which functions should be selected? We decided to examine a selection of activities through which policy is formulated. We selected the key institutions that mediate consensus and conflict: the parties and the cabinet; and those central processes that pull the different parts of government together: policy advice, coordination, budgetary processes and public management and decentralization. Therefore the chapters consider each of the following topics.

- The process of obtaining and maintaining support for government: how is the executive selected on support from parties in parliament and outside (Chapter 3)?
- Collectivity in government; how do the practices of collective government work and influence policy outcomes? To what extent can individual ministers act independently of the collective will (Chapter 4)?
- Policy advice; who provides that advice — civil servants, think tanks, partisan advisers? How are they organized and with what impact (Chapter 5)?
- How are resources allocated and what ability does the core executive have to use the budgetary system as a means to achieve its purposes? How much state activity is outside its powers (Chapter 6)?
- How effective are the processes of coordination? Does the core have the technical or political ability to support the demands of the political executive to enforce cohesion in government policy? What are the values inherent in the coordinating processes (Chapter 7)?
- How do changes in principles of public sector management fit with the desire for government direction? Is cohesion incompatible with managerialism, with its emphasis on devolution, executive agencies and client services (Chapter 8)?

- What impact do changes to core executives have on the political leadership of the nation (Chapter 10)?

Each of these chapters engages significant issues raised in the literature on the functions of core executives and associated institutions. In each case the chapters ask about the impact these functions have on the governments' capacity to ensure coherent policy, and how the institutional and normative arrangements shape outcomes. This task was based on a common set of questions: What is the capacity of the core? How far has it been altered — indeed possibly diminished — in recent years? At a time when the expectations are high, is the centre any more than a set of institutions with limited capacity to achieve those objectives? Is the appearance a sham, a 'hollow crown' that has the appearance of authority, but not the reality? With these common dimensions and themes, the chapters have a similar approach. Within each chapter, and consistent with the common themes, authors were given no instructions on the comparative techniques they should adopt.

These questions build on the research already undertaken by this team of researchers, for example on the position of prime ministers in parliamentary systems (Weller, 1985a), on the changes to cabinet structure (Aucoin and Bakvis, 1993), on ministers (Bakvis, 1991), on coordination (Davis, 1996), on budgetary systems (Forster and Wanna, 1990), on cabinet committees, ministers and cabinet (Andeweg, 1985, 1989a, 1990), on policy communities (Rhodes, 1996), on core executives (Rhodes and Dunleavy, 1995), and on public sector management (Aucoin, 1995; Wanna, O'Faircheallaigh and Weller, 1992). These foundations provide extra benefit: they approach the problem from a number of different theoretical perspectives. The literature on, for instance, budgeting, coordination and policy communities asks different public policy questions and uses different concepts. Here we approach a common problem — the capacity of the core executive to ensure coherence — using and evaluating these several theoretical perspectives.

The conclusion will draw together the threads by considering how the trends, whether towards or away from a 'hollow crown', affect the impact of the leaders. Is their position strengthened or weakened, and what does it tell us about the role of leadership in parliamentary systems?

Yet there is also a need to move one step further — to ask not just what happens, but what has changed, to go beyond the descriptive and catch the dynamic. That requires a common theme or set of ideas against which the changes can be judged. Hence, as noted at the beginning, we have chosen to organize the analysis around the notion of the 'hollowing out of the state'. The concept of the hollowing out of the state is considered in detail in the next chapter; but, stated bluntly here, the hypothesis proposes that the capacity of the centre of government has been undermined by recent developments.

The body of this volume is concerned with the coherence of policy in parliamentary systems and the degree to which the centres there have been 'hollowed out' by developments that put the achievement of coherent policy beyond their capacity.

The evaluation of coherence thus seeks not only to compare the capacity of the central cores of governments, but also to see how and why that central capacity may have changed. Is the centre being 'hollowed out'? That set of theoretical propositions will first be explored and then the ideas will be tested against the experience of the selected nations.

2   In Search of the Hollow Crown

Michael Saward

The American political philosopher Michael Walzer echoed a widespread perception when he wrote recently that 'the state is boring these days, or it is ineffective and corrupt . . . while civil society is an exciting place'. The power of many national states is said to be leaching away from above and below. Short-term actions and long-terms trends, so the refrain goes, all point to a common process — the hollowing out of the state.

How can we make sense of the idea of the 'hollow crown'? The volume as a whole identifies trends and counter-trends in five countries. This chapter is confined to interrogating the idea of hollowing out itself. While a tentative conclusion is reached — namely, that the hollowing out thesis is more credible in terms of international rather than national trends — it is recognized that the debate on the reshaping of states is still in its infancy, and other chapters take a different line. In some respects my central point concerns methodology, and specifically the conceptual frameworks that are most appropriate to the study of the state today.

What Is Hollowing Out?

This question is both unavoidable and unanswerable in the space available. I shall pass over ancient and massive controversies surrounding the question 'what is the state?', and simply posit the following points to anchor my position: the state is a more or less coherent set of institutions with unique authority to impose its will upon other institutions, groups and individuals within a defined territory. It is an institutionalized legal order consisting of the public bureaucracy and its political overseers. This view rules out definitions of the state as (a) the government only, (b) an instrument of the ruling class, and (c) a normative order (Krasner, 1984; Burnham, 1994).[1] This is important, since a hollow state would be something quite different for each definition.

Beyond the definition, my background approach to the contemporary state is built upon the following points.

- The primary brute fact about the contemporary state is the sheer complexity of its structures and functions and the issues confronting it. The modern state is a huge enterprise made up of hundreds if not

16

thousands of separate organizations with multiple and often confused lines of communication, cooperation and accountability. It is not an entity ultimately united by the need to perform some overriding function.

• Far from being a neutral or impartial referee between competing interests, the state is partisan towards certain particular interests within society (Parekh 1994). The object and degree of partisanship will vary from institution to institution (or policy area to policy area), and may include producer, professional or ethnic–religious interests (Lindblom, 1977; Eckstein, 1960; Habermas, 1974; Parekh, 1994). Unless momentarily or accidentally or in exceptional circumstances, the state represents no unified high ideal, and can make no consistent or large-scale claims to embody or represent 'the common good'.[2]

• The state has autonomy, never absolute but always present, from other social and economic interests (see Skocpol, 1985; Nordlinger, 1981). The state's informational, organizational and other resources (not least its ultimate monopoly of the use of legitimate coercion) ensure that its various institutions never entirely lack room for manoeuvre with respect to the wants of societal interests.

In sum, this broadly neo-pluralist perspective portrays the contemporary state as partisan, characterized by three interrelated dimensions of complexity (structural, functional and technical) and never entirely lacking in autonomy from societal forces.[3]

What Changes Occur in a Hollowing Out State?

If the state is hollowing out, what is happening to it? The idea makes most sense as a speculation about a loss of capacity at the heart of the state — in the core executive.[4] In his article 'The Hollowing Out of the State' — an 'avowedly speculative' effort to make sense of the idea, discussed in more detail below — Rhodes writes that 'The phrase "the hollowing out of the state" suggests the British state is being eroded or eaten away' (Rhodes 1994: 138). All such labels are ambiguous, but the bottom line is that things 'erode' from the outside and 'hollow' from within, from the centre or core. Seen in this light, the hollowing out thesis is a thesis about the core executive. We need not debate tensions between the ideas of a 'hollow state' versus a 'hollow core', since the hollow state means a state with a hollow core.

What is it that is hollow about a hollow core? Does the core executive lack coherence, capacity or both? There is a strong case for saying that a loss or lack of capacity is the primary meaning. If the core is hollow but has lost no capacity, then the only sensible meaning for the hollowing out idea can be moral (the state is not pursuing its Rawlsian agenda for social justice, failing to maximize utility, or some such). Capacity can more readily (though not easily) be explored empirically; coherence is a fuzzier notion, where explanation shades into normative concerns about 'good government' (with the theory of good government involved more often than not left implicit). Where coherence is likely to affect future capacity of a certain kind, the two shade into each other, admittedly — other chapters in this volume are not wrong to take coherence seriously, since the pursuit of coherence may represent an effort to counteract a loss of capacity — but here I will discuss hollowing out as a claim about what is happening to the capacity of the core executive in the five countries.

Explaining Shifts in Capacity

Rhodes's (1994) work has helped to clarify the concept and its referents. He identifies some key developments in British politics in the Thatcher and Major years which have had a variety of 'unintended outcomes'. On the internal or domestic front the development of a multiplicity of alternative delivery systems, particularly executive agencies (or Next Steps agencies), has resulted in the fragmentation and increased complexity of British government. The limitation of discretion for public servants through the New Public Management has raised the threat of policy 'catastrophe' (privatization and new limits on public intervention are also mentioned). Rhodes then discusses consequences of these unintended outcomes: fragmentation fosters inefficiency through the overlapping of functions and obscures lines of accountability. Complexity likewise muddies the waters of accountability. Ultimately, this loss of accountability is likely to mean a loss of political control at the centre.

I believe we can add to Rhodes' account of hollowing out in three key areas.

1. We need to consider carefully *intended* outcomes. In Britain, the 'loss' of functions to 'alternative delivery systems' (contracting out, market testing, executive agencies, etc.) was often no loss at all; the Thatcher and Major governments have positively fostered these developments, actively demonstrating core executive capacities in the process. One might reply that what was intended was lower public spending, a smaller state and a stronger role for the market mechanism within and between public institutions. Whether or not these aims were achieved, fragmentation, complexity and a loss of political control were unintended consequences. But fragmentation, complexity and less political control are characteristic of markets.

2. Rhodes adopts the normative stance of the good public administrator without defending it as the best (or at least a good) way to explain hollowing out. In a key passage, he quotes the head of the British civil service on the danger that fragmentation and so on, will lead to there being 'no real working mechanisms for policy coordination'. Future governments, particularly ones with an interventionist bent and redistributive aims, will need to be able to steer service delivery. Fragmentation and complexity will be obstacles to steering.

True as these consequences may be for the state, highlighting them is a consequence of the implicit theory of good government employed. Rhodes cites approvingly the notion that the unelected public administrator can play a role 'roughly akin to the Platonic guardian, standing for integrity and probity against partisan interest and corruption'. This approach is more about condemning what has happened rather than explaining it. It does not get to the heart of the hollowing out conjecture. That is an empirical proposition, which needs to be addressed in a more strictly explanatory framework.

What would be a better framework? I suggest we look first at the interests of those who have initiated these changes. In the 'predatory theory of rule', Levi (1981) suggests that we can explain what states do by assuming that rulers (for present purposes the core executive) seek to maximize their wealth and power. Their success in so doing depends on the nature and extent of bargaining resources they hold *vis-à-vis* their subjects. Subjects will possess an array of resources — economic, political, military — which they can use to constrain the ruler and wrest concessions.[5]

The predatory theory presents an amoral picture of ruling. That is all to the better. If the idea of the hollow state is to have real meaning it must focus on the capacity of the core to impose its will on the rest. The desirability of its being able to do so is neither here nor there; it is an important question, but a separate one that requires a separate, and appropriately grounded, analysis.

3. The 'clearer political control' which Rhodes identifies as one consequence of a sharper distinction between politics and administration in fact suggests the opposite of hollowing out in terms of diminished central capacity. This formulation does suggest that (some parts of) the core may well be strengthened by certain recent shifts in state power and functions. In addition, when discussing the major changes in the British civil service under Conservative rule, Rhodes argues that (a) public bureaucracy has become 'a patchwork quilt of organisations' (1994: 142), and (b) that 'In effect, the job of the individual civil servant is being hollowed out from above and below' (1994: 145). A hollowing out of civil service jobs does not make for a

hollow core. It, too, might strengthen the position of the core by allowing it scope to divide and rule.

In short, while hollowness may be a function of a lack of democracy, accountability and action in the 'public interest', in a more primary sense it should be seen as a thesis about core executive capacities in the contemporary state. Democracy and accountability do not necessarily serve the interests of the core. Because confused lines of accountability may foster a concentration of power at the core, we can expect rational core actors to seek them. Of course, all this remains speculative. We must turn to an examination of key trends in the countries under scrutiny to pursue matters further.

Three Hypotheses

If a 'hollowing out' state is a state with an increasingly weak core executive, three logical hypotheses follow:

1. the core executive is losing or conceding capacities to societal actors;
2. the core executive is losing or conceding its capacity to control other state actors; and
3. the core executive is losing or conceding capacities to supra-state entities.

The following sections examine these possibilities.

Down and Out: The Internal Hollowing Out of the State?

The notion that the state is hollowing out internally relates to the first two of our three hypotheses. It is suggested that either the core of the state is losing control over other societal actors and organizations, or over other parts of the state machine. This is close to what Crook, Pakulski and Waters are getting at when they refer to the transfer of functions 'downwards' and 'sideways' (the third of their possibilities is 'upwards', which I consider in the following section) as part of a broader process of 'disetatization' (1992: 80). I shall consider three general developments which are often (e.g. by Rhodes) linked to the idea that the state is hollowing out internally: privatization, decentralization and 'agencification'.

Privatization

By far the biggest and most profound privatization programme has been that of the Thatcher and Major governments in Britain.[6] Wilks has written that 'With plans to privatise British Rail, British Coal and the Post Office after the 1992 election there is almost literally nothing left to sell' (Wilks, 1993: 235) (though it is worth noting that the sale of the Post Office has fallen through, and that of British Rail — the 'Poll Tax on wheels' — is mired in controversy). In Britain the full gamut of motivations behind industrial privatization has been evident: ideological, economic, financial, managerial and party political (Vickers and Wright, 1988). With 16 major privatizations completed, including gas, water and electricity (Lawson, 1993), it is clear that privatization has fundamentally altered basic structures and functions of the British state.

Cataclysmic comments about the effects of privatization on the basic roles of the state may have some place in Britain, but privatization has played a significantly less prominent role in each of the other countries under study. In (West) Germany, despite strident calls by neo-liberals, backed in the party arena by the Free Democrats (FDP), there has not been an extensive privatization programme. The combination of a persisting party and national consensus about the role of the state in production, continuing *Länder* preference for maintaining public stakes in strategic industries, an overriding concern for national competitiveness, and the fact that '[a]ll those industries and corporations which are in the long run strategically important for the maintenance of key positions in world markets are privately owned' (Esser, 1988: 70–1), has rendered privatization in Germany largely 'symbolic'. The West German government between 1984 and 1987 did reduce or eliminate its stake in over 50 companies, notably ones involved in energy, chemicals and transport, but the programme overall has fallen well short of that of Britain (and indeed of France, the second major privatizer among European democracies).

Like Germany and unlike Britain, multi-party government and a more sympathetic view of the role of the state in production have limited the size, influence and fervour of the coalition of forces calling for substantial privatization in the Netherlands. Kickert (1994: 11) reports that although all four Dutch state companies have been more or less privatized — Postbank, PTT, Fishery Port Authority, Royal Mint[7] — attention came to focus by the early 1990s on 'the increase of administrative independence for organisation units financed or controlled by government, instead of the transfer of government tasks to the market'. As Andeweg and Irwin report, slimming down the Dutch public sector means focusing on welfare provision rather than industrial privatization. There was not a great deal to privatize in the first place, and, as in West Germany, the motivations were pragmatic: 'privatisation was advocated for reasons of administrative efficiency and budgetary reduction; it was not motivated by an ideological crusade for free-market capitalism' (Andeweg and Irwin, 1993: 200).[8]

Since 1983, under the Hawke and Keating Labor governments, Australia has been involved in a large-scale programme of deregulation (notably in banking and aviation), exposing protected industries to international competition (the inside political story of which is told in Kelly, 1994). In Canada, privatization had a lesser impact, not least because there were fewer strategic industries wholly or substantially controlled by the public sector. Canadian reforms have stressed more the need to cull various advisory and regulatory boards, councils and committees.

The extent of state disengagement from direct production has differed enormously in the five countries. Among the many reasons for this, of course, is the fact that the shape, extent and motivations for privatization depend upon the extent and style of public ownership and control of important industries in the first place (see Vickers and Wright, 1988: 11). Further, the state–society balance of power in, for example, Germany and the Netherlands, has meant that rational action by core actors (as in the predatory theory) has been preservative rather than transformative. By contrast, the core executive in Britain could more readily free itself from constraints to transform production fundamentally. It is interesting that neither broad approach offers conclusive evidence of a hollowing out of the state. In the more 'consensual' democracies (Lijphart, 1984b), the core continues to be constrained by more restrictive constitutional structures and standard operating procedures. If *that* represents 'hollowing out', then it was done in the past and is not a recent development. In 'majoritarian' systems, privatization may *appear* to be hollowing out the state, but this trend can equally be interpreted in terms of core actors rationally reshaping the state to suit some of their primary ends (such as power, autonomy, protection from direct responsibility). Where privatization has been extensive, the pressures driving it have come from above, in the core executive or from advisory groups operating through the core executive.

In sum, privatization offers no strong evidence in favour of the hollowing out hypothesis.[9] Indeed, we can see it as core actors flexing their political muscles. Perhaps, as Cassese has argued, privatization and deregulation 'revitalize the center, but not the state' (quoted in Rockman 1989). In a similar vein, Majone (1994: 79) comments that '. . . privatisation tends to strengthen, rather than weaken, the regulatory capacity of the state'.[10] In other words, predatory rulers can enhance their positions by pursuing such programmes.

Decentralization

Are core institutions in the five countries losing functions to other levels of government? The evidence for this is scant; if anything, the opposite trend has loomed larger in recent years. In Britain, a unitary state, a massive centralization of territorial power has taken place since 1979. More than 50 pieces of legislation since 1979 have fundamentally altered the role, powers and style of local government; as King argues, 'The aim of these reforms is to marginalise local government as a political institution by creating alternative local agencies to deliver policy and by denuding its representative function' (King, 1993: 194).

In the Netherlands, there has been little if any recent shift in the balance of power between the three levels of government. The powers of the much-criticized middle rung, the provinces, are limited, while the leaders of more important local government units are appointed from the centre. The vast bulk of revenue for local government comes from the centre. As Andeweg and Irwin have written, 'There is no escaping the conclusion that, relative to most other West European countries, the Dutch policy-making process is highly centralised in territorial terms' (Andeweg and Irwin, 1993: 163).

The three federal systems in the study display markedly different distributions of functions and powers between national and state governments. Australia is considerably more centralized than either Germany or Canada. Throughout much of the Commonwealth's history, the perceived need for central promotion of economic development encouraged an accretion of powers and functions at the federal level. A combination of factors, chiefly sympathetic judicial interpretation of federal powers under the Constitution, unchallenged legislation and the merely conventional status of the state Premiers' Conference, have continued to bolster central power. The persisting 'vertical fiscal imbalance', whereby 'the states lack independent revenue raising capacity adequate to fully fund their expenditure responsibilities, while the Commonwealth has access to revenues in excess of its own-purpose expenditure requirements' (Walsh, 1992: 19; see also Jaensch, 1992: 69ff.), has been especially significant in the continuity of federal power. The federal–state power imbalance looks set to persist; Keating, the then Prime Minister, largely scotched limited plans by former Prime Minister Hawke to address the fiscal imbalance (Walsh, 1992: 31; Galligan, 1992: 3). Australian federalism continues to be largely symbolic (see Lucy, 1993: 293).

Canadian federalism is far from symbolic. In part, this is a reflection of the fact that there are more centrifugal forces working at the core of Canadian government than are evident in Australia — provincial representation and subsequent log-rolling is a day-to-day reality of federal cabinet and budgetary politics (Bakvis and MacDonald, 1993). The distinctive issue of Quebec has been a key factor in curtailing central ambitions. Consider the words of Canada's Leader of the Opposition: 'Every nation has the right to self-government . . . We have no quarrel with the concept of federalism when applied to uninational states. It is a different matter when it comes to multinational states, particularly the Canadian brand of federalism' (Bouchard, 1994). The narrow loss by Quebec separatists in the referendum of October 1995 seems unlikely to resolve these issues. Further, the Canadian Constitution guarantees powers to the provincial governments in the areas of education, health and welfare, civil law, natural resources and local government. The financing of government at all levels in Canada shows a degree of stability and persisting independence for the provinces: 'Both federal and provincial governments tax personal and corporate income and also levy general sales taxes. Both levels of government can constitutionally tap these sources, both now do so, and both are likely to continue to do so' (Bird, 1993: 486).

Germany is perhaps the most territorially decentralized of all the countries under scrutiny. The *Länder* possess considerable constitutional autonomy and a secure source of revenues under national revenue-sharing arrangements. The direct representation of the *Länder* in the federal upper house is significant since the *Bundesrat* 'has absolute veto in matters where the competences of the *Länder* are affected' (Smith, G. 1991: 49). However, the role of the *Länd* governments revolves around policy delivery and administration, not policy formulation — the latter rests with the Chancellor and federal ministers. In practice, even the potential blocking powers of the *Bundesrat* have not proven to be a major constraint on the federal government: most legislative proposals do in fact achieve *Bundesrat* approval without major difficulties (Mayntz, 1984: 161).

Schmidt argues that one of the major political consequences of unification has been the accretion of more power at the centre. The new *Bundesrat* has a majority of poorer *Länder* over richer *Länder*, is more heterogeneous economically, and is dominated by Christian Democrats. Among other factors, these developments 'will impede consensus formation among the *Länder* and weaken their position as a whole relative to that of the federal government'. This new distribution of power 'widens the room to manoeuvre available to federal government' (Schmidt, 1992: 3), especially when allied with the centralization of economic policy brought about by unification.

In all, it seems reasonable to claim that, with the possible exception of Canada, there is no discernible decentralist trend in the five countries. Thus, on the face of it, there is little evidence that the state is hollowing out in the sense that it is losing or giving up capacities to other levels of government. Where central actors have had room for manoeuvre, their strategy seems to have been to maintain or enhance the power of the centre over the periphery.

Agencification

As with the privatization programme, changes in the civil service have been most marked in Britain. Under the Next Steps programme, 60 per cent of civil servants now work to chief executives in 92 executive agencies, with 44 more activities identified as agency candidates in December 1993 (Drewry, 1994). The idea of the Next Steps programme, launched in 1988, is 'to create agencies designed to deliver services entirely separated from policy-making core departments' (Dowding, 1993: 187–8). While still formally under the umbrella of one or other government department — and therefore still in a line of ministerial accountability to parliament — pay, conditions, and operational matters are dealt with autonomously within agencies.

The Next Steps reforms, along with further plans to subject top civil service jobs to open competition, fragment and render more complex the British state. Although there is considerable scope for argument here, there is a strong case for saying that they do not amount to a hollowing out of the core. These are reforms foisted upon a sometimes reluctant bureaucracy from the very top; it is often observed that the reforms would not have been as far-reaching and radical without active prime ministerial backing. Other things being equal, it enhances the security of ministers not to be held directly or fully accountable for bureaucratic shortcomings. They can, in principle, gain a new flexibility, freedom to manoeuvre and a capacity to concentrate on selected issues, dividing and ruling large swathes of the state bureaucracy.

In the Netherlands, there are current plans to create a series of executive agencies in proposals which 'bear a remarkable resemblance to the British example' (Kickert, 1994: 3). A key difference is that the responsibility for honing and implementing the reforms lies with the Ministry of Home Affairs, which has no power to force any other government department to reform its structure (Kickert, 1994: 10). Reform is discussed in terms of locating the 'core tasks' of government and the separation of policy making and policy execution. The paradox, as Kickert points out, is that such reforms, which include reducing the number and size of departments, do not threaten to leach power away from the core; since separation of policy and execution makes policy makers more aware of execution, it 'thus seems to lead to the functional integration of policy-making and execution'.

If anything, recent reforms of the bureaucracy in Canada and Australia represent an opposite trend to the one in Britain and that mooted for the Netherlands. Reductions in cabinet size and the creation of new amalgamated departments has served in effect to enhance the capacity of core political actors to get what they want in policy terms from the bureaucracy. In Germany traditional departmental (and ministerial) independence has persisted. None of these cases arising from the federal countries provides strong support for the hollowing out thesis (though as elsewhere countervailing trends, such as ministers becoming more involved in damage limitation when autonomous agencies get things wrong, are evident to varying degrees).

In sum, the five countries display quite different trends in terms of the organization of government departments: fragmentation on the one side, rationalization on the other. My contention is that a highly plausible interpretation, based on a realistic theory of rule, is that neither is a sign of hollowing out, even where ministers have given up day-to-day control of bureaucratic agencies. Fragmentation can be a sign of leaders in the core executive using their capacities to reshape the state to shield themselves from problems arising from operational and sometimes policy failures.

Style and Substance

My main contention is that the state is being redefined, or reshaped, not hollowed out, at least on this internal dimension. Both theoretical and empirical accounts support this preliminary conclusion. Müller and Wright (1994) are clear that changes in the instruments of policy making should not be misunderstood as shifts in the substance of policy control. Further, by pursuing strategies designed to cope with state complexity, core executive actors are using the key defining characteristic of the state — its monopoly of the legitimate use of coercion (or, more pointedly, *their* legitimate capacity to wield that monopoly) — in a more explicit and directed manner than has been evident for some time (though this is true of Britain more than the other countries).

Dunleavy's (1991) comprehensive critique and revision of public choice approaches to Western bureaucracies suggests that rational bureaucrats will prefer to shape public agencies rather than maximize their size or budgets. For a variety of rational reasons, smaller agencies may be preferred to larger, more unwieldy ones. For Richardson (1994), less government may mean strong government rather than hollowed out government. Metaphors borrowed from quite different contexts have a certain purchase on these developments; as Western economies have shifted broadly from 'Fordist standardized mass production to new manufacturing strategies that emphasise productive flexibility' (Hirst, 1994: 115), so their public sectors have been shaped in a way that might too be called 'flexible specialisation'. Clearly, harnessing specialized expertise effectively is one of the key advantages of agencification (Majone, 1994: 84); its 'flexibility' can be said to increase ministerial discretion to intervene in detailed policy matters.

These speculations can be underlined by looking briefly at the core executives in the states under study. The key questions are: has the core executive suffered a gain or a loss in its capacity to set the agenda; to make and impose decisions; and/or to coordinate the machinery of government?

The transformation of British politics and government since 1979 has occurred largely due to the force, ideological clarity and persistence of Margaret Thatcher as prime minister. She established dominance over the cabinet within two years of assuming office, involved herself more in departmental policy making than previous prime ministers, shunned compromise, and worked effectively through an inner cabinet of trusted ministerial and other colleagues both informally (as a kitchen cabinet) and formally (through cabinet committees). While substantial reductions in government spending eluded her governments, much else that she sought by way of wholesale structural and cultural change in government was achieved. She realised the potential of a powerful office in a centralized polity with few fixed rules of conduct and an undemocratic electoral system. Particularly when they operated with her full support, her ministers could achieve what in the British context were breathtaking changes in health, social services, local government, utilities and other areas.

In West Germany, the Chancellor has always played a central policy role as prescribed in the Basic Law. He is responsible for the 'general guidelines' of policy, appoints and dismisses ministers, and ministers' primary responsibility is to him and not to the *Bundestag* (Smith, 1991: 49). A key development underpinning the Chancellor's role in recent years has been the central role played by the Chancellor's Office. Especially since the rapid expansion of its role under Brandt, the Chancellor's Office has provided an effective 'reporting system' and contributed to 'an increased co-ordinating capacity' (Mayntz, 1980: 165–6). Given the weakness of cabinet committees, the Chancellor's Office has gradually become the clearing house for cabinet proposals, as well as being the Chancellor's general watchdog (Müller-Rommel, 1988: 158). Cabinet in Germany is more a rubber stamp than a decision-making body in the full sense of the phrase, although ministers can take proposals to full cabinet if they wish (Müller-Rommel, 1988: 165–6). There are, of course, constraints on the Chancellor's power. Ministerial autonomy and cabinet vetting of parliamentary proposals reinforce party and coalition constraints (Mayntz, 1980: 143–5). But German unification has enhanced the symbolic importance of the Chancellorship and seems to have bolstered the degree of policy autonomy enjoyed by Chancellor Kohl in the face of major economic and social challenges. Not least due to the widespread legitimacy of the various powers and constraints evident in the German polity, no real hollowing out of the state is evident — if anything the core executive has power increasingly concentrated within it.

In the Netherlands, the prime minister is in a considerably weaker position, but the authority accorded to highly autonomous ministers prevents this fact from representing a lack of capacity at the core. Andeweg and Irwin write that

> Compared with his British, French, or even German colleagues, the Dutch Prime Minister has very few formal powers. He draws up the agenda and chairs all meetings of the Cabinet and its committees. He casts the deciding vote when there is a tie. But the Prime Minister does not appoint ministers and he cannot reshuffle, dismiss or direct them, or arbitrate between them without their agreement (Andeweg and Irwin, 1993: 123–4).

In general terms, despite high degrees of departmental and ministerial autonomy, failed efforts to operate 'inner cabinets' and problems of achieving a sufficient degree of interest aggregation in a functionally decentralized system, the multi-party nature of Dutch cabinets and the difficulties of government formation tend to mean that governments are locked into agreed roles and policies. These and other factors may not represent an obvious concentration of power in the core executive, but at the same time they provide little or no evidence of the state hollowing out.

Since 1983 in Australia, a clique of ministers, centred on Hawke and/or Keating, has achieved major economic reform by gaining effective control of core executive institutions, and through them the more distant arms of the state. In the earlier years after 1983, the use of cabinet committees, and especially the Expenditure Review Committee (ERC) (named the 'razor gang' after an earlier such committee under the Fraser Government), became 'a guillotine for the sacred cows of Labor's *ancien regime*' (Lucy, 1993: 154–5). Hawke himself described the ERC as 'the engine room of the government'. Further, Hawke made effective use of the Department of Prime Minister and Cabinet as a source of independent advice and a watchdog over other departments' plans and activities. The major structural reforms of the cabinet and the bureaucracy in 1987 seem to have further consolidated the capacity of key ministers. Devolving decision making to larger departments took pressure off the core, streamlining decision making, allowing for more effective use of cabinet committees and cabinet time (Weller, 1990: 21–2). Aucoin and Bakvis argue that the reforms fostered 'crossdepartmental loyalties to the government's overall corporate goals' (Aucoin and Bakvis, 1993: 403). They comment further that: 'The success of the Hawke (and later Keating) government in implementing its program can be attributed to the greater influence it had over the recruitment and placement of a moderately sized group of departmental secretaries and cabinet ministers who collectively had authority over the total span of government activities' (Aucoin and Bakvis, 1993: 398).

Canadian cabinets experience centrifugal forces much greater than those in Australia — 'Much as in the nineteenth century there exists in cabinet a set of norms governing the conduct of cabinet business concerning the right of ministers to be heard, if not necessarily enjoying a right of veto, when matters affecting their provinces come before cabinet' (Bakvis and MacDonald, 1993: 61). However, the 1980s and the early 1990s saw a series of reforms, major and minor, which have helped to consolidate the capacity of the prime minister and key ministers to pursue their aims. The development under Trudeau of the Prime Minister's Office, the Priorities and Planning cabinet committees and instruments for effective economic control, 'culminated under Mulroney in the hierarchical cabinet'. The Operations Committee and the Expenditure Review Committee became key tools of core capacity, particularly with regard to spending decisions. Under Trudeau and Mulroney there has evidently been an increase in prime ministerial capacity to shape the cabinet, its agencies and committees, and to select and pursue strategic issues effectively, despite provincial politics soaking up much cabinet time outside these strategic areas (Bakvis and MacDonald, 1993: 67–8).

Despite the fact that Canada possesses the most fully developed cabinet support system anywhere in terms of key central agencies, the sheer size of the cabinet — 39 under Mulroney — rendered it unwieldy (Bakvis and MacDonald, 1993: 49). Only extensive use of cabinet committees, rendering the cabinet more or less marginal in the decision-making process, made this system workable. The reforms of 1993 under Prime Minister Campbell reduced the cabinet to 25; cut down the number of cabinet committees from 11 to 5; and generally resulted in a more integrated structure with a 'reduced number of decision points in the executive system' (Aucoin and Bakvis, 1993: 412). Like the Australian reforms discussed above, these changes concentrate capacity more effectively within the core executive and enhance the capacity of the core executive over other parts of the government machine.

Across the five countries, it is at least plausible to claim that power is not leaking away from, or being given away by, the core executive. Latent and manifest capacities of prime ministers and key ministers have been activated to reorganize and rationalize in the face of structures which perhaps provided too many other potential power centres, for example within federal bureaucracies. As the predatory theory of rule predicts, core executive actors have sought to reduce the degree to which other state and non-state actors can constrain them.

Rationality and Obfuscation

I have suggested that, in the face of fragmentation and complexity, it is rational for core executive actors to reshape the state so that it better suits their own ends. A good deal of what passes for hollowing out can usefully be reinterpreted in this light. We must tread carefully around the concept of rationality. In the public administration tradition, to structure government rationally is to (among other things) maximize clear lines of accountability and responsibility. In other words, to be rational was to seek 'good government' — transparent, accountable, efficient and honest.

In political science today the concept of rationality is rightly and invariably seen in a more tough-minded, unsentimental light. To put the point bluntly, the core executive of the modern state has a much stronger interest in *perceptions* of good government than in the reality of it. We must take fully into account the myriad capacities of the core to foster the impression of commonality and even blamelessness for its partisan actions. In Habermas's (1974) terms, core executive actors often possess the means to prevent a 'rationality crisis' (the state is not doing the good things it says it is) from becoming a 'legitimation crisis' (the people perceive the lie and lose faith in the state). Comprehensive accounts of information and disinformation strategies available to state actors should leave us in little doubt about the extent to which societal perceptions of state success and failure can be manipulated by state actors (see, for example, Edelman, 1977, 1987; Nordlinger, 1981), and why it is rational for them to deploy these strategies as much as they can. Core actors can reshape the state (especially in unitary, majoritarian systems) and mould perceptions of the resulting new order, all to their benefit.

None of this is to say definitively that no form of hollowing out is occurring in some liberal democratic states. It is an argument about how trends can look different when viewed through the lens of a more tough-minded, more strictly explanatory theory. One area in which I happily concede substance to the hollowing out thesis is in the state's international context (Rhodes rightly discusses the effect of 'the Europeanisation of everything'). To show why, I turn now to the third hypothesis.

External Hollowing Out

According to Dirks in *The Hollow Crown* (1987), 'until the emergence of British colonial rule in southern India the crown was not so hollow as it has generally been made out to be' (1987: 4). Under colonial rule, the princely crown did become hollow, as indigenous political structures were 'frozen, and only the appearances of the old regime — with its vitally connected political and social processes — were saved' (1987: 6). Does the idea of hollowing out make most sense if its cause is a layer of political institutions above and beyond the machinery of the national state?

Political scientists are accustomed to viewing national developments in isolation, as if forms of interaction between states have little impact on their internal dynamics. Burnham (1994: 6) rightly argues that: 'A major task for political science in the 1990s is to chart how changes in state form are related to intensified globalisation' (see also McGrew, 1992).[11]

Held (1987; 1991) identifies four major 'disjunctures' between 'the formal authority of the state and the actual system of production, distribution and exchange which in many ways serves to limit the power or scope of national political authorities'. Transnational corporations erode state autonomy in that their activities are increasingly organized on a global scale, a key element in the internationalization of production. Though he is of the view that various 'predictions of the death of the nation-state are premature', Huntington records views such as Barber's that transnational corporations are 'acting and planning in terms that are far in advance of the political concepts of the nation-state', and Ball's that while the nation state 'is still rooted in archaic concepts unsympathetic to the needs of our complex world', the transnational corporation 'is a modern concept evolved to meet the needs of the modern age' (1994: 224) .

The role of transnational corporations is closely linked to the internationalization of finance. The interpenetration of markets has arisen alongside the growth in the number and size of multinationals (Müller and Wright, 1994: 5). A major impact on state capacities, structures and operations arises from its lack of control over information, especially crucial in the realm of finance (Müller and Wright, 1994: 6).[12]

National boundaries are no longer so significant as boundaries of economic activity. The growth and dynamism of the international economy constrains domestic political capacity for economic control and manipulation, a development allied with the emergence of sound economic management as the primary ingredient of sound political management (Sartori, 1991). While these trends are far from uniform across the globe, and in places regional organization does afford new forms of national government leverage over economic development, they do add up to a significant erosion of state autonomy.[13]

Second, Held identifies a major disjuncture in the vast array of international regimes and organizations that have been established to manage whole areas of transnational activity and collective policy problems. To varying degrees, and in different policy areas, the World Bank and the United Nations, for example, now act as more than just a clearing house for multinational decision making, but have developed policy autonomy.

The third disjunction concerns how the development of international law challenges traditional state autonomy. Machinery now exists for the collective enforcement of international rights, most notably perhaps under the European Convention for the Protection of Human Rights and Fundamental Freedoms. Member states of the European Union have successfully been prosecuted for violating citizen rights.

Finally, Held identifies a disjuncture between the idea of the sovereign state and the existence of hegemonic powers and regional power blocs. The North Atlantic Treaty Organization (NATO) is arguably becoming an even more vital factor after the Cold War than during it, as its tentacles reach towards some of the states that were former members of the Warsaw Pact.

According to Parry, we are witnessing an expansive 'interweaving of foreign and domestic policy-making' (Parry, 1993). Of course, this is clearest for the three countries in this study which are members of the European Union, for whom European 'foreign' policy is now effectively domestic policy. As Crowe writes: 'There is now hardly an important area of national economic life . . . which has not been subject to international negotiation, legislation or at least co-ordination and co-operation in Brussels, often with administration, monitoring or enforcement also from Brussels and, even, an international court in Luxembourg' (Crowe, 1993: 176). Pinder notes that the European Union 'has the powers that a federation would require over internal and external trade; and the Maastricht treaty gives it federal powers over money' (Pinder, 1992: 419). Canada is a part of the NAFTA trading alliance, and Australia's economy has been internationalized and linked closely with its ASEAN neighbours.

In sum, evidence suggests that some national governments are — to put the point in its boldest form — becoming local governments (Dahl, 1989). In key areas of policy national governments are much more vulnerable than ever before to pressures and events beyond their immediate control. National economic planning is a task of the state of the past. While caution is in order and countervailing trends are evident (Krasner, 1994), the case that these globalizing developments represent an external hollowing out of core executive capacities remains compelling.

Hollowing and Reshaping: Combining Internal and External Views

Putting together the two threads of the discussion — the internal reshaping and the external erosion of state capacities — suggests that, to varying degrees, core executive actors in the states under scrutiny are reshaping the state in order to: (a) underscore what remains of their distinctive capacities,

(b) foster new forms of selective and flexible policy intervention, and (c) ultimately, to reinforce sources and forms of legitimacy. On the one hand, this is to emphasize the point that core executive actors must be understood as rational actors operating within various structural constraints. On the other, it is to underscore the dynamic nature of links between internal and external factors. Core executive actors today find themselves caught in a maelstrom of pressures, to which they have responded by attempting to redefine and clarify their powers just as those powers are in many respects leaching away to higher authorities and processes.

At the centre of this maelstrom are the capacities of core executive actors to adapt to the demands of a rapidly changing external environment. Political scientists whose primary concern is international relations have been prime movers in developing frameworks to analyze adaptive strategies. Rosenau (1989) argues that

> an inverse relationship between internal controls and external vulnerabilities appears to have emerged as a prime parameter within which the modern state must function. And since the trend line for the future seems likely to involve an ever growing vulnerability to global events and processes, the controls exercised by the state at home appear destined to undergo a corresponding expansion (1989: 35).

To get to the heart of the matter, he says, we must view the state 'as an adaptive entity and its activities as a politics of adaptation' (1989: 37).

Of the four types of adaptive strategy available to states (acquiescent, promotive, intransigent and preservative), Rosenau suggests that 'preservative adaptation' — the effort to achieve equilibrium in the face of extensive internal and external pressures for change — is and will increasingly prove to be the global norm (1989: 42). Something of the terms of this equilibrium may be gleaned from Hirst and Thompson's (1995: 423–35) observations that national states still have crucial roles to play in an internationalized economy where 'governance' is becoming more important than 'government'. They cite, for example, the continuing pivotal role for national states as providers of coherence in links between sub-national and supra-national entities, of stability for financial markets, and more generally of the rule of law.

While dense patterns of interdependence make national states increasingly vulnerable, they bring them both new constraints and new opportunities (Parry, 1993: 145). Campanella argues that rational purposive state actors face an increasing need for 'proactive policies', which go beyond mere domestic adaptation: 'unlike adjustment or reactive policies, proactive policy-making aims not to adapt but to find a comprehensive response to a crisis' (Campanella, 1991: 497). Proactive policy making, in her view, means opening up the domestic economy to international competitive pressures and forging alliances — often regional alliances such as the European Union and NAFTA. 'They are proactive because they are major policies made through cooperative, intra-governmental decision-making' (Campanella, 1991: 497).

Proactive policy making is used in efforts to achieve favourable economic conditions that can no longer be manipulated successfully on the domestic front alone. In this sense, the increasing regional involvement of each of the five countries can be viewed as a rational strategy in the face of limited capacity and powerful economic imperatives. But this time the strategy can plausibly be viewed as arising from the vulnerability of core executive actors due to the hollowing out of their position from 'above'.

The pursuit of proactive policies in this sense requires national state machinery capable of flexibility, decisiveness and perhaps above all of leadership. Arguably at least, it is the core executive in each of these national states which must play this role. Australian opening out to the world economy has been a product of the Hawke–Keating axis at the heart of the revitalized core executive (Kelly, 1994). Andeweg and Irwin suggest that membership of the European Union may have increased the policy autonomy of Dutch prime ministers despite the considerable domestic constraints which bound the occupants of the office: 'European integration does not necessarily weaken national executives. In the Dutch case at least, "Brussels" may have strengthened the decision-making capability of the national political system' (Andeweg and Irwin, 1993: 238).

No longer the foci of relatively independent economic policy making, core executive actors have come to play a mediating role between external forces and internal capacities to benefit from those forces. At the same time, these rational actors look to their own legitimacy, carving out for themselves a more subtle and flexible domestic role — exemplified by agencification, privatization and the 'rise of the regulatory state' — that allows them (in many though not all instances) to enhance domestic control over the remaining, and newly revised, levers of national policy making. Domestically, the evidence points to a conscious reshaping of the state rather than intended or unintended hollowing out. However, this reshaping can be seen to a significant degree as a response to a real hollowing out of core executive capacities in the face of globalizing trends.

Conclusion: Whither the Hollow Crown?

My tentative conclusion is that the evidence points to a hollowing out of core executive capacity due to globalization even while core executives actively seek to shore up their own internal power. I put this forward as a hypothesis with considerable empirical support, though countervailing trends are evident in a number of countries. Other chapters offer more detailed and analytically localized arguments which variously support and reject this line of thinking. My second main contention has been methodological: it is more fruitful to explore the hollowing out hypothesis by regarding core executive actors as rational maximizers of their own power. They may say otherwise, but we must watch as well as listen.

Notes

1. Each of these approaches may well tell us something important about the state, but they are secondary characteristics or simplifying devices which are parasitic on the primary definition.
2. At least, not above baseline provision of law and order. This baseline is consistent with the view that above minimally essential provisions these security values are never evenly distributed. On the idea of the principled state more generally within democratic theory, see Zolo's (1992) critique of Schumpeter (1976).
3. Even recent Marxist theories of the state fit this characterization. Marxists have largely abandoned the search for *a* theory of the state (see Jessop, 1982). Some have relied more on dramatic assertion than empirical demonstration (e.g. Althusser, 1971). Poulantzas (1980) wrote of various divided fractions of capital colonizing parts of an equally fragmented state structure, with working class and other non-capitalist interests themselves represented within the state. He wrote too of the 'relative autonomy' of the modern state. Criticism of 'bourgeois' pluralists strains credulity in the face of such apparent abandonment of the overarching explanatory capacity of the Marxist framework.
4. Dunleavy and Rhodes have defined the core executive as 'all those organisations and structures which primarily serve to pull together and integrate central government policies, or act as final arbiters within the executive of conflicts between different elements of the government machine' (Dunleavy and Rhodes, 1990: 4). However, this definition assumes what needs to be demonstrated — that the core executive does what the textbooks say it should be doing. It is probably more helpful simply to define the core executive in institutional terms, and leave the flows of power to further investigation.
5. This approach is standard in historical studies of the state. See, for example, North (1986) and Rueschemeyer, Stephens and Stephens (1992).
6. The term privatization can refer to such different things as the outright sale of public sector companies, the encouragement of private sector involvement in public companies and public projects, the introduction of private sector management and operational norms to public enterprises, and so on (see Vickers and Wright, 1988: 3). I shall use the term here to refer to the selling off of public companies to the private sector.
7. In the Netherlands, a number of smaller public companies and a 23 per cent share in KLM were also sold off (Vickers and Wright, 1988: 23).
8. The persistence of the corporatist tradition in the Netherlands has played its role. It is reflected in the continuing fragmented and complex network of

In Search of the Hollow Crown

advisory and other bodies in Dutch government, but also in the moderate approach to industrial privatization (see Andeweg and Irwin, 1993: 170–3).

9. As a general point, the effects of privatization, even in countries where it has been pursued successfully and extensively, should not obscure the reach of the state into the national economy. As Vickers and Wright remind us, 'The State, everywhere in Western Europe, continues massively to intervene in the economy by regulating the terms and influencing the environment of public and private industry operations in a number of ways' (see for further detail Vickers and Wright, 1988: 26–7).

10. Arguably 'regulation' should be treated separately from privatization, agencification, etc., though as a modern development in the structure and functions of the state it is closely linked with these other trends. Majone (1994: 80) writes that: '. . . neither American deregulations nor European privatizations can be interpreted as a retreat of the state, but rather as a redefinition of its functions. What is observed in practice is a redrawing of the borders of the public sphere in a way that excludes certain fields better left to private activity, while at the same time strengthening and ever expanding the state's regulatory capacity in other fields like competition or environmental or consumer protection'. It is worth noting that, in Britain at least, regulation for consumer protection (broadly conceived) serves as a direct substitute for public ownership (in the cases of gas, electricity and water). Further, regulation may not restrict ministerial influence. For example, the proposed new Environmental Agency in Britain, although nominally independent of the responsible minister, is being set up under legislation that would allow detailed direction in the area of standard setting by the Secretary of State for the Environment.

11. See Redner (1990) for an extensive effort to generate concepts which might perform this function.

12. Keohane and Nye (1994: 232) comment generally that 'integration of money markets internationally, in the context of governmental responsibility for national economies, has made government policy sensitive both to changes in interest rates by other governments and central banks, and to movements of funds by nongovernmental speculators. These sensitivities are heightened further by the expanding decision domains of transnational organisations such as multinational business firms and banks, reinforced by decreases in the cost of transnational communications' (see also Hirst, 1994: 112ff.).

13. According to Jessop (1994), 'two key transformations in advanced capitalist state during the current global economic restructuring which bear directly on the nature of economic and social policy regimes' are 'a tendential shift from a Keynesian welfare state to a Schumpeterian workfare state; and a tendential "hollowing out" of the national state'.

3 Political Parties and the Core Executive

Patrick Weller

In parliamentary systems governments depend for their survival on continuing support in parliament. The support is organized by parties who nominate candidates, campaign at elections and maintain discipline within the legislatures. Governments in all five countries are recognizable as party governments, whether constituted of members of a single party or a coalition. National leaders and ministers hold office as representatives of their party. Most governments bear, either interchangeably or in combination, the name of their leader and their party.

The core executive includes those leaders and ministers elected by the population or selected as representatives of the party. Their continued existence as a government requires continued party support. Party and core executive overlap because the leaders of the one are necessarily the leaders of the other.

Nevertheless, even if at first sight it might seem self-evident that in a party government the party will always dominate the government, in practice that is an empirial question to be tested. Influence may work in both directions. On the one hand, the party may act as a constraint on the core executive, screening out some alternative policies, creating other imperatives and generally making demands in such a way that policy may appear incoherent, satisfying the diverse needs of the party's different constituencies. On the other hand, the party support may provide the core executive with opportunities, with a means of selling policies to the electorate through the party machine or publicity channels.

A further proposition is that the influence of parties may be constantly changing. For instance, the party's impact on policy may be in decline while its capacity to enforce accountability may be growing more marked. In some respects the party may reduce the power of the core executive, limiting its capacity to act. In other ways, a decline in the ability of parties to determine policy frameworks may cede that power to the centre and make it more cohesive.

These apparent contradictions may be illustrated by the different trends said to characterize political parties in the late twentieth century. There is seen to be a decline of party ideology, and a growth of 'catch-all' parties.

The collapse of communist ideology and the discrediting of much leftist programme orthodoxy has led to a situation where there appears to be little difference between parties of left and right. When Lady Thatcher praises an Australian Labor government for its deregulation, the party labels must surely mean less. Everyone privatizes now.

At the same time parties speak of the need to make bureaucracies more responsive and adopt procedures that will apparently reduce officials' independence. And electorates, disappointed at the failure of governments to deliver on their often extravagant electoral promises, turn on parties with cynicism and disillusion. Membership is declining, with fewer party links to civil society. Social movements, most notably the greens, have sought to capture the idealistic ground deserted by parties. In New Zealand and Italy, the populace have voted for a change in the electoral systems to gain a more responsive and accountable government.

The relationship of political parties to the core executive is central to any debate about the capacity of the centre. To what extent is the core executive, consisting of both the party's ministers and officials, limited in its choices by the ideological or organizational demands of the party at large? Are constraints concerned with general directions or detailed policy prescriptions? And how can the party apply sanctions on the core executive? These questions may give some insights into the independence of the centre to do more than act as a transmission belt for party demands.

The problem of assessing party influence is made more complex by the difficulties of determining which element within the parties is being discussed:

- the ministerial elite who are the essential part of the core executive;
- the parliamentary party which provides the support and which may, or may not, include the ministerial elite;
- the mass party outside parliament, with its organizational leadership of notables.

Within government too there are perceptions of change, as leaders are said to become more influential, more dominant, while ministers cede authority to the leadership or to the collectivity of cabinet.

How then can the impact of parties be assessed?

There are several schemes for determining the degree to which party and government interact (e.g. Rose, 1969, 1974; Lijphart, 1984b). Katz nominates three conditions that have to be fulfilled for a government to be identified as a 'party government'.

1. All major decisions must be taken by people chosen in elections conducted along party lines, or by individuals appointed by or responsible to such people.

2. Policy must be decided within the governing party, when there is a 'monocolor' government, or by negotiations among parties where there is a coalition.
3. The highest officials (e.g. cabinet ministers and especially the prime minister) must be selected from within their parties and be responsible to the people through their parties (Katz, 1986: 43).

Katz suggests these conditions form an ideal type which may be met by some parties more than others. Nevertheless the three conditions provide criteria against which national performance can be judged.

Building on Katz's definition, Blondel tried to develop a model that asked whether the party is dependent on government, or the government on the party. That test provides one axis for locating national systems. A second axis estimates the degree of autonomy or interdependence of government and party (1995: 132). Blondel then examines the factors that affect the government–party relationship — whether broad features of the political system, such as national institutions or electoral systems, or narrow ones, such as party structure or the activities of leadership. He concludes that the European coalition governments provide the best examples of governments which are dependent on parties, while the British Conservative governments reflect the least dependent cases.

Throughout the discussion the different perspectives of the several elements in a party will always raise problems. To a minister, the party may be an unfortunate reality; there is a need to give it constant attention as it restricts policy choices or undermines the stability of government. To the party member, the need to limit the executive may be no more than holding the central government accountable. The desire of the party to reduce the autonomy of the core executive is potentially both constraint and opportunity. It depends who is asked.

The concern in this chapter is to ask to what degree party influence limited, or limits to a greater extent than before, the capacity of the core executive. Are controls now more differentiated than they once were? Because of the integration of party and executive leadership, it becomes difficult to be precise: no prime minister is likely to distinguish in cabinet between party and government roles, the two are fused. However, parties may have greater influence if:

• the parties insist on tighter commitment to party platforms or campaign commitments.

They may have less influence when:

• policy communities draw ministers away from party links to negotiate policy with the active participants;
• the tight circle of the core executive restricts party access; and

- governments are flexible or reactive, with no fixed commitments.

To explore the impact of parties on the executive this chapter focuses on:

- the selection of personnel and the formation of governments;
- policy development: the impact of coalition or single party government;
- the answerability of the core executive to the party.

The Process of Ministerial Selection and Government Formation

Three institutional factors may have a significant impact on the nature of the party system and the potential influence of parties on the capacity of the core executive to act. They are:

1. the existence of coalition or single-party governments;
2. the unitary/federal nature of the constitution; and
3. the nature of class support.

The impact of party will be *different* in single-party and coalition governments.

In Britain, Australia and Canada, the governments have been drawn predominantly from single parties. Although there have been occasions when the government could not command a majority (1972–74, 1979–80 in Canada, 1976–78 in Britain), the solution has been to rely on a third minor party for support and, when that brings parliamentary defeat, to call an election. Formal coalitions have never been attempted. In Australia, the Liberal and National parties are in perpetual coalition. Even when the Liberal party had enough seats in the House of Representatives to govern on its own, it remained in a coalition. The agreement between the two parties settled the number of ministerial positions, but is seldom extended to written policy compacts. Policy problems are settled as they arise. As there has *never* been a question of the National party switching to support the Labor party, or since 1949 of a split in the coalition while in office, the arrangement can be seen as creating a composite party, rather than as two bodies with the capacity to negotiate different terms.

Single parties are not necessarily free from internal tensions. Most single-party governments are themselves coalitions of forces. Intra-party divisions in the British Conservative party have been called 'the only game in town'; the divisions between Eurosceptics and Europhiles has created the greatest tension and was at the basis of Major's decision to throw the prime ministership open to contest. In Canada parties are all a combination of provincial, sectional and personal alliances that require constant trading in terms of ministerial portfolios and public works. Whenever those coalitions collapse — as happened with the Progressive Conservative combination of conservative westerners, Quebec secessionists and traditional Tories that kept Mulroney in office — the governments disappear. Publicly the governments retain support from a single party, even if there is constant internal negotiation. That negotiation tends to be *ad hoc* and movable, with possible understandings about processes but no formal agreements on policy.

Coalition governments develop different imperatives. Parties may campaign as coalition partners, as they do in Germany, or as separate parties with the freedom to negotiate an agreement after the election, as Dutch parties do. When coalitions need to be negotiated before a ministry is formed, parties may have a substantial impact in requiring the ministry to operate within the boundaries of the coalition agreement, rather than being restricted by the demands of the party's electoral policy. In the Netherlands, the process of negotiating the conditions of the coalitions is time-consuming. On one occasion, it took 208 days and nine attempts; the average is 67 days (Andeweg, 1988: 59). It will determine not only what is done but who holds particular portfolios. Once so complex an agreement has been made, it will not be lightly discarded; not only has the programme become more extensive and detailed, it is adhered to more strictly (Andeweg, 1988: 58). Parliamentary leaders may be influential in the formation period because their continuing support is required (Vis, 1983: 150). Consequently, Dutch cabinets have greater stability of personnel and direction because of the need to maintain the conditions of the coalition:

> Under the conditions of multi-party cabinets there is a relentless need to maintain accords at both governmental and parliamentary levels. This results in a continuous imperative towards collaboration between ministers and their parliamentary parties, between ministers and their cabinet colleagues and between the *fracties* in parliament which are expected to sustain the coalition (Gladdish, 1990: 111).

Prior to 1965, coalitions could rise and fall within the Dutch parliament as circumstances changed. Since then the collapse of a government has led to elections because of the view that the 'forthcoming change of partners had to be legitimised by popular vote' (Vis, 1983: 156).

In Germany, the calculation is simpler, with the small Free Democrats holding the balance of power between the two major parties. Unless there is a grand coalition, as in 1966–69, the Free Democrats decide who forms the government. They have twice used their numbers to make and unmake governments, and have managed to ensure that large parts of their programme are implemented. Agreements may be detailed, running to 700 pages. In 1980, it took 60 hours of negotiation to reach agreement. Indeed the electoral promises of the Free Democrats have been seen as the best predictor of German government policies (Hofferbert and Klingemann, 1990). The coalition agreements also identify the ministries to be held by the coalition partners and thus determine a degree of stability for the government. Coalitions may lead to swings between policy immobilism and overproduction (Schmidt, 1983: 51).

Coalitions require extensive discussions that will incorporate not only the executive leadership, but also the extra-parliamentary parties and the party leadership in parliament. Informal coalition talks *(Koalitions-gesprache)* may involve representatives of the Chancellor's Office, relevant ministries and the parliamentary group's leaders, and the last will carry considerable weight (Saalfeld, 1990: 72). Political parties are therefore involved in determining coalition policy and often personnel. Much less is left in the hands of the individual leader.

The dynamics are essentially different. In the single-party government, negotiations are internal. Discipline provides support for the party in government. Certainly negotiations, consultation and duchessing (that evocative Australian term to describe the way leaders ply supporters with perks and drinks to make them comfortable) are required, but the supporters know that their party future is bound up with the success of the party leadership, doubling as the ministerial key participants of the core executive. Only rarely — as with the *Bloc Quebeçois* — does a fraction of a governing party desert the government. In effect, the internal nature of the negotiations allows the cabinet considerable freedom in the development of policy. Initiatives come from the cabinet, who can rely on loyalty, negotiation and self-interest to provide support for the most blatant of U-turns.

By contrast, coalition governments require negotiations between parties. Compacts, once settled, need to be maintained. At the same time, parties need to preserve some form of individual identity for the next election. If cabinet chooses to change direction, it may lose the support of a parliamentary *fractie*. The process is more public, more transparent. The wishes of any individual party may never be fully satisfied — although when the Kohl-led Christian Democratic Union was dominant within the German coalition, its position was particularly powerful. Nevertheless parties as the negotiating bodies may influence more directly the government programme and thus constrain the activity of the core executive.

A second factor is the different effects of *unitary and federal structures*. Unitary states have comparatively fewer veto points, and fewer alternative sources of power. In the Netherlands and Britain, national government clearly has extensive authority over the machinery of central government and those services not delivered by semi-autonomous quangos. Other levels (municipal, provincial or county) hold a subordinate and dependent relationship; the national governments have overriding authority, even if the picture of united purpose is an overstatement (Rhodes, 1996).

In federal systems, the dispersal of authority, and the strength of provincial/state/*Länder* governments, requires the national government to negotiate outcomes in many policy areas. Even the presence in government of a leader from the same party does not guarantee easier cooperation. Provincial politics live by different dynamics. In Canada, federal and provincial parties tend to have totally separate organizations. In Germany, the route to the party leadership is more likely to come through experienced provincial government than through federal ministerial office. The premiers of *Länder* therefore have career and territorial incentives that are different from those of the Chancellor. Besides, as the *Länder* are directly represented in the *Bundesrat*, the support of leading *Länder* ministers is required to pass legislation. This party 'polycentrism', based on territorial dispersion, often muffles ideological differences (Smith, G., 1991: 51).

In Australia, the parties are federal and compartmentalized in character; the national entity is made up of the six state and two territorial branches which are interested in success at state level. Whereas there is a trend to give greater authority to the national branches of the party, state premiers from the same party as the prime minister are by no means subservient to the national leader.

The consequence is that the concept of party government becomes more complex in a federation because the party may govern at different levels in different interests. Where the national government does not have extensive authority, negotiation is essential *between* party notables. Federation fractures party unity and cohesion as readily as government power.

Federalism has a further impact that shifts power away from any single level of government. Federal governments must negotiate with the states/provinces/*Länder* on a government to government basis. Executive federalism bypasses normal party channels. The *Bundesrat* in Germany may act as the vehicle for *Länder* interests; its support — and hence the support directly of *Länder* governments — is needed for legislation. In Canada and Australia, the regular meetings of prime ministers and state or provincial premiers (known in Australia as the Council of Australian Governments) may determine policy directions that require cooperation in a forum far distant from the interests of supporting parties which will become directly concerned only where legislation is required.

But what do the parties essentially stand for and what scope or freedom does this give to the executive? Parties of course are concerned to aggregate votes and represent people in parliament. The more precise and identifiable the constituency, the more the parties may have to respect their interests.

At one end of any spectrum are the catch-all parties of Canada; they may have regional strengths, but the governing parties have usually drawn support from all provinces (with the exception of the weakness of the Trudeau government in western provinces after 1979). The parties have few clear ideological differences and with a few shifting points of dispute, like the North American Freetrade Agreement, Canadian politics is often concerned with the delivery of services to the members' regions (Bakvis, 1991). The principal German parties are also described as *'Volksparteien'* (Smith, G., 1991: 49), but they depend on party identification and a broad appeal, particularly after unification. They have divisions on socio-economic and regional lines that lead to internal conflicts that must be managed (Saalfield, 1990: 75).

Class parties — in Britain and Australia — may have become more blurred at the edges, but nevertheless their support can be broadly classified in social and economic terms. 'Safe' constituencies, always held by one party or the other, constitute well over half the parliament (compared to virtually none in Canada). Professional politicians can develop long careers. But class need not define policies. The Hawke and Keating Labor governments in Australia have pursued policies that were often at odds with party traditions; deregulation and privatization were strongly rejected while the party was in opposition. Since the parties have platforms that provide a *smorgasbord* of promises, they are not rigidly beholden to particular constituencies, but rather have to maintain a balance across all interests.

Even though pillarization[1] in the Netherlands has declined as a direct force in elections, its legacy ties the parliamentary party to a much more distinct group. The support is continuing and constant and it reflects divisions in society. The expectations of tying performance to sectional needs became more clear, and this position is represented in the careful negotiations that precede the formation of Dutch coalitions. Precise policy initiatives are often incorporated in the agreement. Ministerial portfolios are negotiated on the basis of particular party interests. Commitments are more public and specific. The room for manoeuvre, while not entirely constrained, is lessened.

Policy Development

Who makes policies and to what extent are they regarded as sacrosanct? The attitude of parties to policy differs between single-party and coalition governments. In the former, policy is largely determined by the cabinet — or even the leader alone; in the latter the party may have a separate involvement in policy development.

In Canada, Britain and Australia, all but the Labor[2] parties regard the detailed policies as primarily the prerogative of the cabinet and the electoral platform as the responsibility of the leader. The extra-parliamentary parties are concerned with party organization and finance. In Canada, with the election of leaders by a broad convention, the extra-parliamentary parties are often dominated by the machine created by the successful leader. The British Conservative party and Australian Liberal party will hold regular conventions where policy is discussed. But any resolutions are essentially advisory, often presenting views that appear more extreme than those of the political centre to which a government must appeal. Leaders, whether prime minister or leader of the opposition, determine the policy. It may be carefully cleared with the parliamentary party in opposition to ensure support, or discussed with leading ministers in government. But those consultations are options, not requirements. Every policy speech will include its share of surprises that no one outside the inner circle knows.

In government, policy is the responsibility of cabinet. Since ministers must be members of the parliamentary party, there is an expectation that the latter will support cabinet policy. In Australia and Canada that discipline is almost always maintained. Politics is adversarial; criticism is kept within the party. In Britain, the Conservative backbenchers have a longer history of revolts, particularly with the Eurosceptics in recent years. The larger size of the House of Commons provides a wider range of dissidents who may be prepared to criticize the government. As yet they have not brought the government down. John Major's difficulties — and his decision to put his leadership to a ballot — were caused by his inability to maintain cohesion over Europe in a fragmenting party with an overall majority of one.

But the parliamentary parties are essentially reactive. They may criticize and berate. They do not initiate or introduce legislation (apart from the symbolic private members' bills in Britain which still require government approval to proceed). Committee hearings may bring amendments, but they are parliamentary, not party, forums. In Australia and Canada, legislation may be cleared with the parliamentary party that meets weekly in session and includes all ministers and backbenchers. Within the Canadian parties are further regional and provincial caucuses; the Quebec caucus has been particularly influential. Occasionally legislation may be changed in response to party criticism. The British Conservatives have no equivalent opportunity. Parties depend for survival on the success of the government.

Labour parties in Britain and Australia claim to have greater input into party policy. In Britain, party policy is regarded as significant but not binding. Labour prime ministers have been quick to distance themselves from any notion that governments should be limited by party policy if broader interests required different directions. In Australia, cabinets are supposed to be bound by party policy as decided by the national conference of the Labor party. For many years the belief was, at least publicly, accepted. The wartime prime minister actually convened a special national conference of the party to gain the approval of the party to a government proposal to introduce a limited degree of conscription for overseas service.

But, while the symbolic policy supremacy of the party conference has been maintained, the initiative has passed to the parliamentary party, whose members had the time and facilities to develop policy. In the late 1960s and 1970s the change was largely the consequence of the strategy of the party leader Gough Whitlam, who developed policy and then embedded it in the official platform as a means of later binding a cabinet to his proposals. When Whitlam demanded that the party platform be sacrosanct, it was because that platform was largely his initiative. In the 1980s, cabinet became ever less concerned with the formal lines of authority. Conferences of the Labor party in office were primarily symbolic, often bringing party policy into line with government action. For instance, Labor policy forbade the export of uranium to France, because of its practice of nuclear testing in the South Pacific. The government announced its decision to export uranium first, and asked the party to change its official policy later.

In essence the position is substantially the same in all Westminster-derived parties. When governments and parliaments are integrated with ministers required to be members of parliament, authority over policy is ceded to cabinet. There is little capacity for policy input or initiative, and only limited means of altering policy within some party meetings. Policy belongs less to parties than to the governments whom parties support.

The very pace of government makes this situation inevitable. Crises in economics require constant attention. Prime ministers commit their nations in foreign dealings. Detailed or innovative policy may be developed in conjunction with the experts and the committed in the policy community and presented to parliament essentially as a *fait accompli*. Cabinets and core executives initiate, sometimes within accepted limits of party policy, sometimes outside.

Indeed the decline of ideological divisions between parties reduces the direct link between parties and obvious policy solutions. As Labor parties have rejected nationalization, public ownership and high levels of public expenditure, so policies have tended to become managerial and 'economically rational'. Privatization and deregulation are no longer exclusively policies of the right. Social justice as an objective can be reached by a variety of policies. If it is no longer possible to move logically from ideology to policy solution, the policies are more obviously a matter of choice for cabinets, freed from the shackles of symbolic party doctrine.

The contrast with coalition governments is marked. In Germany changes of coalition have been rare, but as long as the Free Democrats are able to provide the crucial votes in the *Bundestag*, some negotiated policies are required. At election time the coalition may require a detailed coalition agreement, even though times and policy change. The rapidly evolving circumstances, most obvious in circumstances such as German unification, which could not have been predicted, the Chancellor has the ability — and indeed the constitutional responsibility — to set the general policy directions, the *Richtlinienkompetenz*. There are few official constraints. The parliamentary party is a separate organization, with its own elected leader, but it responds to the initiatives of the Chancellor and his ministers. Nevertheless conflicts may need to be settled beforehand. The *Bundestag* is reactive; 'its power depends on the constraints it is capable of placing on the policy-related activities of the executive, rather its independent policy-making capacity' (Saalfield, 1990: 69).

In the Netherlands, party involvement in determining policy at the formation of a government is greater. The parliamentary groups have a greater role in establishing the government. Because the selected policies are a key point of the coalition negotiations, and because the parliamentary *fractie* have an existence that is independent of the ministers, their impact on policy may be more significant. The distribution of portfolios is part of the coalition deal, with parties taking the ministries in which they have the greatest interests. Ministers have much greater independence to act and therefore the implementation of the accepted policy becomes a much greater responsibility. But the involvement of the leaders of the *fractie* is essential. Ministers from each party often hold a dinner the night before cabinet meetings; the parliamentary leader of its government party, and sometimes the party chairperson, may attend to discuss business coming to cabinet (Andeweg, 1988: 62). Further, the parliamentary parties have withdrawn support when they were dissatisfied with policy — thus bringing down the government and forcing an election. Their policy support cannot be taken for granted, even if it is asserted within the constraints of a coalition agreement.

The Answerability of the Core Executive to Parties

The picture of cabinets and ministers operating in comparative freedom from detailed constraint may suggest limited party influence. But that poses a different question. If parties are unlikely to influence policy, can they make the core executive answerable for the general standard and success of government? It is quite feasible, as the problems of government become more complex, that a declining capacity to monitor detail is coupled with an increasing awareness of the need to protect the standing of the government in the polls and hence to make leaders directly answerable to the party. That answerability may be applied directly through internal party procedures (in the selection and removal of prime ministers and ministers) or indirectly through the increasing influence of parliament. Leaders become prime ministers only after they have reached the top of their party. Ministers need their parties to win a majority before they can take office. But what sense of obligation is created by this link? And how is that obligation asserted?

The question can be put in the opposite way. If parties are unhappy with the performance of leaders, can they remove or replace them *while* they are prime minister or chancellor? If they can, then there is clearly a line of answerability that makes leaders respond to demands or sensitive to changes of mood.

Some prime ministers are vulnerable to internal revolt. In Australia, prime ministers are elected by a vote of the parliamentary party. They can be removed by the same group — at any time. All it requires is a meeting of the party. Usually the meeting will be held for that purpose, but a vote 'spilling' (declaring vacant) all the leadership positions can in theory be moved without notice. Two prime ministers have been removed by their parties (in 1969 and 1991); another was unsuccessfully challenged after being pushed to a vote (1981). But the frequency of the challenges is not an adequate indicator of the impact of the procedure; leaders are always under scrutiny, always liable to have their performance tested with the knowledge that if they are seen to be weak their position will be challenged. The consequence is a constant need to deliver electoral victory, or at least the perception that the next poll is winnable. The implications are ·immense, for when the leadership of a government is in doubt (usually reflected by a poor performance in the polls), every policy issue becomes judged in terms of leadership. This perception can lead to sudden lurches, as prime ministers seek to satisfy the only constituents who matter — the parliamentary party.

A similar situation developed in the British Conservative party. The 1973 rules, allowing the removal of a Leader of the Opposition, were activated in 1990 to defeat Thatcher. The rules are more restrictive than in Australia. A Conservative prime minister is only required to stand for re-election at the beginning of each parliamentary session and there is no vote unless there is a second candidate, which is rare. But when a prime minister's standing is low, there is the possibility of a nominal challenge by a backbencher to test the level of disapproval. If enough dissent is illustrated, more serious candidates may enter the field, either in a second ballot or a year later.

Initially, the Thatcher defeat was regarded as a fluke; an event caused by a conjunction of circumstances that would not be repeated. That position no longer seems tenable. Rather, it created a precedent that will be followed if the party regards any leader as likely to lose. The undermining of Major, leading to his decision to put his leadership on the line, was caused by the knowledge that a formal opportunity to remove him was due in a few months. Regardless of whether supporters agree with the policy, they will be driven by electoral expediency, by the need to survive (Weller, 1983, 1994).

In Britain and Australia, a limited constituency allows action against prime ministers. Where the constituency is broader, action is probably impossible. Canadian prime ministers become party leaders by election at a national convention of their party; a Liberal prime minister notionally had to face a vote on whether to hold a leadership convention — not a vote on the leadership itself. Presumably a decision to hold a convention would require a period of campaigning in which the prime minister would use all the available powers of patronage to bolster the incumbent's position. It is almost inconceivable that a party would try to depose a prime minister by such a process of attrition. Rather persuasion is the only weapon — and in effect prime ministers have gone at the time of their own choosing — often rather too late for their parties. The successors to long-serving prime ministers Trudeau and Mulroney were both defeated a few months after their succession.

In Germany, a national election for the Chancellor gives the incumbent credibility and standing based on electoral victory. The choice of candidate may be that of the party, confirmed by the *Bundestag* after the election; the endorsement from the people provides an independence from internal party pressures. But leaders can still be removed, even if with difficulty. Erhard was forced out by internal opposition, while the parliamentary group leader 'seems to have acted very brutally when ousting Brandt' (Von Beyme, 1983: 33). To an extent it may depend on whether, like Kohl, the Chancellor is successfully head of the party as well as of government, and can thus control the party machinery and influence the selection of candidates. Indeed the German leadership has been stable with only three chancellors in the last 25 years. The *Bundestag* can only remove a government with a 'constructive vote of no confidence' that nominates an alternative candidate. Internal revolt is less easy. As the party did not elect them, there is no easy means of removing them, so there is less pressure from the party and transient unpopularity may be less fatal.

The Dutch prime minister's relations with the party are likely to be affected by the nature of the painfully and slowly negotiated coalition agreements. The partners to the deal accept the leadership of a particular person. The direct reliance on party support thus becomes one step removed. To remove the leader would bring down the coalition. In practice, the splits between leaders and parliamentary party have occurred between junior partners, such as the VVD in 1989. But the effect is the same. If a party leader is repudiated, the coalition collapses and an election ensues.

Limited dependence may not mean limited contact. The need to consult, discuss and persuade the party to adopt legislation still exists; cooperation is always necessary. Besides, leaders have other options. They may bypass the parliamentary parties by appealing directly to the electorate, developing an image and standing that bolsters their position within the party (Foley, 1993). They may be regarded as embodying the party's *Zeitgeist*. But even so, as both Hawke and Thatcher (winners of four and three elections respectively) discovered, public support may not always be translated into parliamentary loyalty. Leaders are always conscious of the capacity to withdraw consent; it is a significant calculation for leaders and led that will shape how both act.

So it is for ministers. Their party debts are likely to create the need to modify their behaviour in the light of internal demands. Career politicians, for whom the ministry is the ambition, will be conscious of those whose support was necessary for promotion. In an Australian Labor government, ministers are *elected* by the parliamentary party. The prime minister is often influential, but the three well-organized factions will decide precisely who is promoted, and whose time is up. Over five election victories, from 1983 to 1994, only two ministers have served cabinet continuously. The factions select, the factions dismiss. Factional links are essential for almost all ministers. And the parliamentary party is the only route to the ministry. Although in one or two cases people have entered the ministry immediately they enter parliament, rapid promotion is rare. However, all ministers are likely to have a history of party involvement prior to their election to parliament and thus some commitment to the party as an organization. Party identification — rather than particular expertise — has brought them to the ministry.

In the British parliament, the prime ministers select their ministers, but primarily from those who already have developed a reputation in the House of Commons. Politics again is seen as a career within a political party. In Canada, there is the possibility of recruiting notables with little party background and providing them with a riding (constituency) from which they can be immediately given ministries. Ministers too are required to represent geographical areas and provinces; thus there is a need for a balance in the composition of a ministry. Given the volatility of the Canadian system, it is not surprising that many ministers — or even prime ministers — have little parliamentary or ministerial experience; and that their commitment to their party may be less than complete (Sutherland, 1991).

How much independence do they have? Even though the cabinet process may in places become more extensive, departmental business will often be maintained almost in independence of party scrutiny, particularly by those powerful ministers so colourfully described by Anthony King as 'the big beasts of the jungle' (1994: 219) who develop considerable autonomy.

Even so, the requirement to be elected to parliament (nominated senators excepted) remains in Canada. By contrast, the legislatures in the Netherlands or Germany are not necessarily seen either as a career or as a stepping stone to the ministry. Dutch ministers are selected through seniority in party lists and the process of coalition negotiation; they do not sit in parliament and may not have any parliamentary experience — indeed, half of them do not. In 1989 five out of eighteen cabinet ministers and in 1994 seven (or 50 per cent) still had no parliamentary experience, even though it can be argued there is a 'gradual but irreversible colonisation of the government by the political parties' (Andeweg, 1988: 63). There has always been some distinction between those selected for their expertise and those who have administrative/political experience, even if the balance is now tipping towards the latter. The more technical the expertise and the less commitment to the party, the less party influence for partisan purposes there is likely to be.

German ministers are often drawn from the *Länder* where their executive experience is already proven or they may be selected for technical expertise (Müller-Rommel, 1988: 156). This capacity to be independent of the parliamentary party means that there are lfewer debts or obligations, and perhaps less of a personal commitment to the party rather than the portfolio. It means less dependence on the continued support of the party.

What concessions do governments need to make to their parliamentary parties? There is clearly a contrast between parties dominated by and integrated with the executive, where cabinet ministers are legislators and where there is a tight link between ministry and supporters, and the parliamentary parties that are separate from the government. In the former adversarial chambers, to adapt Polsby's distinctions (cited in Andeweg and Irwin, 1993), parliament is an arena in which politics is fought out; in the latter there is a greater chance that it may have some institutional impact on policy outcomes.

This is not to deny that *all* parliamentary parties have the potential to discipline governments or to force concessions on them. But the internal structures of integrated parliamentary parties have meant that no government has been brought down in the last 50 years by internal revolt. In Britain, when the Callaghan government did not have a majority, discipline within the party declined and the government was defeated several times on legislation by defecting backbenchers — but the backbench never defeated the government on a vote of confidence or on an issue which the government declared to be an issue of confidence. Indeed a distinction was made between minor defeats and issues of confidence in order to prevent the need for resignation that constitutional theory had previously seemed to demand when a government lost control of the Commons. The Eurosceptics have brought the Major government to the brink and had the whip withdrawn, but have not destroyed it. In Australia and Canada, discipline remains much tighter, with party endorsement likely to be at stake if individuals pursue constant revolts.

But public discipline should not be taken to mean automatic private obedience. The role of the weekly meeting of the parliamentary parties allows backbenchers to discuss policy with ministers and to question them on policy intentions. Legislation may be debated by party committees, and will have to be approved before the full party or even cabinet gives it a final stamp of authority. Criticism of government policy may be internal, but can be strident. In the Australian Labor government, the faction leaders may combine to settle issues and force a compromise that meets some of the demands. Canadian caucuses may seem less influential, but they play a significant role because of the regularity of their meetings. Regional influences and interests are voiced loudly. Prime ministers and ministers will take their parties seriously. External discipline may mean internal voice, particularly where the size of parliament and hence the party majorities are small.

In Britain, the parliamentary party meets rarely, if ever; in the Conservative party, there is no mechanism for the backbenchers to meet the ministry on an even footing. The 1922 Committee provides an opportunity for backbench views to be expressed and ministers may appear by invitation to answer questions, but the whole cabinet never does. Other mechanisms are available; early day motions are signed as expressions of opinion; the whips maintain contact with members and backbench opposition is duly noted, even if in the last resort there may be demands for loyalty. Backbenchers are more inclined to buck the whips, for there is greater scope for maverick behaviour. British parties in government have more often faced revolts on the floor of the Chamber, even losing legislation at times. The parliamentary parties need to be managed, not merely regimented. But internal dissidence has not yet brought down a government.

Yet in all Westminster systems, parliamentary discipline provides an opportunity for the cabinet to present and sell its policies; it is a transmission belt along which the cabinet's initiatives pass, with guaranteed support, from the internal procedures of the cabinet to the public area. By the judicious use of parliamentary and media opportunities, and supported by a publicly loyal majority, parliament provides a means to press home an advantage, even where there are internal divisions.

In Germany and Holland, the parliamentary parties are separate organizations, with their own leaders. While this division of responsibilities will always require negotiation with the party, it may not mean that the government is in danger. The parties in the *Bundestag* have not threatened the existence of their own government; indeed they have generally been subservient to government policy. On occasion there have been organized defections to allow a vote of no confidence to be passed, in order to create the conditions for calling an election (Mény, 1993: 218–19). But that is not indicative of frequent unrest. There is an 'internal pluralism' in the parties that takes account of socioeconomic and regional differences in the parliamentary parties; the existence of these factions usually necessitates bargaining and serves to prevent 'a total domination of intra-party decision-making by the cabinet' (Saalfeld, 1990: 76). Working groups can exert influence on the shape of policies and a high degree of voting cohesion is achieved only after extensive intra-party negotiations. But the 'atmosphere of a working parliament is not conducive to active revolt' (Smith, G., 1991: 52). Coalition pressures assist, as MPs are conscious of the need to maintain the arrangements that keep them in power. Smith notes: 'Were it not for the necessity to govern through coalition — and the desire not to weaken the Chancellor's authority — then one might expect the Chancellor to have far greater difficulty in keeping his parliamentary party in order' (Smith, G., 1991: 52). Steering the coalition relies on its parliamentary leadership and informal talks (Saalfield, 1990: 69).

Difficulties are greater in the Netherlands. Precisely because the coalition governments there consist of two or more parties, the need to satisfy the caucuses may become far more complex, since the links are between coalition parties and between each of those governing groups and their parliamentary caucus. It is possible the caucus may feel that its interests are inadequately considered by its selected ministers. In 1966 the parliamentary *fractie* withdrew support and forced a period of renegotiation and then an election. In the face of increased parliamentary activity, such a reaction from a junior coalition partner may not be entirely surprising. It occurred again in 1989, when an election was caused by the defection of the VVD *fractie*. The CDA leader, Lubbers, was returned as prime minister, but in coalition with PvdA, rather than the VVD (Wolinetz, 1990). By 1994 it was the VVD and PvdA in coalition.[3]

Further, the separation of cabinet and parliament means that the States-General is less overtly dominated by the executive than elsewhere. The parliamentary *fractie* have their own elected leaders and cohesion depends on group pressure rather than on party whips. Although governments seek to have their legislation accepted, they are often prepared, or required, to make amendments to allow their proposals to pass. The bridge between executive and parliament is provided by the presidium. As Gladdish has noted:

> The key point here is that the cabinet governs, to a greater extent than in other systems, with the consent of the parliamentary groups. As a leading commentator has put it, 'because the key to cabinet stability is in the hands of . . . the parliamentary parties, the Netherlands has become an exceptional case of 'rule by parliament' (Gladdish, 1990: 109–10).

Precedents encourage activity; the Dutch government can certainly not take its parliamentary support for granted — it never did.

If the parliaments will maintain governments without any great threat, what of their capacity to scrutinize? Here there is no doubt that activity is increasing. Parliamentary committees have seen a renaissance in Australia in the last 20 years, primarily as a consequence of the inability of the government to win a majority in the Senate, which is elected by proportional representation. As a House with equal powers, it has the ability to reject any legislation in practice, and fundamental pieces of legislation, including the 1993 budget and the legislation recognizing native title, have to be negotiated through the Chamber, and concessions must be made.

The once quiescent Dutch parliament is now more active. The Dutch parliament saw a massive growth in activity and scrutiny, with many of the scrutiny procedures used far more frequently. The legislation does not need to be defeated on the floor; opposition from within parliament is often enough. But the statistics make the point. The number of questions to ministers doubled between 1971 and 1981; as did the proposed amendments to bills and the budget (Gladdish, 1990: 114). Even if activity declined again since the early 1980s, parliament is certainly more probing than it was 30 years ago.

The German parliament too is more influential on the detail than on the principles. Its committees carefully consider legislation, but are unlikely to dismiss it in general. The *Bundestag* committee system is non-partisan in its approach, while the government's willingness to make concessions means that about 60 per cent of bills are amended by committees. But the consent of the government is needed.

> The chamber's ability to scrutinise and influence the government largely depends on the permeability of decision-making within the majority parties and the extent to which minority rights exist and enable the opposition to fulfil its function of criticism and presentation of alternatives (Saalfeld, 1990: 82).

Since 1972 the *Bundestag* has moved closer to the 'competitive adversarial model' (Saalfield, 1990: 81). But does greater activity mean greater influence? Andeweg and Irwin (1993: 151) suggest that the dogs may be barking more because it is the only activity allowed. Public activity may hide a declining private influence.

Party, Policy and the Core Executive

In summary then, what constraints are imposed on the core executives by party and what opportunities are provided? The point must be made that any comparative advantages or disadvantages must be relative. All systems are parliamentary, with well-disciplined parties. None have the fragmentation of the USA, nor the volatility of Italian politics. Stability is the norm. Comparative findings must be understood within that framework.

Second, party remains all-pervasive. In a recent volume, Laver and Shepsle sought to identify the impact that the allocation of ministerial portfolios had on policy. They predicated their approach on departmental autonomy, and eventually concluded, after a number of independent specialists had applied their concepts across a range of countries, that

> the real reason cabinet ministers are not as autonomous as we have alleged is that they are heavily constrained by party politics . . . What the portfolio-allocation approach has hitherto not emphasised enough, therefore, is that cabinet ministers are for the most part also members of political parties, subject to party discipline if they wish to retain their positions after the next election (1994b: 308).

They suggest a need to 'concentrate upon the role of cabinet ministers, acting as agents of their party, in the departmental processes of policy formulation and implementation' (1994b: 308). The departmental perspective will direct attention away from party to policy communities, to the interests with which ministers must negotiate policy. Ministers may have restricted autonomy there too, but the policy community will provide a counterweight to party input because it brings direct interest and expertise to the policy analysis. Detailed policy development cannot often be guided by broad party commitments.

Such a statement may have been a useful corrective to all too easy assumptions of ministerial autonomy. Party, particularly when the consequences of elections are considered, remains the basis that ties ministers to governments. But party shapes the general rather than the particular. Yet within that framework what is the distinction between parties? There is a clear contrast between the countries with single-member

electorates, majority governments (usually) and integrated executives/
legislatives and those with coalition governments and separate legislatives.

In the former, the party depends on the cabinet or the leader to
determine policy, within the broadly defined limits of what the party
believes it stands for. The parties — or more precisely the parliamentary
parties — may advise, warn and be consulted, but they seldom initiate. The
leadership has internal constituencies to satisfy; but as long as the leader
retains support in the party and the polls, that allows scope for policy
innovation, or indeed U-turns. Internal party discipline will usually deliver
the necessary support, for all are conscious that only through the party can
an ambitious politician rise to the ministry. The party is gatekeeper to
office.

In coalition governments, the process of forming — or maintaining — a
coalition requires greater party involvement in policy debate. Because
policy is negotiated *between* parties, the process is more open and explicit,
with written agreements defining what governments stand for, and who gets
what position. Where the parliamentary and national leadership is in
different hands there is a need for continual negotiation and consent.
Because more than one party is involved, calculations broader than its
electoral fortunes will need to be taken into account. There is consequently
less emphasis on policy innovation than upon consensus and accommodation (Gladdish, 1983: 170). Ministers, some of whom have no parliamentary experience, have different agenda as their futures are not based on
their standing in the parliamentary parties. The closer links between
coalition governments and an extensive input to party policy are a
consequence. But there is another agenda: that of answerability.

In coalition governments the arrangements may be so tight that
governments stand or fall on their maintenance. If a cabinet group defects,
or if the parliamentary *fractie* votes against its ministers, the government
falls. The coalition must be renewed — usually after an election. Of course
this potential vulnerability may also discourage the *fracties* from forcing an
election where they will do badly. Coalitions may provide cautious
government and thus assist the cabinet. Accountability may be tightly
related to specific policy outcomes. Where the party has a means to hold
the leadership accountable, it is possible to renew the government without
the recourse to an election. The falls of Thatcher and Hawke both allowed
their successors to win the next election by presenting a 'new' government
without a change of party. Whether *neither* occur (as in Canada), the
leadership may become particularly alienated from broader feelings in the
community, yet survive.

The distinction is between a capacity to constrain on the *detail* of policy
— more marked in coalition governments — and the capacity to make
leaders answerable for the *general performance* of governments, that is

increasingly occurring in some parliamentary systems. In the former, policy may be coherent, or at least consistent, because much of it was declared in the coalition agreement and because it must always be negotiated by the coalition partners. In the latter, policy may swing more dramatically as the cabinet, answerable *in the last resort* to an otherwise pliant supporting majority, seeks to maintain its status. In the former, parliament may negotiate the detail, in the latter the process is more adversarial.

Federalism will further mute the party capacity to direct, because the policy agenda is contested in a number of arenas and the same parties at different levels will still often have contradictory agenda. The greater the number of veto points, the less the direct influence of parties.

In assessing party impact, Blondel noted that single-party governments, such as those in the UK, made parties dependent on government, while in the European coalition governments, governments were dependent on parties. Cansino (1995: 172) suggests that coalition governments indicate a high degree of party penetration in government and high degrees of party influence, while single-party 'fusion' situations reflect a high degree of penetration, but a low degree of influence of parties on government.

This chapter suggests that these calculations are too simple, because in each case other dynamics may be at force. Certainly the Canadian parliamentary or electoral parties have the least influence on policy because of the limited sanctions available but they survive in an established tradition of governmental patronage and provincial pork barrel, rather than in any clear ideology. In Britain and Australia, detailed policy input from the party may have declined, particularly in governments of long standing, but the parties have gained the ability to use the sanction of dismissal against leaders without necessarily leading to the immediate loss of office for the party. In European coalition governments, the more binding coalition agreements provide parties with an initial detailed input. They clearly restrain the freedom of action of core executives to a greater extent.

Notes

1. Pillarization (*verzuiling*) involves the identification of subcultures in Dutch society which are highly segmented. Lijphart (1971) identified a range of criteria which measured pillarization, including ideology or religion, the density of the organizational network, cohesiveness of the network, a degree of social apartheid and the encouragement of pillarized behaviour by the subcultural elite. See Andeweg and Irwin (1993: 28–32).
2. The Australian *Labor* Party and the British *Labour* Party spell their titles differently. The British spelling has been used where both are being discussed.
3. The VVD is the neo-liberal party, the PvdA the Labour party and the CDA is the centrist Christian party that combined earlier Catholic and Protestant parties.

4 Collegiality and Collectivity: Cabinets, Cabinet Committees, and Cabinet Ministers

Rudy Andeweg

As cabinet government is sometimes depicted as the answer to the quest for coherence and control, as a 'government against sub-governments' (Rose, 1980b), it is deplorable that it is such an ill-defined topic. The problem does not seem to be that scholars and practitioners of cabinet government have put forth conflicting or widely diverging definitions of the concept, but rather that we lack a definition of cabinet government that is both reasonably precise and suitable for comparisons across political systems.

In his search for a definition of the related concept of 'executives', King (1975: 174–5) explored three perspectives: '. . . one in terms of the functions of the various institutions, another in terms of their operating procedures, a third in what one might call (inelegantly) their "historical/ normative" development'. For cabinet government, this last approach is dominated by Bagehot's famous definition of cabinet as 'a combining committee — a hyphen which joins, a buckle which fastens, the legislative part of the State to the executive part of the State' (Bagehot, 1965: 68). In this structural approach to a definition, cabinet is the most senior effective committee of politicians, directing the governmental apparatus and responsible to parliament. In practice, however, it is difficult to delineate this committee of politicians, as there are often several tiers of committees of which the members meet the three criteria of being politicians, being in charge of (parts of) the civil service and being accountable to parliament. The first 'twilight zone' consists of junior ministers (Johnson, 1983: 77). We may perhaps exclude them on the grounds that their position *vis-à-vis* both the civil service and parliament is a derivative of the position of other, more senior, politicians to whom they are subordinate. They belong to the government or the ministry, but not to the cabinet, and in Australia (Weller, 1991a: 140) and Canada (Theakston, 1987: 168) this is symbolized by slightly more relaxed rules of collective responsibility for junior ministers. It is more difficult to find the definitional criteria for the distinction between cabinet ministers and other senior ministers whose access to cabinet is limited to discussions affecting their own portfolio, but who are not subordinate to another politician within that portfolio. This was the case in Australia until 1987, and still is the case in the UK. A further problem is presented by the phenomenon of 'inner cabinets'. These may be an expression of a certain hierarchy within the cabinet, but in certain cases they may also have come to replace it, relegating the nominal cabinet to the status of ministry. Such a development seems to have occurred in Canada under Trudeau, Clark, and Mulroney (1969–93), but the borderline between an inner cabinet within the cabinet and an inner cabinet as the *de facto* cabinet is not clearly demarcated. So, the structural approach to a definition of cabinet government leaves us with grey areas and fuzzy borders.

In the functional approach to a definition, cabinet government is defined in terms of what it is supposed to accomplish. The function that is most often mentioned in this respect is that of coordination: 'We define the core executive functionally to include all those organizations and structures which primarily serve to pull together and integrate central government policies, or act as final arbiters within the executive of conflicts between different elements of the government machine' (Dunleavy and Rhodes, 1990: 4; Rhodes, 1995: 12). It is not self-evident, however, why coordination should be the defining function of cabinet government, rather than functions such as the provision of democratic legitimation to government, or the creation of a channel for political accountability, or simply decision making: the 'authoritative allocation of values'. And even if we accept the subjective choice of 'coordination', it is not clear what is and what is not to be included in that term. We may assume that coordination results in a low proportion of unresolved conflicts within the government, but so does 'negative coordination' — an extreme form of division of labour whereby ministers and officials scrupulously avoid trespassing on their colleagues' policy territories — or 'log-rolling' — the combination of unrelated policies into a single package deal. It is also not clear whose policies are to be coordinated: those of the various government departments and agencies, as is implied by most of the literature, or also those of the various factions or political parties making up the government? The functional approach to a definition appears to be no more successful in dispelling the fog around the edges of the concept of cabinet government.

A procedural approach to a definition is suggested by Weller (1991b): cabinet government is a '*principle* of government and barely an institution at all', in the words of Seymour-Ure (1971: 196). It is 'due process', a set of procedures for arriving at binding governmental decisions. As Weller recognizes, however, the value of this approach is limited by the fact that procedures, while not completely arbitrary, are always contingent. Furthermore, not only does the content of the procedures vary widely from one political system to the other, so does their stability. Despite the growing bureaucratization of cabinet government everywhere, the procedures seem much more institutionalized in Germany and the Netherlands, than in Australia before the 1987 reforms, or in Canada, where they can change substantially with the coming to power of a new government.

The underdefined nature of the cabinet has led some scholars to prefer other concepts: the 'cabinet system' (Burch and Holliday, 1995), the 'core executive' (Rhodes and Dunleavy, 1995), or the 'central executive territory' (Madgwick, 1991). In doing so these authors seek to incorporate the grey areas surrounding the concept of cabinet government. This may prove useful, but it does not provide more precise definitions. The structural, functional and procedural approaches highlight different aspects of the concept: the who, what and how of cabinet government. The core of the concept is to be found at the crossroads of these three approaches, but its boundaries remain vague. It is not a satisfactory answer to the question 'what is cabinet government?', but it will have to suffice; the variety of cabinet practizes across countries precludes more precise definitions.

Two Dimensions of Cabinet Government

Interestingly, there is much less variety and ambiguity over the constitutional conventions that are relevant for decision making within the cabinet: ministers are collectively responsible to parliament for government policies, and they all have one vote in cabinet.

The norm of collective responsibility implies that 'The Chancellor of the Exchequer may be driven from office by a bad dispatch from the Foreign Office, and an excellent Home Secretary may suffer for the blunders of a stupid Minister of War' (Morley, 1889: 18). In theory, as David Ellis points out, 'it is not necessary for the preservation of collective responsibility that each minister . . . should be given the opportunity to discuss governmental policy. The critical fact is that once the decision has been made there should be no sign of dissension' (Ellis, 1989: 49). However, analogous to 'no taxation without representation', collective decision taking is assumed to follow from collective responsibility: cabinets are *supposed* to meet regularly (Weller, 1991b).

The norm that each cabinet member's vote counts equally is not without formal exceptions. In case of a tie, the prime minister eventually casts the deciding vote. In the German cabinet, the Ministers of Finance, Interior and Justice cannot be overruled on proposals affecting their portfolios, provided the Chancellor sides with them (Johnson, 1983: 71). For the Minister of Finance in particular this provision is potentially important, as his or her role touches on all other ministers' portfolios, but until now this power has never been invoked (Sturm, 1994: 89–90). Even the clichéd title of the prime minister as *primus inter pares* underlines that all members of the cabinet are *supposed* to have an equal voice, to be colleagues.

Cabinet government can thus be characterized as collective and collegial decision taking, but it should be emphasized that this is a normative, rather than an empirical, description; such a 'golden age' of cabinet government probably never existed. However, as the norms of collective and collegial decision taking can be found in all five political systems in this study, we can use them to construct a (Weberian) ideal type of cabinet government as a common standard with which real-life cabinets can be compared empirically. Deviations from the ideal type can be away from both collectivity and collegiality, or from only one of the two characteristics. In other words, real-life cabinets can be plotted against two dimensions of cabinet government: they can be more or less collective, and they can be more or less collegial (Andeweg, 1993). Collegial decision taking stands opposite monocratic or hierarchical decision taking, and the dimension between these two poles gauges the concentration or dispersion of power in cabinet. Collective decision taking can be contrasted with individual decision taking, with the two extremes connected by a dimension indicating the centralization or fragmentation of decision taking in cabinet.

Much the same dimensions are proposed by Aucoin in his analyses of Canadian cabinet government, although he uses the term centralization for the dimension measuring the degree of collegiality:

> In order to appreciate the different modes of decision making within cabinet government, it is important to recognize that the cabinet is an executive organization in which formal authority (or informal power) can be distributed in ways that are more or less centralized–decentralized and responsibility (or spheres of influence) can be assigned in ways that are more or less integrated–differentiated (Aucoin, 1994b: 110).

In their study of the British cabinet system, Burch and Holliday (1995: 142–6) also use two similar dimensions (prime ministerial style (active/passive) and mode of cabinet system relations (more or less collective)) to distinguish the 'tone of administration' in postwar British cabinets. Aucoin dichotomizes both dimensions to arrive at four 'modes of cabinet government decision making' whereas Burch and Holliday trichotomize them. For the purposes of this chapter the two dimensions have been trichotomized also, resulting in a three-by-three table (see Figure 4.1). Such decisions are essentially arbitrary, however, as both dimensions are continua.

The lower right-hand corner represents the case of the ideal-type cabinet with both collective and collegial decision taking. As noted before, this cell is probably empty. The upper left-hand corner is furthest removed from the ideal type: a monocratic prime minister takes decisions after consulting cabinet ministers individually. Historically, cabinet government in the UK, the Netherlands and Germany (Prussia) originated from this cell (ministers as individual advisers to the monarch), but today it too is probably empty in parliamentary systems (the US presidential 'cabinet' would nicely fit into this category).

COLLECTIVITY

COLLEGIALITY	Fragmented (individual minister)	Segmented (cabinet committee)	Collective (cabinet)
Monocratic (prime ministerial)			
Oligarchic (inner cabinet)			
Collegial (ministerial equality)			

Figure 4.1 *The two dimensions of cabinet government*

The existing literature generally fails to make the distinction between collegiality and collectivity. Thus, Baylis finds 'collegial leadership' where 'significant decisions are taken in common by a small, face-to-face body with no single member dominating their initiation or determination' (Baylis, 1989: 7). Rose apparently uses collective and collegial as synonyms in his own attempt to arrive at an ideal type of cabinet government (Rose, 1980b: 344). So does James when he asserts that: 'in Britain, the collegiate ethos remains potent: all ministers, including the premier, are expected to behave as part of a collective group' (James 1992: 6).

It is true that collectivity and collegiality are related, if only because the convention of ministerial equality is sometimes seen as a corollary to the fact that all ministers share equally in the cabinet's collective responsibility. Yet, it is important to distinguish the two dimensions. First, because the failure to do so may well be the cause of inconclusiveness in the debate over 'prime ministerial' versus 'cabinet' government that dominates British cabinet studies, and is an important part of the literature on cabinet government in Australia, Canada, Germany *(Kanzlerdemokratie* v. *Koordinationsdemokratie)* and the Netherlands. As Weller puts it, the debate posits a dichotomy between prime ministers' individual decision making and cabinets' collective or collegial procedures. Yet this distinction may not accurately reflect the exercise of power because prime ministers are part of cabinet. If, by contrast, it can be illustrated that prime ministers dominate decision making *through* the use of the collective processes of cabinet, as a *consequence* of following established procedures of consultation, then the distinction loses analytical force. Prime ministers may not be dominant only when they pursue individual decision making (Weller, 1991b: 132).

Or in terms of our two dimensions: prime ministerial ascendancy refers to a particular position on the dimension of collegiality, but it does not automatically entail a particular position on the dimension of collectivity.

Second, the distinction between the two dimensions is simultaneously a distinction between two strategies for the provision of coherence in government policy: hierarchical coordination (i.e. low collegiality) and horizontal coordination (i.e. high collectivity). By establishing the position of various cabinets on both dimensions, we discover the various mixtures of coordination strategies pursued.

This chapter is devoted to horizontal coordination, to the prospects for *collective* government. It attempts to ascertain to what extent the full cabinet is the primary arena for decision taking compared to other arenas of executive decision taking, such as cabinet committees and individual ministers within their portfolios. Before we turn to these questions, two caveats are in order. First, our analysis seeks to gauge the *relative* weight of these arenas: all of them exist in all five countries, but their role and function varies. Second, our discussion will suffer from over-generalization: the prospects for collective government differ not only between but also within political systems. Some are more institutionalized than others, but there is always room for changes over time, related to the parties and personalities involved (see Burch and Holliday (1995: 142–6) for such changes along the dimensions of cabinet government in the UK). Even within a single cabinet there may be differences related to policy area. The focus of this book is on cross-country comparison, but these within-country and within-cabinet variations should be kept in mind.

Collective Government: The Full Cabinet

The literature is not encouraging about the prospects for collective government. Country-specific studies often cite particular historical or political reasons why the full cabinet has ceased to be the primary arena. Blondel looks for a more fundamental cause of this general malaise. In his view, truly collective decision taking in cabinet is logically impossible. Without conflicting views dividing the cabinet, collective decision taking is unnecessary, but in order to survive, cabinet must avoid internal conflicts: 'If the principles of cabinet government were applied to the letter, the system would not merely be grossly inefficient, but truly not viable' (Blondel, 1988: 4); or elsewhere: '. . . cabinet government can function effectively only if it abandons to an extent its basic principle of organisation' (Blondel and Müller-Rommel, 1993: 2). Blondel suggests that the dilemma between collective decision taking and cabinet stability is solved everywhere at the cost of collectivity, by reducing the number of potential conflicts. In single-party cabinets this is done through party discipline and the underwriting of a common party programme by all cabinet ministers. In coalition governments it is achieved by the acceptance of a coalition agreement, and by hiving off controversial issues to extra-governmental arenas, such as summits of party leaders. As a result, in both single-party and coalition government, the scope for collective government is, according to Blondel, confined to 'low politics'.

Blondel makes a valid point, but there are (at least) two objections to his pessimistic conclusion. First, as Blondel acknowledges, it narrows cabinet government to joint decision *making*, ignoring the fact that cabinet meetings serve other functions that are vital to the coherence of policy-making in the core executive, but are less affected by the collectivity/ stability dilemma (see Mackie and Hogwood, 1985: 10–12). The most important of these functions is that of information exchange: through their submissions to cabinet, through their reports on developments in their policy sector, and through their gossip about party politics, cabinet ministers brief their colleagues about their activities. This may alert some of these colleagues or the prime minister to the need for interdepartmental or political coordination in specific cases. The lack of this information is most acutely felt by non-cabinet ministers, who are only allowed to join the meeting when an item within their remit comes up for discussion. Interviews with Dutch cabinet ministers who had been junior ministers before revealed that this is a considerable source of frustration among non-cabinet ministers. A similar frustration among British junior ministers has been registered by Theakston (1987: 113–17). However, in the Dutch and German core executives, at least all policy areas are represented in the cabinet: since the 1950s and 1960s respectively, there have been junior ministers in both countries, but no junior departments. The function of information exchange is less well performed in the UK, where some departments' chief ministers do not have cabinet rank. The same situation existed in Australia for most of the period between 1956 and 1987, but since 1987 all departments have been represented in the cabinet, with junior ministers outside the cabinet. As we shall see shortly, Canada is a rather special case in this respect. Another function for the full cabinet, apart from decision making, is to act as a court of appeal when no consensus between the ministers concerned has been reached in other arenas within the cabinet system. As Mackie and Hogwood assert: 'Even where largely symbolic, the right-of-appeal role of the cabinet is important in maintaining the constitutional myth of collective decision making and responsibility' (Mackie and Hogwood, 1985: 11). In Germany, this is the only function of the cabinet that is explicitly mentioned in Article 65 of the constitution. As we shall see in the next section, cabinets vary in the extent to which they are allowed to perform this function, most notably with regard to cabinet committees, but nowhere is it completely absent. Finally, even when it merely rubber-stamps decisions taken elsewhere, the cabinet's plenary session gives such decisions legitimacy. This too contributes to the coherence of the government. Given such other functions of meetings of the full cabinet, Blondel's emphasis on decision making is therefore too restrictive.

The second objection to Blondel's pessimism concerning the prospects for collective government concerns his assessment that internal conflicts threaten the cabinet's survival. Many conflicts in cabinet, however, do not have the potential to develop into a full-blown cabinet crisis. Inter-departmental conflicts, for example, carry fewer risks than partisan or factional conflicts, if only because a department cannot leave the government. Yet, these appear to be the most numerous conflicts, even in coalition cabinets. For Germany, Mayntz observes: 'Conflicts which do become manifest in cabinet discussions are rarely of a purely partisan nature (for instance, FDP ministers against SDP ministers); more often they are structurally determined, reflecting the conflicting interests and orientations of the departments and their clientele' (Mayntz, 1980: 156). In the Netherlands, a study of 96 cabinet conflicts that were reported by the national press between 1973 and 1986 showed that 67 per cent of these conflicts were interdepartmental. It also showed that only 2 per cent of interdepartmental conflicts resulted in a crisis, and 5 per cent in non-decision making, compared to 13 and 25 per cent respectively of all party-political conflicts (Timmermans and Bakema, 1990: 178–88).

Moreover, Blondel assumes that cabinets resolve conflicts by majority decision. Even if that were true, it need not threaten the government's survival as long as ministers who lost feel confident about winning the next battle. When a majority in cabinet consistently outvotes a minority, it will not be long before that minority withdraws from the government. This result is certainly possible for coalition government, but even in single-party governments the common bonds of party loyalty are unlikely to overcome a consistent division between a majority and a minority for long. This potential outcome, however, turns into a self-denying prophecy, because ministers realize the danger. As a result, taking votes is rare in cabinets (Laver and Shepsle, 1994b: 299). It appears to be non-existent in Australian coalition cabinets, and even in Labor governments votes are exceptional (Weller, 1985a: 125). In the UK, the Wilson cabinets came close to having votes through the Prime Minister's practice of going round the table 'collecting voices', but other prime ministers have not followed that example. In Dutch cabinets there have been occasional votes, especially in the 1950s, the record being 51 votes during one year, but that is exceptional. Steiner and Dorff (1980) argue that in face to face groups such as cabinets, manifest conflicts are often not resolved (non-decision making), but when they are, the decision tends not to be formalized, precisely to avoid identifying winners and losers. They call this 'decision by interpretation'; in cabinets it is known as the prime minister's 'summing up' of 'the sense of the meeting'. In Harold Wilson's words 'summing up is vital: it is the fine art of cabinet government' (Wilson, 1976: 55). The controversy over whether this fine art includes rigging the outcome, also dating back to Wilson's days, need not concern us. Here it suffices to note that decision taking in cabinets resembles the practices of consensus democracies, even in otherwise majoritarian political systems.

Blondel's argument remains valid, but the potential for collective government is still considerable, given that cabinets perform other vital functions besides decision taking, that many conflicts by their nature do not threaten the government's survival, and that the dominant mode of decision taking in cabinet emphasizes compromise and face-saving rather than 'winner takes all'. In practice, however, not all cabinets realize their potential for collective government to the same extent. The same secrecy that is necessary for collective decision taking makes it difficult to ascertain its occurrence, but we can use indirect evidence such as the frequency of cabinet meetings, which is documented in some and can be estimated for most countries.

The full cabinet is convened at least once a week in the five countries of our study. If some cabinets have a higher average number of meetings than one per week, it is because of *ad hoc* meetings being convened in addition to the regular weekly ones, or because the regular meetings are not confined to a morning or afternoon, but last for several parts of a day.

Between 1945 and 1979, the regular Thursday morning meeting of the British cabinet was often supplemented by a meeting on Tuesday morning, but since 1979 it has become exceptional for cabinet to meet more than once a week (although this weekly meeting lasts longer in the Major cabinets than in the Thatcher cabinets) (James, 1992: 71, 79, 82). The frequency of cabinet meetings declined from the 80–100 per year in the 1950s mentioned by Jennings (Jennings, 1969: 249). In the 1960s and 1970s, Wilson is reported to have convened a total of 472 cabinets, averaging 60 meetings per annum, whereas Thatcher presided over a total of only 394 cabinets, which comes down to an annual average of 34 (Madgwick, 1991: 53).

This is in marked contrast to the Dutch cabinet, especially if we take into account the length of its meetings. If we count each morning, afternoon and evening as a separate meeting, the frequency of meetings gradually increased to just over 100 per year in the 1950s. It stayed at that level, with the exception of the 1970s, when it reached a record of over 150 meetings per annum. The Den Uyl cabinet (1973–77) became legendary for its marathon sessions, starting on Friday mornings, and often lasting until the early hours of Saturday morning. In 1976 this cabinet met 163 times, for a total of 478 hours (Andeweg, 1990: 20)!

In Australia, not all governments have distinguished between cabinet and ministry, but when the distinction was made, the full ministry too sometimes met (on average seven to eight times per year). In order to compare the frequency of cabinet meetings across time, we have to combine the two. The available figures for the 1970s show that the Whitlam government met an average of 45 times per year, but the Fraser governments (1975–83) met more than twice as often (on average 110 meetings per annum), albeit with wide fluctuations (Weller, 1985a: 110). Since then, the frequency of meetings has dropped again to an average of 61 for the Hawke governments until 1988 (Weller, 1990: 19). This is probably largely due to the more important role given to cabinet committees in this period. Although it is claimed that the 1987 reforms led to 'a steady decline in the total of cabinet meeting, cabinet papers lodged and cabinet minutes recorded since 1987' (Keating, 1993: 10), there seems to be more fluctuation than structural decline (Keating, 1993: 15, Appendix 1.2). From July 1990 to June 1991, for example, cabinet *cum* ministry met 67 times (Jaensch, 1992: 153), compared to the 61 meetings per year of the Hawke governments before the reforms. Finally, it is worth pointing out that Australian cabinet ministers are likely to meet informally more often than their colleagues in the other political systems in this study, as they all work in Parliament House rather than in their respective departments (Davis, 1994: 53).

The Canadian and German cases are more difficult to interpret. In Canada the number of meetings fluctuates, but seems to have declined from about 70 meetings per year in the 1970s (Weller, 1985a: 109) to a mere 26 in 1987 (Jackson and Jackson, 1990: 300). However, this number is misleading because, until recently, no distinction was made in Canadian government between cabinet and ministry, although parliamentary secretaries gradually developed into a kind of junior minister (Aucoin, 1994b: 274). The Canadian cabinet was a much larger body than its counterparts in the other countries. As we shall see below, this gave rise to the development of a complex system of cabinet committees. Among these committees, the Priority and Planning Committee (P&P) enjoyed a special position. In 1979 Prime Minister Clark renamed P&P the 'Inner Cabinet'. Clark also reduced the number of meetings of the full cabinet (Campbell, 1985: 70). Even though the title stuck for only a short time, P&P continued to play the role of the functional equivalent of the full cabinet in the four other countries: during Mulroney's premiership P&P 'assumed the functions that are assigned to the cabinet in political systems where the cabinet and ministry are distinguished' (Aucoin and Bakvis, 1993: 410). In 1987 P&P met 44 times. If we combine that figure with the 26 meetings of the full cabinet, and even if we leave out the meetings of P&P's increasingly powerful Operations Committee (Bakvis and MacDonald, 1993: 58), there was no decline in collective government in Canada (Jackson and Jackson, 1990: 300). Today the size and structure of the Canadian government is more comparable. In 1993, Prime Minister Campbell abolished P&P (but kept the Operations Committee) and, emulating the 1987 Australian amalgamation of portfolios (Aucoin and Bakvis, 1993), reduced the size of the cabinet to 25. Her successor, Chrétien, completed the reform by discontinuing the Operations Committee and by introducing a two-tier system in his cabinet through the appointment of eight junior ministers (Secretaries of State) (Aucoin, 1994b: 271, 282–3). It is too early to tell what effect this restoration of the full cabinet as 'the senior forum for collective decision making' (1993 press release by the Office of the Prime Minister, quoted in Aucoin 1994b: 283) has on the frequency of its meetings.

In Germany we also have to take into account a functional equivalent of meeting of the full cabinet. Reliable figures for the frequency of meeting of the German cabinet are not available, but one author estimates that it meets once a week when parliament is in session, and at most twice a month during the summer recess (Müller-Rommel, 1988: 165). From a comparative perspective, this frequency is surprisingly low, and many authors have concluded that policy is primarily made in bilateral discussions between the Federal Chancellor and the individual ministers. However, a note of caution is in order, as in the German cabinet system a low frequency of cabinet meetings does not necessarily indicate a lack of collective government. Many items that need cabinet approval never reach its agenda, because they have already been approved in the *Umlaufverfahren*, a procedure in which written proposals are circulated to all ministers. If all ministers approve of such a proposal in writing, it is never discussed by the full cabinet (Sturm, 1994: 103). Apparently, a similar system is used by the European Commission to filter out non-controversial proposals (Donnelly and Ritchie, 1994: 37). Brauswetter estimates that 75 per cent of all submissions to Brandt's cabinet were approved through what is in fact a cabinet meeting on paper, reducing the need for 'real' cabinet meetings (cited in Mayntz, 1980: 154).

From these data it would appear that the Dutch and to a lesser extent the Australian cabinets are nearest to, and the British cabinet furthest removed from, collective government. The Canadian and German cases are more difficult to interpret, because much depends on the weight one is prepared to attach to functional equivalents of cabinet meetings.

Segmented Government: Cabinet Committees

Despite the occasional occurrence of both *ad hoc* and standing committees in cabinets in earlier times, the literature for all countries concerned is in agreement that a committee system can only be said to have developed during and immediately after the Second World War. As this period was also one of rapid expansion in the scope of government, the development of cabinet committees is generally seen as a logical answer to the increased workload. In Canada it is also interpreted as a consequence of the increase in the size of the cabinet (reaching a record of 40 members in Mulroney's 1984 government), and the reluctance, until recently, to distinguish cabinet from non-cabinet ministers.

Whatever gave rise to their existence, cabinet committees have given rise to controversy about their role within the core executive. One such controversy concentrates on the membership of civil servants in some cabinet committees, but more important for the purposes of this discussion is the debate on whether cabinet committees weaken or strengthen collective government. On one side of the argument we find Walker (1970), Jones (1975) and Weller (1985b), who argue that cabinet committees serve to strengthen or at least maintain collective government: cabinets would be swamped by a plethora of submissions if committees would not deal with minor issues. Because of the work of cabinet committees, the full cabinet is free to concentrate on the truly controversial items. Other observers, such as Seymour-Ure (1971), Mackie and Hogwood (1985) and Lord Hailsham (1987), are less optimistic, and argue that momentous decisions are sometimes taken by *ad hoc* committees, composed by the prime minister with an eye to the desired outcome, without the rest of the cabinet being aware of the committee's existence, let alone its decision. The decision, under Attlee, to build the first atomic bomb in the UK, has become the most notorious example of such a procedure (Hennessy, 1986: 123–62).

So far, it is primarily a British debate, but not without relevance for the other countries in this study. Whether cabinet committees support or erode collective government depends first of all on the situation before their establishment. Those who see committees as diminishing collective government can only be right in so far as collective government can be said to have existed in that particular political system. If, however, the core executive was highly fragmented, with individual ministers largely autonomous within their portfolio, cabinet committees may have provided a step towards integration rather than disintegration of the core executive. Second, there is too much variation in the powers and composition of cabinet committees to allow easy generalization about their contribution to coherence in government policy. Where cabinet committees serve to prepare or even pre-empt but not to supplant discussion in cabinet, they still fit the mould of collective government.

Segmented government can be said to exist when a cabinet committee is a 'partial cabinet . . . a number of ministers who constitute part only of the cabinet but act for a time as if they were the cabinet. A partial cabinet is different from an inner cabinet in that it is an organized part of the cabinet system. Typically a partial cabinet is a standing or *ad hoc* committee presided over by the prime minister, which may — in matters of great moment and secrecy — prepare policies in detail and sometimes take decisions without prior consultation with the cabinet as a whole' (Walker, 1970: 88). To distinguish 'ordinary' cabinet committees from 'partial cabinets', we may look at the powers of committees, their composition and the frequency of their meetings. With regard to the powers it is important to ascertain whether committees have the authority to take decisions autonomously, and whether non-members and members have a right-of-appeal to the full cabinet. Two aspects of the committees' composition are relevant: whether or not all ministers have access to all committee meetings, and the degree to which the composition reflects the composition of the full cabinet. Finally, even if committees have formal authority and exclusive membership, but rarely meet, they will do little to affect the prospects for collective government.

In the UK the importance of cabinet committees has steadily increased. Walker (1970: 42–3) mentions the 1944 Education Bill as an important example of the principle that a committee's conclusions had the same authority as those of the cabinet, but were still subject to cabinet challenge. This right-of-appeal is important because the 'law of anticipated reactions' keeps committee decisions roughly in line with the views of the full cabinet. This link between committees and cabinets became attenuated by Wilson's 1967 ruling that a minister may only appeal to the full cabinet against a committee decision if that committee's chairman or the prime minister allows it. Under Prime Minister Thatcher the right-of-appeal was further restricted, and was one of the objections raised against her style of leadership, particularly when, in 1986, Heseltine resigned from the cabinet over her refusal to allow him to present his views on the Westland Affair to the full cabinet (Hennessy, 1986: 106–11).

The composition of British cabinet committees is generally decided by the prime minister, but in the case of standing committees, the choice is largely determined by the need to have the departments most concerned represented on the committee. A curious exception is the 'Star Chamber', discontinued in 1988 (Madgwick, 1991: 227). It was responsible for adjudicating budget conflicts between spending departments and the Treasury; for obvious reasons this committee excluded those most concerned (Mackie and Hogwood, 1985: 45). If the prime minister manipulates the composition to influence the committee's decision, it has to be done at a much earlier stage, through the assignment of specific portfolios to particular persons. There is more room for manipulation in the composition of the MISCs or GENs, those mysterious *ad hoc* committees whose existence or composition is yet declassified. It is through such committees that Attlee got his famous atomic bomb. Non-members are not allowed to participate in committee meetings. Moreover, 'there is no evidence of concern to ensure that committees are balanced in terms of ideology or any other basis of representation' (Mackie and Hogwood, 1985: 45). Although the exact frequency of committee meetings is unknown, ministers seem to spend considerably more time in cabinet committees than in the full cabinet. Under Major, the British cabinet has probably become more collegial, but not more collective: 'Major's cabinet meetings may be more discursive than Thatcher's, but not more frequent. The focus for decision making remains at committee level' (James, 1995: 85).

The Canadian and Australian systems of cabinet committees show a more curvilinear development. In Canada, under Pearson, the full cabinet dominated decision taking and reviewed all committee decisions (Jackson and Jackson, 1990: 297). Ministers who were not members of a particular committee could attend those committee meetings, an exception being the P&P (Aucoin, 1991a: 141). Under Trudeau and Clark the committee system grew more and more elaborate, and the committees also became more powerful. In 1968 cabinet committees were given the authority to take decisions in lieu of the full cabinet, but ministers could appeal to the cabinet through the Privy Council Office (Campbell, 1985: 65). The use of this right, however, was not encouraged by the prime minister (Bakvis and

MacDonald, 1993: 55). Trudeau also strengthened cabinet committees, by giving their members advice on the submissions from central coordinating agencies, in addition to the advice from their own departments. By giving the committees their own budget, the 'envelope system', Clark completed the development.

The composition of committees is decided by the prime minister, but his or her room for choice is limited by the need for the representation of the departments most concerned, and by the Canadian practice of having all regions and ethnic communities represented (Mackie and Hogwood, 1985: 22–3). Moreover, the composition is less important because some ministers are deemed so central to cabinet coordination that they have the right to attend all cabinet committees, or send a civil servant to replace them. Even 'any ministers vitally concerned with a specific matter before a committee other than the one under which their portfolio fell could exercise their right to attend any policy sector meeting on an ad hoc basis' (Campbell, 1985: 66).

The Canadian committee system did not live up to its expectations. Ministers continued to define their role in terms of departments and regions rather than in terms of committees, and felt frustrated rather than supported by the central agencies. Some committees became very large, and when the envelope system proved to be an obstacle to keeping the budget deficit down, the cabinet committees lost some of their ascendancy (Campbell, 1985). The envelope system was abolished and the number of committees reduced. Mulroney's 'brokerage style' preferred bilateral contacts over cabinet committees (Bakvis and MacDonald, 1993: 62), all major committee decisions had to be ratified by either the cabinet or P&P (Jackson and Jackson, 1990: 297), and the frequency of committee meetings has declined from 232 in 1982 to 147 in 1987 (Jackson and Jackson, 1990: 300). This trend was continued by Prime Ministers Campbell and Chrétien who reduced the number of standing cabinet committees to its current number of four (Aucoin, 1994b: 281).

In Australia the role played by cabinet committees has also varied considerably from one government to another, although Weller claims that they became more institutionalized under Fraser (Weller, 1985b: 111). When they were first introduced by Chifley, no less than 19 standing committees were set up, which may explain why committees were not much used by Menzies (1949–66) and his successors, and why Whitlam (1972–75) had only five committees in his brief attempt to remodel the committee system on the Canadian example (Jaensch, 1992: 157). Fraser (1975–83) empowered standing cabinet committees to take final decisions against which appeal was only possible with the prime minister's consent (Weller, 1985b: 97). One of the standing committees, the Coordination

Committee, enjoyed relatively broad terms of reference, and was being accused of usurping powers from the full cabinet after Peacock's resignation in 1989 (Weller, 1989b: 130–3). During the first four years of Hawke's reign, the committee grew so important that there was a significant drop in the number of decisions made by the full cabinet (Weller, 1990: 19). Since then the role of committees in the Australian cabinet has decreased somewhat. After the 1987 reforms, committees continued to be important, but the Coordination Committee is no longer listed among the eight standing committees, and cabinet committee decisions are, with few exceptions, printed on blue instead of white paper, indicating their need for endorsement by the full cabinet (*Cabinet Handbook*, 1988).

The committees' compositions are dictated by the need for both departmental and regional representation (Mackie and Hogwood, 1985: 24), as in Canada. In addition, the need to achieve a party balance in Liberal–National coalitions, or a faction balance in Labor governments, also enters into the considerations. Moreover, ministers who are not members of a committee receive its agenda and its minutes, and can sit in on committee meetings, except those of the Security Committee and the Expenditure Review Committee (*Cabinet Handbook*, 1988). The frequency of meetings varies considerably from committee to committee, but the annual number of meetings for all committees combined indicates that the average committee meets considerably less often than the cabinet itself (Weller, 1985b: 89; Weller, 1990: 19; Jaensch, 1992: 153).

The Dutch cabinet committee system is highly institutionalized, and occasionally a committee may play a role of some importance, such as the Council for Economic Affairs (REA) in the aftermath of the Second World War, or the Council for European Affairs (REZ) in recent governments. In general, however, the importance of cabinet committees should not be over-estimated. With the exception of the Committee for Intelligence and Security and the Honours Committee, cabinet committees can only 'prepare' items for submission to the full cabinet; they cannot take decisions autonomously. Committees play no role in budgetary matters. The prime minister nominally presides over most cabinet committees, but does not decide their composition: that is part of the coalition building negotiations. In addition to cabinet ministers, some junior ministers, a few senior civil servants, and even outsiders such as the President of the Dutch Bank, may be members. Departmental representation is most important, but party balance also plays a role. In 1952, Social Democrat ministers had obtained most portfolios in the socioeconomic area. The Catholic party objected, and the REA was subsequently enlarged to restore the balance. The REA eventually became so large that it is now bigger than the cabinet itself. Its role in policy making was then taken over by an informal committee, the 'socioeconomic triangle' of the Ministers of Finance, Economics and Social Affairs. Partly for reasons of coalition balance, the Social Democrat prime minister joined the triangle during the 1973–77 Den Uyl cabinet. Again for reasons of political representation, the Liberal Minister of Internal Affairs (who was then the deputy prime minister) completed the transformation from triangle to pentagon during the Van Agt I cabinet (Andeweg, 1985: 144–50). During the three Lubbers cabinets (1982–94) the pentagon seems to have given way to largely bilateral consultations about socioeconomic policies. The importance of committee membership is largely symbolic as agendas and minutes of committees are sent to all ministers, who are allowed to participate in any cabinet committee meeting. With the exception of the REA, most committees meet only a few times each year.

In Germany cabinet committees are not considered important. They developed only recently. In the mid-1960s only an Economics and a Defence Committee existed (Müller-Rommel, 1988: 159), but by the 1980s 16 committees were operative (Mackie and Hogwood, 1985: 19). Only ministers in the Christian Democratic–Social Democratic Grand Coalition (1966–69) report that committees played an important role in the decision making process (Müller-Rommel, 1994: 155). For Brandt's cabinets, Brauswetter estimates that only 20 per cent of cabinet submissions were filtered through cabinet committees (cited in Mayntz, 1980: 155). The lack of importance is further illustrated by the fact that the Chancellor, who formally presides over all committees, often relinquishes the chair to one of the ministers most concerned, and by the fact that ministers often deputize civil servants to committee meetings (Müller-Rommel, 1988: 159). Ministers who are not members can attend any committee's meetings (with the exception of the Defence Committee), and will receive its minutes (Sturm, 1994: 95). In 1985 Kohl reformed the cabinet committee system, so that there are now six committees. They did not become more important, however. When, occasionally, a committee does play a significant role, such as a finance committee in the late 1960s, or the committee on German reunification more recently, this is regarded as an exceptional and temporary phenomenon (Johnson, 1983: 72–3; Sturm, 1994: 95–6).

Among our five cases, the British core executive is the clearest example of segmented government; here the development of partial cabinets has been at the cost of collective government. The experience with segmented government in Canada, and to a lesser extent in Australia, has been shortlived, but cabinet committees continue to provide an important arena of decision making in these two political systems. Committees cannot be said to be a significant part of the Dutch and German core executives.

However, especially in these last two cases, it should be emphasized that we have confined our discussion of segmented government to cabinet committees, that is, to sectoral or functional segmentation. Most coalition cabinets will have some form of political segmentation. In the Netherlands ministers and junior ministers from each governing party will meet with their own parliamentary leader and chairperson on Thursday evening, primarily to discuss the next day's cabinet agenda. Occasionally, party discipline is enforced and the decision taken by the cabinet differs from the one that would have emerged had all ministers followed their own judgement. In Germany, under the Brandt and Schmidt governments at least, the FDP ministers had their own breakfast meetings. Ministers from the Bavarian CSU are regularly summoned to Munich to coordinate their party's position in cabinet. It is also evidence of political segmentation that mechanisms have been developed to counterbalance it. In the Netherlands this has become institutionalized in the 'turret meeting' (so named after the building in which the prime minister is housed), a weekly luncheon of the prime minister, the deputy prime minister(s) (i.e. the other governing party's most senior minister(s)) and the parliamentary leaders of the governing parties (Andeweg, 1988: 135). In Germany similar practices exist: there are regular meetings of the coalition parties' leaders in cabinet and in parliament, which became famous as the *Kressbonner Kreis* during the Grand Coalition (Mayntz, 1980: 155, 159; Müller-Rommel, 1988: 158). Under Kohl, the *Koalitionsausschuss* (coalition committee) meets weekly. When the problems are particularly difficult to solve, the *Elefantenrunde* of party leaders is convened (Wewer, 1990: 147). Compared to Dutch and German coalitions, Australian coalition cabinets are ideologically more homogeneous, but there is a mechanism for the resolution of party conflicts in the form of joint caucus meetings (Stewart and Ward, 1992: 107).

In itself, political caucuses within cabinets do not lead to segmented government, because such meetings are never authorized to take decisions. All they can do is coordinate a party's strategy in the coming cabinet meeting. They may even strengthen collective government: through its junior ministers, a party's cabinet ministers are informed about plans in departments that are led by another party's cabinet minister. The meetings of the coalition committee are more of a threat to collective government to the extent that they replace the cabinet as the effective decision centre, as seems to have been the case during the German *Grosse Koalition* (Mayntz, 1980: 159). This danger is real, as the experience in Italy shows, where the 'political summit' has evolved into a separate and distinct power centre, of which the prime minister is the only member representing the cabinet (Criscitiello, 1994).

Fragmented Government: Individual Ministers

There can be no doubt that individual ministers enjoy a considerable degree of autonomy within their portfolio in all core executives. The sheer size and scope of government intervention makes it impossible for it to be otherwise. This autonomy is also sanctioned by the existence of a doctrine of individual ministerial responsibility in addition to collective responsibility.

> The doctrine of individual responsibility gives [ministers], in effect, a warrant for keeping other ministers off their turf. As in other countries, there is a tacit agreement in Britain that individual departmental ministers will not gratuitously interfere in each other's affairs. To try to deprive other people of their autonomy is to risk being deprived of one's own (King, 1994: 207).

In Germany, parliament can only censure the Chancellor (as *pars pro toto* of the collective cabinet), not the individual minister, but there the position of the individual minister is protected by the *Ressortprinzip* ('Within [the general policy of the government], each minister conducts the affairs of his department independently under his own responsibility') mentioned by the Constitution in the same article as *Kabinettprinzip* and *Kanzlerprinzip*. The question can only be to what extent ministerial autonomy is constrained by collective or segmented government.

One — rational-choice — approach to decision making in coalition cabinets starts from the assumption that ministerial autonomy is unfettered. Portfolios within cabinets are treated as analogous to committees in legislatures: the party leadership determines the policy outcome through the composition of the committee or the allocation of the portfolio to a particular politician, whose views are known (Austen-Smith and Banks, 1990; Laver and Shepsle, 1990a, b). According to Laver and Shepsle, in a footnote to their paper, 'In effect, we are assuming that cabinet ministers are policy dictators in their respective jurisdictions. This assumption is actually defensible in some polities . . .' (Laver and Shepsle, 1990a: 888). Although the portfolio-allocation approach deals with coalition governments only, the assumption of ministers as policy dictators applies to all core executives. However, after a rare and courageous confrontation of their deductively arrived at propositions with empirical evidence from 14 political systems (including the UK, the Netherlands, Germany and Canadian provincial government), Laver and Shepsle conceded that they had to 'accept that sweeping assertions about the autonomy of cabinet ministers are ill-founded' (Laver and Shepsle, 1994b: 308). The main reason for relaxing the assumption of ministerial autonomy was, interestingly, that they had underestimated the volume of collective decision making that apparently constrains individual ministers: 'ministerial discretion, in short, must result from the minister's ability to shape collective cabinet decisions rather than to defy them' (Laver and Shepsle, 1994b: 297–8).

Still, the rejection of any notion of *absolute* ministerial autonomy says little about the potential for *relative* fragmentation of cabinet government. The nature of this relative ministerial autonomy, however, is diametrically opposed to what it was supposed to entail in the portfolio-allocation approach. Beatrice Webb did not despair that 'all cabinets [are] congeries of little autocrats with a super-autocrat presiding over them' (cited in Mackintosh, 1977: 477), because ministers continued to press upon their departments the views they held before kissing hands. On the contrary, with the possible exception of Australia (Butler, 1973: 34), the literature abounds with complaints about ministers 'going native', exchanging their party's political ideology for their department's sectoral interests (Andeweg and Bakema, 1994: 71), notwithstanding occasional 'Big Beasts of the Jungle' (King, 1994: 220), as a result of exceptional personality or political circumstances. As noted at the beginning of this chapter, even in coalition governments, most conflicts tend to be interdepartmental rather than partisan. Fragmented government would be departmentalized government. It should be emphasized that this does not necessarily mean that ministers are 'captured' or 'house-trained' by their civil servants. This undoubtedly occurs too, but it is probably much more common that ministers start to identify with their department because their reputation in cabinet, in parliament, in the press, as well as within their own department, depends almost exclusively on their performance as head of department: 'ministers are expected to go to bat on their department's behalf' (King, 1994: 207).

The degree to which ministers seek to defend their departmental cabbage patch against cabinet trespassers depends on a variety of factors. Ministerial autonomy *vis-à-vis* the cabinet or its committees is, for example, strengthened in countries (and in policy sectors) with (neo-corporatist or otherwise) strong policy networks, such as the Netherlands and Germany. In these two countries, and in the UK, European integration may also contribute to fragmentation of national governments. Dutch Ministers of Agriculture, for example, have been eager to transfer powers from The Hague to Brussels. After all, in the European Council of Ministers, they meet only other Ministers of Agriculture, who are all convinced of the importance and needs of that particular sector, whereas in their national cabinets they confront ministers with other portfolios, and considerably more scepticism.

The tendency of ministers to protect their departmental turf is reinforced if the pattern of ministerial recruitment favours specialized ministers. In the UK, Canada and Australia ministers are exclusively drawn from parliament, and selected primarily for their political clout, their parliamentary experience, or — in the two federal countries — their regional affiliation. In Australia, the short electoral cycle (three years) makes ministers more interested in political developments than in departmental detail. In Germany and the Netherlands, recruitment is not confined to the benches of parliament. Only 73.6 per cent of postwar German ministers and merely 52.9 per cent of their Dutch counterparts had parliamentary experience when they were appointed ministers (De Winter, 1991: 48). There is more opportunity to recruit ministers with technical experience within the portfolio with which they are to be entrusted, especially where the parliamentary pool is relatively small (the Dutch Second Chamber has 150 seats). Blondel calculates the per centages of 'ministers who lasted nine months or more in government [who] have been allocated to posts corresponding to their prior training, provided these posts cover a particular field of administration for which a given training is relevant' for 1945 to 1981 as 13 in the UK, 16 in Australia, 17 in Canada, 34 in the Netherlands and 43 in (West) Germany (Blondel, 1985: 195, 277). The figures for Germany and especially for the Netherlands probably underestimate the technocratic nature of ministerial recruitment in these countries (Bakema and Secker (1988) estimate the per centage of specialized ministers in the Netherlands after 1945 at between two-thirds and three-quarters). Another indication of the degree of ministerial specialization is the proportion of ministers who stayed in one department throughout their ministerial career. The figures are 79 per cent in the Netherlands and 63.5 per cent in Germany, compared with only 38.4 per cent in the UK (Bakema, 1991: 90). Blondel also includes Canada and Australia and puts the per centage of one-post ministers at 78 in the Netherlands, 70 in Germany, 54 in the UK, 55 in Australia and 53 in Canada (Blondel, 1985: 277). Specialized ministers are less likely to have the general knowledge and interest needed to engage actively in collective government, and more likely to be able to ward off any interference from cabinet colleagues.

Even generalist ministers with a political background, however, will find it difficult to participate in debates on issues outside their portfolio if they are not briefed in advance about submissions from other ministers. However, in most countries ministers have to rely largely on their departmental officials, who will often confine the advice to their minister on other department's proposals to possible conflicts with their own department's policies. Canadian ministers may be an exception in this regard, being equipped with political advisers and getting non-departmental advice from the central agencies. In practice, however, the exempt staffs concentrate on liaison work with the minister's constituency and party, and with parliament, and we already noted that ministers feel frustrated rather than supported by the central agencies.

On the other hand, ministerial autonomy is limited by the growing interdependence between policy sectors. Some departmental boundaries have been drawn with the intention of creating countervailing powers (e.g. with regard to the police or economic policies), but even where they were once intended to create autarchic portfolios, the original boundaries may no longer be as logical as they once seemed. As departmental reorganization is notoriously difficult such boundaries are rarely redrawn, and collective, or at least segmented, arrangements are necessary to achieve a modicum of coordination. The need for interdepartmental consultations probably affects all core executives equally, but it does vary from department to department. According to King, there are four factors that may account for relative departmental autonomy: (a) a relatively self-contained portfolio, without much need for contact with other departments; (b) a portfolio containing few politically controversial issues; (c) a tradition of autonomy; and (d) few internal pressures to expand the departmental budget, and few external pressures to reduce it (King, 1994: 214–17). King actually lists the UK departments according to their degree of autonomy. Although his four factors may produce different lists in different political contexts, the factors themselves are not country-specific: it is not self-evident that any of the five countries in this study 'suffers' considerably more or less from them.

If we look at the other variables discussed in this paragraph — strong policy networks, ministerial recruitment and rotation — as a first and rather impressionistic conclusion, it would seem that fragmented government is approximated most by Dutch and German executives, with the Westminster systems, and the Australian government in particular, furthest removed from this type of decision taking.

Collective, Segmented or Fragmented Government: Causes

Having surveyed the structures of cabinets for their emphasis on collective, segmented or fragmented government, we have found very different mixtures in the five countries in our study. Because of their recent reforms, the Australian and Canadian cabinets are difficult to characterize. The Australian reforms, more or less copied in Canada, were intended to strengthen both the collective cabinet and the individual minister. This may have introduced some fragmented government, not yet reflected in Figure 4.2. It is also worth reiterating that we have attempted to classify countries on the basis of their cabinet's structures, that the style and personalities of the politicians involved may result in variation across cabinets within a

country, and that the nature of issues considered by the cabinet may even
result in variation within a particular cabinet.

	Collective government	Segmented government	Fragmented government
Australia	++	+	
Canada	+	++	
Germany	+		+
The Netherlands	++		+
United Kingdom		+++	

Figure   4.2 *Collective, segmented and fragmented government in five
countries*

With such caveats in mind, it is clear that the relative emphases on
collective, segmented or fragmented government do not correlate with ready
classifications such as Westminster versus continental, unitary versus
federal, or single-party versus coalition government.

One potential explanatory variable would be the size of cabinet. C.
Northcote Parkinson, better known for Parkinson's Law, has also written
'an extensive study of national cabinets, over space and time', no doubt also
tongue-in-cheek.   In this essay he presents a 'coefficient of inefficiency',
the maximum number of members above which a cabinet ceases to function
efficiently, and disintegrates into smaller bodies.   This coefficient is
between 19.9 and 22.4 members, 'the decimals represent partial attendance;
those absent for a part of the meeting' (Parkinson, 1957: 48).   Baylis sees
cabinet size as one of the factors that help determine what he calls the
collegial nature of the cabinet (Baylis, 1989: 154–5).   In our sample,
however, the size hypothesis seems to be contradicted by the Canadian case,
where collective government has not atrophied completely, despite a cabinet
of 25 members, down from Mulroney's original 40, but well above all
other cabinets in our study (14 in the Netherlands, 17 in Australia, 19 in the
UK and Germany).   The relative sizes of the British and Canadian cabinets
especially make it hard to see size as the only determinant.

An interesting explanation would be the quality of ministers.   Some
authors on the Australian cabinet suggest that this country suffers from a
more than average number of weak ministers, who seek collective guidance
and endorsement to compensate for lack of self-confidence (Butler, 1973:
27–8; Weller, 1985a: 86–7).   The collective cabinet takes on an additional

function to those mentioned earlier in this chapter: that of a security blanket or 'comfort stop'. In Australia the supposedly low quality of ministers is associated with the limited pool from which ministers can be selected: a parliamentary party of about 100 members. Hawke and others have proposed to allow extra-parliamentary recruitment to 'increase the level of ability within a ministry' (Jaensch, 1992: 141–2). Even if the quality assessment is correct, other factors must be at work as well. Australian ministers seek cabinet approval not only out of their own free will, but also because the *Cabinet Handbook* contains such a wide-ranging list of items that need to be considered by the cabinet or its committees. Moreover, the other core executive with a relatively strong emphasis on collective government (and with at least as wide ranging a list of items for cabinet discussion in its standing orders), the Dutch cabinet, does not suffer from the same kind of restrictions on ministerial recruitment.

The most important difference with regard to the prospects for collective government is between the segmented British cabinet, on the one hand, and the other countries' cabinets, with at least some collective government, on the other. What do these other four have in common? The common denominator is representation. Dutch and German cabinets invariably are coalition governments in which at least two, in Germany up to three, and in the Netherlands up to five parties have been represented. Australian Liberal–National governments are also coalitions, although they probably put slightly less emphasis on the minister's role of party representative, because this coalition is a semi-permanent alliance that does not bridge a social or ideological cleavage. Since the institutionalization of the factions within the Australian Labor party in the 1980s, Australian Labor governments, although technically single-party governments, have become more like coalitions. As Labor ministers are chosen by the caucus, not by the prime minister, factional representation in the cabinet is ensured.

Canadian governments are composed of a single party, but they too face the representation imperative. The federal nature of Canada, and of Australia, requires that the cabinets in these polities include representatives from most regions or provinces. In Canada, the current Chrétien cabinet is the first to govern without a representative from one province (Prince Edward Island). Until now, 'regional ministers' have exerted their influence in different ways as the nature of the cabinet system evolved, but that influence has declined but marginally (Bakvis, 1991). When the Atlantic Regional Opportunities Agency and other regional agencies were set up, ministers even had some help in preparing for cabinet as regional ministers, as one of them told parliament: 'What you get . . . now is an agency almost as a department to those Atlantic Ministers . . .' (quoted in Aucoin, 1991a: 145). At first sight, representation of the various *Länder* does not seem to play an important role in German cabinets. However, the inclusion of the CSU assures the representation of Bavaria in the cabinet, and Kohl has appointed junior ministers from the north and from the former East Germany in order to achieve a regional balance in his government (Sturm, 1994: 84).

In addition to the regions or provinces, other interests may also be taken into account. In Canada the various ethnic/linguistic and to a lesser extent religious communities have to be represented in the cabinet. In Germany and the Netherlands, the representation of social interests in cabinet is only thinly veiled. Sturm's description of the German cabinet could just as easily apply to many Dutch cabinets:

> The minister of agriculture, for example, has to come from the farmers' lobby, whereas the job of employment minister goes to a union representative. A justice minister should be trained in law, while a minister responsible for the family and the young should not be a bachelor. As a rule defense ministers should have served in the armed forces . . . (Sturm, 1994: 82).

A gender balance has not yet been achieved, but there is a constant pressure to increase women's representation in the cabinet in most countries.

In contrast, most of these considerations do not come into play in the UK: with few, but significant, exceptions (such as Eurosceptics and Euroenthusiasts in Major's cabinets), neither political, nor geographic, nor any other form of representation plays a significant role in the British cabinet. The little regional representation that exists is departmentalized in the Welsh, Scottish and Northern Ireland Offices, and thus does not provide ministers with a second focus of representation. Representation of other than departmental interests is a strong incentive for collective government because it provides ministers with more than one hat. If their only role is that of departmental chief, interdepartmental coordination is the only reason for bilateral or at most segmented consultations. British prime ministers seem to prefer segmentation to the more chaotic world of *ad hoc* bi- or tri-lateral discussions. In the other countries ministers are forced to take an interest in other ministers' portfolios, not merely for reasons of interdepartmental coordination, but primarily because they have a legitimate reason to interfere: party ideology, regional interests. As Hockin testifies for the Canadian case: 'When issues arise respecting a particular region, the minister representing that area will be expected to get involved in those issues regardless of the department under whose purview they come' (Hockin, 1991: 163). Theoretically, this involvement can be done in cabinet committees as well as in the full cabinet, provided cabinet committees meet all the representational criteria. In practice, multiple representation leads to collective rather than segmented government. When there are many regions or parties or interests to be represented, this creates a pressure to enlarge the committees, as we have seen in both the Dutch and Canadian cases. The committees then become unwieldly and gradually give way to the full cabinet. As Hockin states: 'The principle of regional representation enhances the importance of the cabinet as an institution' (Hockin, 1991: 163).

From our overview, it would seem that cabinet government is not necessarily Rose's 'government against sub-governments', mentioned at the beginning of this chapter. Looking at one of the two dimensions, the prospects for collective government are brightest where cabinets not only bring together the various departments of state, but also various parties or factions, regions or social interests. We end on a counter-intuitive, paradoxical note: multiple representation strengthens instead of weakens collective government.

5 Advising the Executive: Think Tanks, Consultants, Political Staff and Kitchen Cabinets

Herman Bakvis

The question of who has the ear of the Crown has long fascinated journalists, historians and political scientists. Personalities such as Cardinal Wolsley at the time of Henry VIII, Grigory Rasputin in the court of Tsar Nicholas II, Woodrow Wilson's 'dear, dear friend', Edmund House, and Harold Wilson's political secretary, Marcia Williams, are perhaps some of the more intriguing examples of advisers said to have had unusual sway.

The rise of representative and democratically elected government and, especially, the advent of the modern administrative state, means, some might argue, much less scope for these kinds of advisers. Representative government assumes that once a party is elected (or re-elected) on the basis of some specified platform, the focus shifts from consultation and making choices to the implementation of those choices, which is said to be the responsibility of the state bureaucracy. The rise of the administrative state, in turn, with the attendant professionalism and expertise of civil servants, also leaves less room, and need, for such advisers. Yet it can also be argued that, in the late twentieth century, formally constituted cabinets, legislatures and bureaucratic support agencies are no longer, or perhaps never were, fully up to the task of melding technical and political advice. Certainly in the present era of populist democracy, advice giving and receiving 'has now acquired a more continuous character' (Peters and Barker, 1993: 1). And while the emphasis in recent years has been more on management reform and rolling back the state rather than on new policy initiatives, ultimately the process of de-inventing government, and the dismantling of the welfare state in particular, are tasks of political management rather than administrative proficiency (Pierson, 1995).

In any event, in part as a response to a more demanding and politically complex environment, the upper reaches of the bureaucracy have become more politicized (Aucoin, 1995), indicative of the need of the executive for more partisan advice.

All this suggests that the demand on the part of executives for special, more political and less formal advice is increasing rather than decreasing.

84

Yet the response of present-day executives has not been to revive the practice of relying on a single trusted adviser. Nor has it necessarily meant reverting back to a reliance on traditional pressure groups (Hall, 1986). Rather a quick glance at the crucial advisory space enveloping core executives in a number of countries suggests that this space is increasingly being populated less by key bureaucrats, pressure group representatives and close partisan advisers and more by gurus from think tanks, polling firms and management consulting organizations (Lindquist, 1990; Plowden, 1991). As well, discussion of the advisory function often relates more to the structures and processes used by the executive to organize and apply advice received from diverse sources to the problems of governance than to whether reliance on non-bureaucratic advisers is appropriate or inappropriate.

This chapter briefly surveys advice from the bureaucracy but then focuses on advice received by the executive from sources other than the bureaucracy and the process and structures by which it is delivered. These sources include external bodies such as non-governmental think tanks or policy institutes, professional management consultants and staff hired directly by members of the executive to assist them in their political tasks and to provide analysis of policy problems, often as a counterweight to the advice provided by the bureaucracy. Many of these sources often come together in a small circle of advisers and confidants close to the minister or premier and consulted on a regular basis, their 'kitchen cabinet' if you like. The main issue is whether the rise in the importance of non-bureaucratic advisers and related advisory structures have helped to strengthen the capacity of the core political executive to direct the affairs of state or whether it undermines the capacity of the executive to do so, that is, contributing to its hollowing out. Linked to the hollowing out thesis is the possibility that, given their international connections, think tanks, management consultants and the like represent the impact of globalization; that is to say, power from the core may be flowing not to the domestic civil society but to an international community composed of managerialists and neo-conservative thinkers. Not only may globalization limit what governments can do by way of manipulating economic and political levers but it is possible the use of the levers that remain to them are increasingly being conditioned by ideas emanating from this international community.

This chapter, then, bears directly on the capacity of elected governments to exert authority over, and give direction to, the apparatus of the state, particularly at that crucial juncture when a government-in-waiting is about to take power (Savoie, 1993). It relates to the ideas and strategies that parties, governments or ministers may adopt and subsequently implement as actual policies (Budge and Hofferbert, 1990). And, finally, it relates to the possibility that the impact of globalization on the nation state may well be manifesting itself directly within the core of the state through the role of outside advisers.

In keeping with the comparative design of the hollow core project, evidence will be drawn from Australia, Britain, Canada, Germany and the Netherlands. The advisory needs of executives in the different systems are not identical. The first part of the chapter briefly discusses existing bureaucratic arrangements for policy advice and from there moves to a discussion of non-bureaucratic advice in terms of seven categories of 'needs' that advisers and advisory structures fulfil. The role of think tanks, management consulting firms, political advisers and kitchen cabinets in the five countries will then be examined through the lens of the sevenfold model.

Executive Support Agencies

Before discussing alternative sources of advice we should pay some attention to those bodies that are formally tasked with assisting the executive in providing advice, weighing alternatives, helping the executive relate to political realities and so on. Here we have in mind those agencies that are expected to assist the executive, cabinet and the prime minister collectively and the support staff who help individual ministers, even when that may well put them into conflict with staff in central agencies. The basic distinction in support models lies beween what Campbell and Wilson (1995) have labelled the Whitehall model, on the one hand, and the European model, on the other. The UK epitomizes the former, but the Whitehall model has been adopted, in altered form, by the two other Westminster countries in our analysis. Its hallmark has been its alleged strict separation of the political from the bureaucratic realm in contrast to the European model where the executive and the bureaucracy have found ways to bring the two realms more closely together. It is the Whitehall model that is seen as the more problematic in terms of meeting the needs of the executive. As will be seen in subsequent sections, it is also the model which, in the UK, has undergone the greatest challenge in recent years. According to Campbell and Wilson (1995), the central feature of the Whitehall model is a senior civil service — a career bureaucracy — schooled in the notion that they are the primary if not sole providers of advice. They are expected to be not so much politically neutral but, to use Richard Rose's (1987) felicitous phrase, politically promiscuous; that is, they are expected to serve to the best of their abilities whatever party is in power. With regard to supporting individual ministers, speech writers and personal secretaries are all drawn from the ranks of the career bureaucracy. Thus, in the case of the British prime minister, the people with whom he or she has the most regular contact, are the Principal Private Secretary (PPS) and four or five additional private secretaries, all of whom are drawn, on secondment, from regular line departments for periods of up to three years. In terms of formal structures supporting the PM and cabinet, a distinction is drawn between the Prime Minister's Office and the Cabinet Office. The former is comprised of the Private Office, the Policy Unit (originally created in 1974 by Harold Wilson), the Press Office, the Political Office, Special Advisers (up to seven or eight specialists drawn from outside government) and the Efficiency Unit (created by Margaret Thatcher in 1979) (Madgwick, 1991). All told, approximately 100 people work in the Prime Minister's Office, of whom about 30 are senior staff. The Cabinet Office has approximately 750 staff, of whom 35 are senior officials (assistant secretary and above) and another 200 are of intermediate rank. There are about another 200 or so senior officials in the departments supporting the work of ministers. Within the Cabinet Office work is organized around five secretariats, headed by deputy secretaries and each corresponding to major cabinet committees. A committee comprising the deputy secretaries, the prime minister's PPS and the cabinet secretary acts as a steering committee for cabinet business. In the words of Peter Madgwick it is involved in 'policy management', but 'not, please, policy determination' (1991: 98). This 'policy management' is not without significance, however, since this sort of 'influence through process' can result in some options being promoted while others are quietly dropped. The Cabinet Office has housed a variety of other units, such as the Efficiency Unit and the Central Policy Review Staff (CPRS, created by Heath in 1970 and killed off by Thatcher in 1983). The Treasury remains as a separate entity and its Secretary, along with the Cabinet Secretary, is seen as one of the two most powerful senior officials in the British government. What ought to be stressed, once again, is that the Cabinet Office is staffed in the main by career civil servants. As will become evident in our discussion of political staff, it is only in the Prime Minister's Office that there has been scope for bringing in outsiders.

Canada and Australia loosely follow the British model. In Australia the Department of Prime Minister and Cabinet (PM&C) provides the logistical support for the prime minister and cabinet and it houses the cabinet offices. As of 1995 when Keating was still prime minister, it has 544 staff, approximately half of whom are involved in policy work and including roughly 35 people at the assistant secretary level or higher. It has a much more explicitly policy focus than the British cabinet office, although given what some consider to be its rather limited size there is worry about the lack of depth (Campbell and Halligan, 1993). It is organized around four main policy divisions — international affairs, economic policy, social policy and trade and industry — in addition to those dedicated to parliament, the status of women and multicultural affairs. John Howard, elected in 1996, created a small unit of Liberal policy advisers within the department. In the main PM&C is staffed by career civil servants, though, as will be noted later, changes in recruitment practices have led to PM&C staffers being more closely identified with the view of their political masters than was perhaps the case previously. The Prime Minister's Office (PMO) is staffed by roughly 30 personal advisers. These are political appointments but at least half are drawn from the bureaucracy seconded to the PMO. On the surface their task is more process than substantive policy, yet many crucial decisions will be made in the small circle surrounding the prime minister. Campbell and Halligan (1993) and Aucoin (1995) have argued that the PMO is in fact far more influential than its Canadian counterpart. The sway of this small circle is enhanced by a small yet crucial feature — the physical segregation of the PMO, located in Parliament House, from PM&C, located down the hill several blocks away. The opportunity for interaction is simply much more limited. At the same time the importance of officials in the Treasury and the Department of Finance should not be discounted, given the importance of managerial and economic issues in Australia in recent years. And increasingly many of these officials will have served an earlier apprenticeship in PM&C.

In Canada the main central agencies supporting the political executive are the Prime Minister's Office (PMO) and the Privy Council Office (PCO). The Department of Finance (the equivalent of the Treasury in Australia and Great Britain) plays a crucial role in supplying financial advice to cabinet. The Treasury Board Secretariat supports the Treasury Board in carrying out its responsibility for overseeing the expenditure function of government, but it is generally seen as less influential than its counterparts in other jurisdictions (e.g. the Department of Finance in Australia). The PMO is seen primarily as a partisan agency, its 60-odd staff composed of administrative support staff and partisan appointments, which has little policy capacity. The Liberal Chrétien government has sought to reinforce the policy capacity of the PMO, while at the same time reducing its size compared to that under the Conservative government of Brian Mulroney. Under Mulroney the Deputy Prime Minister's Office became influential in supporting the Operations Committee of cabinet, the key gatekeeping committee. This role, and most of this office, disappeared with the Operations Committee in 1993 upon the arrival of the new Chrétien government. On the whole the PCO remains as the primary agency supporting the deliberations of the Canadian cabinet. The PCO comprises some 625 staff of whom roughly 75 fall into the senior executive category with another 150 falling into the professional and administrative category. The PCO supports the work of the two main committees of cabinet, social and economic — plus a number of *ad hoc* committees such as programme review and national unity. It is also responsible for providing support to the

Minister of Intergovernmental Relations, a crucial position given the sensitivity of the Quebec issue. There used to be a separate federal–provincial relations secretariat until it was incorporated into the PCO in 1993 as part of the machinery of government reforms. One of the main features of the Canadian system of executive support has been, at least in the past, the penchant for elaborate organizational designs. According to Colin Campbell, the Canadian government has probably gone furthest in 'fulfilling the canons for institutionalized executive leadership' (1983: 351). This unfolding of the institutional logic of Canadian central agencies reached its zenith in the early 1980s when cabinet had not only the PCO but also two separate ministries of state directly responsible for providing advice on economic and social matters. The whole edifice of central agencies heaped upon central agencies threatened to collapse under the weight of its own design and in 1984, with the departure of Pierre Trudeau, the incoming prime minister John Turner eliminated several agencies, including the two ministries of state, and streamlined the cabinet. The main point to keep in mind, however, is that the intent had been, and to a large extent still is, to provide cabinet and cabinet committees with countervailing sources of advice, to help them avoid being captured by departmental interests, through the creation of labyrinthine agencies staffed by high-powered civil servants.

The Whitehall model is typically contrasted with the continental model, where the latter is perceived to provide the executive with bureaucratic support more attuned to its political needs and preferences. Two points need to be made. First, the two continental systems in question here are not as prime minister centred as the three Westminster systems, a function in part of the coalitional nature of their cabinets. The style of governance in these systems is much more likely to fall in the 'fragmented' category (see Chapter 4), where individual ministers enjoy significant autonomy over their portfolios and where the prime minister has concomitantly less influence. Structurally, the Chancellor's Office in Germany bears a resemblance to its counterparts in the three Whitehall–Westminster systems, except that it combines the function of Cabinet Office and Prime Minister's Office, including what in Australia and Britain is considered the PM's personal office, into a single unit. It is staffed by over 500 employees. Of these, approximately 140 are higher civil servants, with 70 of them at the level of section head or above. The Chancellor's Office is organized into six divisions that replicate the basic structures of the government. According to Murswieck (1993: 88), 'its major functions lie less in the field of policy development, which is accorded mainly to the ministries, but rather in the co-ordination of government policy and the management of conflict between the ministries and the partners in a coalition government . . . [I]ts ability to serve as an advisory unit is restricted'. If we turn to the offices of individual ministers, however, there too the number of staff directly supporting ministers tends to be quite small. There is nothing like the French cabinet system — that is, a large staff personally loyal to the minister drawn from outside the ministry — despite the fact that in Germany the ministries are the sites in which the more crucial policy decisions are made. As we will see later, however, there are built-in mechanisms within the bureaucracy that allow a significant role for more direct partisan advice.

In the Netherlands we also find a paradoxical case. More so even than in Germany the Dutch system can clearly be labelled a fragmented core executive with ministers jealously guarding control over their departments, brooking little interference from others in cabinet, and where the prime minister, more than anywhere else, simply acts as a chair of the board (Andeweg and Irwin, 1993). Ministers serve with, rather than under, the prime minister. The prime minister has only a very small staff — 10 to 12 — who act as advisers and who all tend to be drawn from the bureaucracy. The Cabinet Secretariat, according to Andeweg and Irwin (1993), is part of the Department of General Affairs, and has a semi-independent position. In other words, it is not directly managed or controlled by either the prime minister or other ministers. All this reflects the multi-party coalitional character of Dutch cabinets, where the prime minister has little influence over who occcupies which cabinet position or what policy initiatives ought to be undertaken in any one domain. Yet if the real power lies more in the hands of individual ministries then we would expect to see more advisory capacity under the direct control of ministers lodged in ministers' offices. But this is not the case. Like the prime minister, individual ministers have small personal staff and are dependent almost entirely on career civil servants from within their own department.

The paradox concerning Germany and, especially, the Netherlands, is that both systems have a reputation for strong party government, that is, where the partisan dimension, as articulated through party programmes and policies developed within parties, is seen to have much more influence over what government does. Yet the formal advisory structures appears to leave most of the advising to career civil servants. How the political executive taps into sources of non-bureaucratic advice and to what extent this type of advice is necessary for the development and implementation of policies based on political preferences in these two systems is one of the issues addressed in this chapter.

Before turning to the need for and sources of external advice, it is worth asking what functions executive support agencies are expected to perform, particularly with respect to advice giving. According to Weller (1991a: 363–4), the roles in which the cabinet generally and the prime minister in particular need support are: 'managing the administrative process, managing the political processes, influencing and/or controlling the policy content'.

It is the last that is most crucial in relation to the advice-giving function, although political process management invariably tends to overlap with policy issues. Advice giving can be crudely divided into two categories. The first is simply the process of keeping the advisee informed. If he or she is expected to intervene in a policy matter, if only by gently nudging a decision in one direction or the other, then that individual needs to be up to speed on what is or is not transpiring in the policy domain in question. As well, as Weller (1991a: 373) notes, 'if not properly informed, their involvement is likely to be ineffective or even dangerous'. The second issue is what to do. Here the process can be conceived of as 'analysing problems and proposing solutions' (Halligan, 1995: 139). If intervention is called for, what are the alternatives and which should be chosen? While often a distinction is drawn between substantive and political policy advice, in practice the distinction tends to become cloudy. The advice given by technical experts will often have embedded within it, consciously or unconsciously, certain political preferences and values. Political advisers, on the other hand, need to have a modicum of knowledge of often complex technical issues in order to assess the political implications stemming from a decision. In addition, advice intended for the prime ministerial consumption must bear on the broader picture, one that takes into account the collective, long-range goals of the government (Weller, 1991a).

The Need for Non-bureaucratic Advice

Under conditions of what Aberbach, Putnam and Rockman (1981) have termed the 'Image I' model of relations between politicians and civil servants, where the bureaucracy acts in an ostensibly neutral role, substantive or technical policy advice would most certainly be seen as the prerogative of civil servants. Even external scientific advice — from scientific agencies, for example — can still be seen as advice tendered to a government agency where bureaucrats would play a key part in both contracting for and subsequently interpreting the advice received. The Image I model, however, is generally held to portray a non-existent world (Campbell, 1988a). Many will allow that even in Westminster systems of cabinet government, which have adhered more closely than other systems to the principal of a neutral civil service, the executive and individual ministers need to obtain ideas for programmes and policies from a variety of sources, particularly when it comes time for either governing or opposition parties to begin formulating election campaign platforms. It is also recognized that there is a range of activities, relating mainly to partisan matters, where advice from the bureaucracy would be inappropriate.

Thus recognizing that, in general, political leaders do have a need for policy advice beyond that tendered by the bureaucracy, and that this need has expanded in recent years, what are the most likely sources of such advice? Second, what are the specific needs served by different actors or bodies advising members of the executive, as well as their strengths and weaknesses in serving these needs?

There are eight sources of external advice.

1. *The political party.* The role of political parties in developing election platforms, providing advice to a newly elected or re-elected government, recruiting staff and the like is a topic sufficiently important in itself to warrant a separate chapter in this volume. Some points to note here are that: the party proper will often develop outside linkages and seek outside advice in developing party platforms; and there is a necessary grey area between the formal party and less formal networks extending into various communities and to the executive itself.

2. *Governmental advisory bodies.* These advisory councils and boards are fully funded and appointed by government but draw on outside experts and interest-group representatives and tender advice either to specific departments or to government as a whole. Canadian examples include the National Council of Welfare, mainly advising the Department of Human Resources, the former Economic Council of Canada and the Science Council (both abolished in 1992), providing more general advice and research, and the National Advisory Board on Science and Technology. Jarman and Kouzmin (1993) have compiled a list of what they label 'public sector think tanks' in Australia, such as the Advisory Committee on Home and the Community and the Australian Science and Technology Council (see also Marsh, 1992). These bodies, however, typically have a reporting relationship to a government department or agency, a relationship that invariably predates the arrival of any current minister who may have only limited control over the tenor or makeup of such an advisory body. Furthermore, such bodies may interact much more directly with bureaucrats, and information or research generated by these bodies will be shared with or, more likely, filtered through the bureaucracy. The reports made by these bodies may also be public documents. Hence, many if not most such bodies are not really under the control of, or beholden to, the executive and may not really qualify as external or non-bureaucratic sources of advice.

3. *Task forces and commissions.* These bodies examine and make recommendations on specific issues. In Canada royal commissions are frequently used to handle controversial issues, to depoliticize them or simply to delay them. They have wide-ranging powers of investigation and can conduct extensive research to support their recommendations.

The results of a royal commission can be used by the executive to support a particular course of action. The Canadian Royal Commission on Economic Union and Development Prospects, which reported in 1985 with a recommendation for free trade with the USA, had an important influence on the Conservative government of the day. The irony here is that the commission was originally set up in 1983 by the previous Liberal government, which underscores the possibility that the policy advice may end up being quite different from what the minister would like to hear; it may also be a long time in coming. Task forces, at least in the Canadian setting, perform many of the same functions, investigating and making recommendations on particular problems, but tend to be of much shorter duration and, more importantly, can be controlled more directly by the minister or executive. In the hands of a minister, it can be an effective instrument to bring into play the ideas and influence of outside advisers in whom the minister has confidence and to expose the bureaucracy to alternative points of view.

4. *Interest groups.* These groups include business associations, professional bodies such as medical societies, and professedly non-profit public interest groups. The last in particular may well be highly dependent on government for funding. Many of the comments made above on governmental advisory bodies apply here as well. In most cases, ministers cannot claim (nor would they necessarily wish to do so) to have a privileged or exclusive relationship with an interest group. More often than not, interest groups will interact much more extensively with the bureaucracy. At times, a particular group may have the ear of a minister on a specific issue; but it would be extremely rare for a group to claim such a role on a permanent basis or as its primary *raison d'être*. In so-called corporatist systems (e.g. with well-organized peak organizations), the advice tendered by the business or trade union sectors may carry more weight, but again advice from these sources would not necessarily be exclusive to, or primarily intended for, the executive. Key elements of the bureaucracy will also participate in the process of corporatist concertation. Even in non-corporatist systems, and the three Westminster systems fall into this category, many professional bodies have been influential. The design and implementation of medical policy, for example, has frequently involved the direct participation of the medical profession. But in light of recent developments in government retrenchment, governments have sought to disengage these actors from the policy process, often seeing them as part of the problem rather than the solution.

5. *Think tanks.* These organizations purport to do research on public issues, are independent, though they may receive either sustaining grants or research or consulting contracts from governments, and have

some claim to intellectual credibility. Following the title of James Smith's book, they are best visualized as 'idea brokers' (Smith, J.A., 1991). While claiming not to represent specific interests, they will often have a particular ideological slant on public policy issues. What differentiates them from most pressure groups is that they will actively seek to advise rulers on broad programmes of action as well as on particular policies. There is evidence from Britain that certain think tanks have at times exercised considerable influence over key political decision makers or legitimated decisions being taken.

6. *Management consultants.* While their role is ubiquitous in virtually all areas of public sector management — in evaluating programmes, designing new organizational structures, auditing — management consulting firms, typically one of the big six such as Price Waterhouse or KMPG Peat Marwick, are not generally thought of as playing a critical role in advising the core executive. However, with the advent of managerialism, particularly in the English-speaking countries under investigation here, and with its accompanying stress on using the tools of financial management to achieve good and above all economical government, it is inevitable that members of political executives and senior officials of management consulting firms are brought closer together. Furthermore, even beyond the issue of managerialism, these firms appear to have the capacity to bring together in one integrated package generalist as well as highly specialized skills ranging from forensic accounting to assessing the viability of whole industrial sectors. If one conceptualizes the hollowing out thesis in terms of governments contracting out many of their key functions, including ones at the highest level such as advice giving, then management consulting firms would appear to loom large indeed. The extent to which these firms have actually played such a role and in which countries is uncertain because relatively little has been written on them. However, there is enough evidence to suggest the role of such firms is more prominent than generally acknowledged.

7. *Political staff.* In virtually all systems, and certainly in the five systems under investigation, both the first minister and cabinet ministers have a staff to support them recruited from outside the normal public service channels. They can be a mere handful, an executive assistant and a party liaison person, or an extensive staff of several dozen, including high-powered advisers with expertise in the minister's area of jurisdiction. Having a large staff is no guarantee that such staff will play a critical role in policy analysis and development. They might well be concerned primarily with the nitty gritty of distributing political patronage or party matters.

8. *Kitchen cabinets.* This category of people have a close and often long-lasting relationship with the minister or first minister. They play an important albeit informal role by acting as a sounding board or as a critic of courses of action proposed by the bureaucracy or the minister him- or herself. The setting for tendering such advice is often outside of the office or normal working hours, a discussion after dinner in the family kitchen, for example. It cuts across a number of categories in that close 'kitchen' advisers may be from a minister's political staff or a think tank; but they may also be relatives or close friends who would not normally be considered to have an important role in the political realm. To constitute a meaningful category, however, one would have to say that these 'kitchen' advisers are consulted by members of the executive on a regular basis and they have been shown to have had influence in initiating or altering a course of action undertaken by the minister.

In this chapter I am interested primarily in the shift from bureaucratic to non-bureaucratic advisers who work for and were controlled by or beholden to the executive collectively or individually. This grouping also includes those institutions or individuals who have succeeded in capturing the ministers with their ideas, or where there is a symbiotic relationship. The most important sources of advice are: external think tanks, management consulting firms, political staff and 'kitchen cabinets'. There is overlap between these categories — key political staff may well be members of a minister's kitchen cabinet, for example, and there will be movement of people between them — but they are analytically distinct.

I will examine each of these four categories below, but before doing so I will explore the needs such external advice fulfill.

1. *Mandate.* First and foremost there is a need for advice in formulating the platform or, if you like, proposed mandate of the executive or executive-in-waiting (Budge and Hofferbert, 1990; Savoie, 1993). This task is primarily the responsibility of the political party; in most systems the bureaucracy would be reluctant to become involved in drafting campaign statements and promises. In Image I type systems civil servants might be reluctant even to provide basic information, statistical data, for example, to an incumbent government preparing its election statements.

2. *Implementation/Transition.* The second critical need relates to the implementation of a mandate. Again, a new government would need to be well prepared in order to give directions to the bureaucracy, have a good sense of the feasibility of implementing the promises made during an election campaign, and have a strategy in place to ensure that the bureaucracy will follow through on implementation. This assumes that

governments know what they want to do, which is not always the case. The Australian Labor government under Hawke from 1988 to 1991, the Mulroney Conservative government, 1988–93, in Canada and the Major Conservative government in the UK would be examples of parties successfully elected but unsure of their objectives once in power.

3. *Partisan tasks*. The third need relates to the handling of partisan matters. These range from: the administration of the political appointments process (i.e. patronage-type positions to boards, and commissions for the party faithful); to ensuring that the appropriate political spin is placed on new programmes or decisions in relation to their timing or packaging (including alerting the appropriate party officials should their constituencies or political domain stand to be affected by particular decisions); to advice on more broad ranging decisions that could affect the party electorally (i.e. the role played by pollsters in interpreting polling data).

4. *Evaluation*. The fourth need concerns the evaluation of bureaucratic advice and proposals: the provision of countervailing advice. Assessments, for example, of whether a proposed course of action recommended by the department fits with the government's agenda, what alternative courses ought to be considered and so on. In this area, advisers need much greater expertise in the substantive policy areas in question.

5. *Legitimation*. Fifth, advisers can also play a role in supporting the executive's efforts to provide leadership in different arenas and particularly departments. This means providing the government or minister with vision and ideas on policy matters and managerial issues, to help create a climate for the acceptance of the ideas or proposals that the minister seeks to promote, what Andrew Johnson (1981) has labelled the 'legitimation function'.

6. *Mobilization*. The sixth need concerns supporting the smooth functioning of the political–bureaucratic interface. This relationship is frequently depicted in adversarial terms — us versus them — but often, indeed perhaps in the majority of cases, the two levels need to cooperate closely in order to achieve mutually beneficial objectives. If ministers are to make headway in achieving some of their goals then the task involves mobilizing the bureaucracy, or at least critical segments of the bureaucracy, to get them onside. Here advisers can play a critical role, if only by not alienating key bureaucrats.

7. *Reflection/Rejuvenation*. Finally, every politician needs some opportunity for reflection, to receive intellectual stimulation and to be able to bounce ideas off others in a setting that is removed from the strategic calculations and pressures of normal politics on a day to day basis. Political parties should, but often do not, provide such

opportunities for reflection and recharging one's batteries, particularly when the party is out of office. This function also relates to the agenda-setting process, particularly when parties, perhaps after a defeat, are exploring new issues and ideas as possible pathways back to power.

This discussion assumes that the needs of individual ministers and the collective executive are the same. It should be recognized that the interests, and the activities undertaken in pursuit of them, by individual ministers may well be at odds with the collective or corporate needs of the executive. At the same time, there is more at stake than a simple distinction between collective and individual aspects of ministerial leadership. As Chapter 1 points out, the executive operates in different settings or conditions, which require different means of achieving a collective identity and modes of collective action.

Thus, each model of cabinet decision making may require different kinds of advice or expertise delivered in different ways (Bakvis, 1994). A cabinet characterized by a corporate management style will depend upon a rather different kind of non-bureaucratic advice regime compared to a monocratic or fragmented style. The relative importance of such advice will also vary.

Think Tanks

The definition of think tanks best suited to our purposes is that of James (1993: 492): 'a think tank is defined as an independent organization engaged in multi-disciplinary research intended to influence public policy'. Emphasis should be placed on the relative independence of think tanks, particularly from government, and on their policy advocacy role. This rules out so-called 'public sector think tanks' and many university-based ones. My use of the term think tank is also consistent with that of Weaver (1989).

Although seen largely as an American phenomenon, think tanks have existed elsewhere for quite some time. The influential Institute of Economic Affairs in Britain, for example, was founded in 1955. The stereotypical view of the think tank is that of a large, well-funded research organization producing trenchant studies of social problems and government policies. While often characterized by a distinct orientation, whether liberal or conservative, it is seen to carry weight by virtue of its independence from government funding and to a degree from other interests, especially if it is well endowed. The Brookings Institution in the USA comes closest to fitting this model; but as James Smith (1991) points out, this body is more the exception than the rule, particularly with regard to the research function. Even those which are well funded tend to spend many of their resources on education, publication and, above all, publicization of ideas. And while many think tanks tend to be prolific publishers, most of their more substantial works represent the efforts of university-based scholars as opposed to original research conducted by a think tank itself. In this sense such institutes are often seen by academics as a useful publishing outlet rather than the stimulus or creator of new research.

This factor also underscores the role that many think tanks see themselves playing, namely shaping the policy agenda. They attempt to do so, in part, by shaping public opinion and the intellectual climate in which decision makers operate through the provision of 'one-pagers' and 'backgrounders' to the media and by holding well-publicized conferences and seminars drawing together intellectuals and practitioners. They can also be seen as brokers of information or, as Evert Lindquist (1990) puts it, 'a third community' of professional intellectuals. According to Allan Tupper (1993: 543), they constitute 'actors who commission research, who mediate between experts and officials, and who develop strategies for the dissemination of arguments'. More important, think tanks also attempt to capture directly the ear of key decision makers, particularly politicians, when the opportunity presents itself, but again they attempt to do so by cleverly packaging and publicizing their ideas rather than through behind the scenes manipulation. How do they accomplish this? How do they bring their influence directly to bear on the executive?

Britain, where think tanks operate on modest budgets, provides one of the more notable examples of policy influence by think tanks. According to Simon James (1993), it was the Centre for Policy Studies (CPS), founded by Mrs Thatcher and Sir Keith Joseph in the 1970s, that was the primary vehicle for changing the course of the Conservative party: 'significantly the Centre for Policy Studies, not the Conservative Research Department, produced the "stepping stones" policy documents for the Shadow Cabinet' (p. 495). Furthermore, the CPS and other Conservatively oriented think tanks — for example, the Institute of Economic Affairs — provided doses of rejuvenation when the Thatcher cabinet appeared to falter, especially after the general elections of 1983 and 1987.

In many respects the important role played by think tanks in the UK can be credited to Margaret Thatcher. She broke new ground by deliberately fostering links with think tanks outside the party and, through the Prime Minister's Policy Unit, bringing into her inner circle intellectual entrepreneurs who helped set the party on a new course (Willetts, 1987). And in doing so she effectively helped put in place a new paradigm of how to impart direction to the affairs of state. James (1993: 505) points out that 'had Labour won the 1992 election the Institute of Public Policy Research [IPPR, a Labour-oriented think tank] would probably have exercised an influence similar to, if less potent than, the Centre for Policy Studies'. He also noted that the deputy director of this institute had been 'pencilled in as head of the No. 10 Policy Unit'. In 1994, David Miliband, an IPPR research fellow, was placed in charge of policy in Tony Blair's private office. More generally, IPPR 'has proved a haven for frustrated [Labour] parliamentarians who want to talk policy with experts' (Milne, 1994: 25). While IPPR has the closest connection with Labour, it is not the sole provider of intellectual stimulation. The century-old Fabian Society, the Social Market Foundation, the European Policy Forum and the two year old post-modernist Demos all put ideas and studies in the hands of Tony Blair giving him the opportunity to demonstrate that he is not simply waiting for the Tories to self-destruct but also that he and his new head of policy are in the market for new ideas. In general many politicians, or at least those with leadership aspirations, find some convenience in being associated with think tanks. Thus, John Redwood, the former Welsh secretary and challenger to Prime Minister John Major's leadership, at about the same time as his attempt to depose Major in the summer of 1995, became involved in the founding of the 'Conservative 2000 Foundation', headed by his political adviser and leadership campaign organiser.

All this ferment and interaction between the parties and think tanks in Britain suggests that the role played by the latter is not a temporary one. Nor is it restricted to just the Thatcherite period. And while James suggests that, overall, think tanks in Britain are less influential than those in the USA, his analysis indicates that under certain circumstances the British think tanks are not only enormously influential but can be used to good effect by the executive. Rather than developing an in-house capacity for policy development, party leaders in the UK appeared to have developed a technique for outsourcing the need for new ideas while maintaining strong control over how those ideas are to be used and incorporated into the party's policy agenda. The ability to do so largely derives from the Westminster model, which provides the opportunity for (but certainly does not guarantee) strong executive governance. Certainly Thatcher's leadership style and use of think tanks fit monocratic decision making, being highly centralized and integrated. Thatcher, in her use of think tanks, also underscores a point made by Michael Foley (1993), namely, that, in addition to making direct appeals to the populace, prime ministers increasingly distance themselves from their government.

Canada is blessed with a number of more or less independent think tanks. They are more numerous compared to those in the four other countries under examination. There are at least two reasonably well funded such institutes with a claim to national prominence and a fairly broad orientation to economic and social issues, the C. D. Howe Institute and the Institute for Research on Public Policy (IRPP). Of the two the former is rather more conservative and focuses more on economic issues. The Vancouver-based Fraser Institute has carved out a significant niche for itself by offering a distinct neo-conservative, and sharply edged market-oriented view of issues. There are also institutes with distinct regional identities, the Canada West Foundation and the Atlantic Provinces Economic Council (APEC). Both APEC and the IRPP are more dependent on government funding than the others. The Fraser Institute eschews such funding. Then there are a host of smaller, often more specialized organizations, such as the Ottawa-based Institute on Governance, the Atlantic Institute of Market Studies, the Caledon Institute and the Centre for Policy Alternatives. The last is the only one offering a distinctly left perspective on a wide range of issues, while the Caledon Institute, also to the left of centre, is concerned mainly with the protection and promotion of social programmes. The main ones, including the Fraser Institute and the regional bodies, are quite prolific. APEC is most directly dependent on government funding and does have in-house economists conducting research. Most, however, follow the classic description of idea brokers, relying on external researchers for their feedstock and adding value through the packaging and selling of ideas and proposals.

Canadian think tanks have helped to structure the broader policy agenda and have served as an important conduit for the distribution of academic ideas on policy problems to government and the media. Certainly the well-established outfits such as C. D. Howe, the IRPP and Fraser Institute have mastered the art of extracting maximum publicity out of even relatively thin publications. Yet the direct impact of these institutes on political decision makers has probably been less compared to Britain and Australia where, ironically, they are both fewer in number and less well financed. In the main, they lack the direct connections with ministers and prime ministers. None of the Canadian think tanks can be described as 'havens for frustrated parliamentarians'. Except perhaps for the Reform Party, Canadian politicians have not attempted to cultivate such connections; and institutes in turn have also been reluctant to develop them. Part of the reason lies in the tax regime: think tanks which become involved in politics risk losing their status as charitable institutions for tax purposes (Lindquist, 1993). There is also a climate in Canada, which makes it unseemly to become too directly involved in politics. The net result is that much of the criticism of government policies made by or through such institutes often has a curious apolitical cast to it. Furthermore, while a number of institutes have been asked by government in recent years for help in organizing conferences and public meetings as part of the government's consultative process, no one think tank has succeeded in putting its imprint on a party's election platform, in placing specific items on a government's legislative agenda, or in having key figures from an institute move into a prime minister's or minister's policy entourage. In short, there has been nothing comparable to the relationship between the Centre for Policy Studies and the Thatcher government in Britain, and as a direct source of advice to ministers and governments think tanks remain weak in Canada. They have, however, played an important role in shaping the broader policy agenda. In particular institutes such as C. D. Howe and the Fraser Institute have helped to promote and legitimize the objectives of deficit reduction and government retrenchment, especially at the provincial level.

Think tanks in Australia have a more distinct ideological cast than those in Canada. Marsh (1992) and Stone (1992) note that the rise of Australian think tanks parallels American and British developments. Thus on the right of the political spectrum are the Institute of Public Affairs, the Tasman Institute, the Sydney Institute, the Centre for Independent Studies and the Australian Institute for Public Policy; on the left is the relatively new Evatt Foundation, 'which champions social democratic values' (Marsh, 1992: 35). None of these, however, appears to have had the same direct impact on mandate formation and implementation as the British Centre for Policy Studies, not even the Evatt Foundation, which does receive substantial funding from the Commonwealth government. There is little evidence of party leaders having used think tanks as spring boards or sources of ideas on policy. Both the Liberal and Labor parties have affiliated research centres, the Menzies Centre and the Whitlam Institute, but they do not have a high profile or impact on party policies. In the case of the latter, it could be that advice from this body, which would lead to spending more money on new programmes, did not fit with the then Labor government's managerialist agenda.

There has at the same time been a growth in what in Australia are referred to as 'public sector think tanks'. Thus, bodies such as the Australian Bureau of Agricultural and Resource Economics appear to have a more prominent role. However, they are government created or dependent bodies and their advice and influence is channelled in good part through individual line departments. This development is consistent, therefore, with what Oliver (1993: 134) describes as the 'iron triangle of bureaucracy, industry and executive government' in Australia, making for a 'closed, non-porous, policy-making system'.

In Australia, therefore, the role of independent think tanks and the capacity of political leadership to make use of their expertise appears to be limited. This may not always have been the case, however. Walter (1986: 45) notes that the birth of the Institute of Public Affairs in the 1940s served as a rallying point for non-Labor forces after the collapse of the United Australia party, and subsequently this institute played a role in the formation of the Liberal party. From the late 1940s until 1972, however, executive governance was characterized by 'bureaucratic dominance of ministerial offices' (Walter, 1986: 48). Subsequently, ministers and political staff have gained more influence in relation to the bureaucracy.

And, as will be noted below, the political parties in Australia do appear to have the capacity to tap into less formal networks of expertise, lodged within the parties, in universities and in consulting firms. None the less, in Australia the influence of the independent think tanks lies much more in shaping the intellectual climate in which the debates over the role of the state and the importance of markets occur.

If among our five countries Britain represents the case of where think tanks have been inordinantly important in the advisory process, then Germany and the Netherlands represent the two countries where independent think tanks appear to have the least weight. Mayntz, writing on Germany, notes: 'There are some policy research institutes which serve the government collectively, but the influence of these bodies on government policy is mostly rather indirect and it would be difficult to trace specific policy decisions to their advice' (quoted in Gellner, 1990: 3, n. 8). Furthermore, many of these research institutes receive extensive government funding; it is difficult, though not impossible, to point to bodies that play a more autonomous role comparable to those found in the UK and the USA. Some of the more autonomous institutes are found at the *Länder* level where frequently they have links with politicians. The *Institut für Wirtschaft und Gesellschafts*, for example, is linked to the Premier of Saxony, Kurt Biedenkopf. On the other hand, one can point to certain bodies in Germany and the Netherlands that carry out some of the functions performed by independent think tanks elsewhere. In Germany, the Council of Economic Experts (CEE), created in 1963 and consisting of five academic economists, is by law supposed to be independent of both government and interest groups, though two of the current appointees are typically seen as having links with trade unions and employers respectively. Its role is to provide the government 'with the views of senior academic economists on economic policy' and to help educate the broader community on economic matters (Singer, 1993: 82–3). While allegedly not enjoying direct influence, government policies have nevertheless been consistent with, or followed, the views of the CEE and changes in them. Essentially, the CEE has played a role in signalling changes in economic heterodoxy comparable to that played by think tanks elsewhere. Thus Singer points out that in the United Kingdom think tanks were critical in countering orthdodox Keynesian assumptions operating within government circles, while in Germany it was the CEE that broke new ground by advocating a 'moderately monetarist approach' in the early 1970s, which was accepted by the government and followed by more explicit money supply targetting by the *Bundesbank*. Keynesian heterodoxy, it should be noted, was never that pronounced in the German bureaucracy.

Keynesian heterodoxy is likely to have held greater sway in Dutch government and advisory circles. The Central Planning Bureau (CPB) was created in the early postwar period, with Jan Tinbergen as its first director, originally as part of the Labour Party's socialist vision but it evolved as a macroeconomic forecasting agency. The Scientific Council for Government Policy (*Wetenschappelijke Raad voor Regeringsbeleid* (WWR)) has provided more specific applied policy advice, though its influence began to wane in the 1970s. The Dutch government has an in-house equivalent to the German CEE, namely the Commission of Economic Experts (CEE) *(Commissie Economische Deskundigen)*, which brings together the top economists from the Ministries of Finance and Economic Affairs and yet a further body, the Social and Economic Council (SER).

The SER in the Netherlands, and the informal links between the ostensibly independent CEE in Germany and employers and trade unions point to other aspects of the advisory systems in place in Germany and, especially, the Netherlands, namely the presence of neo-corporatist bodies and practices. In the Netherlands, until changed by parliament in 1994, the government was required by law to consult the SER, a body which draws on representation from organized labour and business as well as expertise from universities and other sectors. The main actors in the SER, including the trade union federation, the employers' federation, agriculture, small business and the government's own experts from the CEE, have their own research and analytical capacity, and their advice will often feed in to the deliberations of the political parties and policy-making networks more generally (Van Delden, 1993: 155–6).

Finally, and perhaps the most important point of all, political parties in both countries have in-house think tanks in the form of party institutes or foundations. The ones in Germany, such as the Konrad Adenauer Foundation linked with the Christian Democratic Union (CDU) and the Friedrich Ebert Foundation linked with the Social Democratic Party (SPD), are exceptionally well financed and perform a role that goes well beyond what one might normally expect of such bodies; for example, they serve in part as vehicles for German foreign aid. Thus both the CDU and SPD had budgets of approximately DM140 million each in 1986, of which some 95 per cent came in the form of government subsidies and of which about 60 per cent was allocated for foreign aid projects (Pinto-Duschinsky, 1991). Dutch party foundations are supported on a much more modest scale, in the thousands of guilders rather than millions of marks. None the less, according to Wolinetz (1990), while the range of activities of Dutch party foundations is necessarily narrower, they are still quite effective in what they do.

In both countries they serve many of the functions performed by outside think tanks in Britain and the USA. In Germany emphasis of the party foundations is much more on education than research and policy advice; in the Netherlands, even though the institutes are smaller, they do have

relatively more emphasis on research. Because of the manner of government subsidies, the Dutch parties have separate research bureaus and
educational institutes; these research bureaus are in addition to the research
staff of the parliament parties. The literature on German party foundations
suggests that the research and policy advice function is much less important
than the extensive training and educational work they undertake. One
suspects, however, that these party foundations still provide an important
anchor for networks of experts who at the same time have a partisan
affiliation to the executive or executive-in-waiting. These networks can
then become quite useful in developing the party's election platform. These
networks and party foundations appear to be less important in the
implementation phase, although it varies from ministry to ministry.

The notion of networks is also critical in the functioning of the Dutch
party foundations. On the research side, the foundations prefer to
concentrate on those issues 'with which the party will have to grapple in
the next three to five years', although they will entertain requests from the
party for short-term advice (Wolinetz, 1991: 11). More critically, 'regular
staff can normally draw on the assistance of party members (and others) in
universities, trade unions, business, or government with expertise or
interest in particular areas. The CDA [Christian Democratic Appeal]
Scientific Institute, for example, maintains a "bank" of some 400 experts
on different fields' (Wolinetz, 1991: 12).

The second point, stressed by Wolinetz in the case of the Netherlands
but also applicable to Germany, is a more general political culture that
places a high value on expertise. Considerable weight is placed on the
substantive expertise of prospective candidates for ministerial portfolios, and
lists used for balloting purposes under proportional representation are
constructed with the need for such expertise in mind (Andeweg, 1988).
Furthermore, since constitutionally in the Netherlands there is no requirement that cabinet ministers be drawn from elected members of parliament,
they are often drawn from universities and other institutions.

So, what are the actual and potential functions of think tanks? First, in
developing a political party's mandate, think tanks would seem to be ideally
situated to provide the intellectual fodder for the development of party
platforms, particularly if the party is shifting to a new course. Such
institutes, or at least their key personnel, can also become directly involved
in drafting party manifestos, as appears to have happened with the Conservatives under Thatcher.

Second, think tanks are useful in the critical transition phase, when an
opposition party becomes, or becomes part of, the government or governing
coalition, by preparing briefing books and specific proposals for new
policies and strategies for implementing them. Think tanks are less useful
on the actual implementation, unless personnel from the think tanks in

question move directly into government, either in ministers' offices or into key bureaucratic positions.

Third, think tanks are less relevant for meeting partisan needs. Personnel recruited for lower level 'political administration' type positions — liaising between the ministers and different segments of the party, dealing with constituency matters — are typically more likely to come up within party ranks or, at higher levels, to be concerned primarily with process rather than substantive political ideas.

Fourth, as sources of countervailing advice, think tanks are useful in challenging prevailing assumptions, as well as specific policies, held by line department bureaucrats. On a day-to-day basis, however, it would be difficult for think tanks to perform this function, again unless the personnel in question were to move directly to a minister's office or into the bureaucracy itself.

Fifth, the legitimation role of think tanks should be seen primarily as breaking ground for new ideas, not as directly assisting the minister or party leader in championing these new, often radical, ideas. Sherman's metaphor is evocative of this role: 'think tanks are outriders who, if they win the preliminary skirmish of ideas, allow politicians to move onto the new ground' (quoted in James, 1993: 500). In any event, it may be misleading to hypothesize a too direct linkage between the activities of think tanks and the adoption of specific policies (Denham and Garnett, 1994). With regard to new ideas, it is worth stressing the international character and origin of many proposals on privatization and the like and the international links between many of the right of centre think tanks. Many of these links go back to the first conferences of the Mont Pèlerin Society organized by Friedrich Hayek in the late 1940s (Cockett, 1995), and they still persist in the form of regular exchanges, communications and the like among institutes such as the Heritage Foundation in the USA, the Adam Smith Institute in Britain, and the Fraser Institute and Atlantic Institute for Market Studies in Canada. Certainly in Canada the New Zealand experience in government downsizing has been actively promoted by bodies such as the Fraser Institute.

Sixth, the mobilization function is the task of ministers who infuse the bureaucracy with new ideas and persuade them to adopt some new course of action. The value of think tanks lies in their capacity to provide exogenous shocks to the bureaucratic system, not in providing the wherewithal for managing the bureaucratic politics that invariably accompanies the introduction of new initiatives.

Finally, think tanks play a strong reflection and rejuvenation role. By virtue of being some distance removed from party and cabinet actvities and the demands of the portfolio, a think tank provides an ideal venue for ministers to think about larger issues and longer term strategies. This might be in settings such as seminars or retreats, or even informal gatherings where a politician can discuss or be exposed to interesting ideas without being put in the position of being seen as pronouncing on policy matters.

Management Consulting Firms

If think tanks are about developing, brokering and popularizing ideas, then management consulting firms can be said to be about the actual implementation of decisions based on those ideas, designing the appropriate organizational structures and programmes, and evaluating their performance after implementation. An additional, and crucial, distinction needs to be drawn between think tanks and management consultants. The former are concerned primarily with pressing their ideas on governments, the latter are essentially hired guns, willing, for a price, to do the government's bidding: that is, to design appropriate policies or to examine carefully a subset of government operations and make recommendations on their improvement. The distinction is not hard and fast — much like traditional public servants, management consultants can be far from neutral in their advice, having developed their own ideologies and ways of doing things. Nevertheless, management consulting firms can be seen as instruments that astute executives potentially can use to bypass reluctant civil servants or simply to tap into expertise not generally available within the bureaucracy.

There is much greater variety among and between management consulting firms, particularly in terms of size, than between think tanks. Virtually any former civil servant with a cellular phone, fax machine and computer can set themselves up as a consultant, ready to sell their specialized expertise to former employers and others. At the other extreme we have what are generally referred to as the 'big six' — Arthur Andersen, Coopers & Lybrand, Deloitte Touche Tohmatsu, Ernst & Young, KPMG Peat Marwick and Price Waterhouse (Stevens, 1991). On a global basis, Arthur Andersen (or specifically their consulting arm, Andersen Consulting) is the largest player. These six all have their roots in accounting; indeed, in formal terms, they still are accounting firms often with a consulting branch organized as a separate subsidiary. However, in recent years well over half their profits derive from non-accounting services, and a good portion of those services are delivered to governments. In between the two extremes we have more specialized firms, specializing in areas such as economic analysis or information systems. The McKinsey Group and, especially, the Boston Consulting Group, for example, specialize in strategic brain storming and economic analysis. Towers Perrin is focused more on human resource consulting. EDS, currently in the process of being spun off from its parent, General Motors, specializes in the design and management of complex information systems. Significantly, however, EDS is becoming increasingly involved in providing advice on broader management and strategic concerns to both governments and corporations, more than tripling its revenues to in excess of US$600 million in 1995 after acquiring A. T. Kearney, a Chicago-based consultancy. In other words EDS is more and more occupying terrain covered by the big six. By and large, therefore, it is the big six and some of their competitors, such as EDS, in which we should be interested. They are best positioned to provide advice on major issues, by virtue of their detailed knowledge of particular sectors or departments, and they stand to have significant impact when they bring their integrated knowledge to bear in particular decisions made by both bureaucrats and the political executives. And the knowledge in question is typically that acquired on the basis of previous work for government and from experiences around the world. This latter point brings into play a further aspect of their role: the globalization and diffusion of expertise in the area of administrative reform. While there are international links among think tanks, especially among those right of centre, it is the large management consulting firms that really have the organizational wherewithal to distribute and diffuse specialized knowledge around the world and, more crucially, be in a position to implement their ideas and knowledge. Although local branches tend to be owned by the principals in specific countries, they are all essentially multinational firms operating globally.

With respect to advising core executives, in what ways are or can these firms be important? How and why did they develop such a role? One dilemma is that there has been relatively little concrete research done on the policy/advisory role of management consulting firms. A 1976 work by Guttman and Willner, published under the auspices of Ralph Nader's Center for Study of Responsive Law, lumps management consultants in with think tanks as part of a 'shadow government' that has effectively taken the policy-making function away from elected and appointed public officials. This argument represents an early if crude version of the hollowing out thesis. This particular analysis of the role of management consultants in the USA has not been pursued, however. Recent works such as Ricci (1993) focus more on think tanks as the agents primarily responsible for usurping the policy function, paying virtually no attention to management consulting firms. However, with regard to management practices and implementing bureaucratic reform, Halligan (1995) suggests that in the UK, New Zealand and Australia management consultants have been actively involved in implementing these changes. And Saint-Martin's (1996) detailed study of management reform in Canada, Britain and France argues that, certainly in Canada and Britain, the big six firms have had extensive involvement in

diffusing and implementing managerialist ideas. How do these developments bear on policy advice at the highest levels?

William Farlinger, chairman of Ernst & Young in Canada and close
confidant of the leader of the Conservative party in Ontario, Michael Harris,
became head of the transition team for Harris when the latter was elected
premier of Ontario in June of 1995 on the basis of a distinctly right of
centre platform emphasizing deficit reduction and extensive cuts to social
programmes. Subsequently, Farlinger was appointed chairman of Ontario
Hydro, North America's largest electric utility. Ernst & Young had
previously conducted a study on the feasibility of, and recommended, the
privatization of the utility.

The well-publicized Australian Liberal party's *Fightback!* manifesto of
1991, which became the centre-piece of Liberal leader John Hewson's
election platform, was drafted not within the party or by think tanks closely
affiliated with it but by an outside consulting firm, Access Economics.

In Britain, the Conservative government has not only handed out several
million pounds worth of consultancies to Andersen Consulting, Booz Allen
and others, but John Major himself has hired a consultant from McKinsey
to head his policy unit. Also in Britain the links between management
consulting firms, think tanks and politicians are quite close. Within both
Labour and Conservative circles there is considerable movement between the
three arenas. Furthermore, in the case of the think tank closest to Labour,
the IPPR, 40 per cent of its funding comes from corporate sources, and a
good portion of that comes from consultancies such as Andersen Consulting
and Price Waterhouse. As well, of the 50 per cent of funding from
'charitable sources', a good amount is likely derived from charitable
foundations established by consulting firms such as Andersen Consulting
(the remaining 10 per cent comes from trade unions). Money through these
channels is both for core funding and specific projects.

In these three countries at least, there is strong circumstantial evidence
of close connections, and the exercise of influence, between management
consulting firms and governments at the highest level. Management
consulting firms can be especially useful with respect to the development
and implementation of new policies. The evidence is less clear for Germany
and the Netherlands. In the latter country, consulting firms such as
McKinsey were used extensively during the government's economic
restructuring as well as in the reorganization of its bureaucracy and
government organization, especially with regard to the allocation of
responsiblities between local, provincial and central levels of government.
Cuts to the bureaucracy during the Lubbers centre-right coalition period
meant that a fair bit of specialized government expertise was lost thereby
forcing government departments to resort more to outside consultants for
advice on restructuring issues. The Ministry of Economic Affairs, the main

source of internal expertise on such matters, has always been rather thin on the ground. Evidence of the increased use of consultants by government departments lies in an interdepartmental task force of officials set up by the government in 1993 to assess problems in the use of consulting contracts.

Germany has done least in applying managerialist solutions to its public sector problems, the main calling card for the big six in the three Anglo-Saxon countries. It is not that management consultants were not active, but many of their services were delivered not to government but to banks and other non-government agencies involved in economic restructuring issues, especially with regard to East Germany.

So what accounts for the increasing importance of management consulting firms in the policy process? Over the past decade the views of management consulting firms have increasingly come to penetrate governments. Although governments may initially have invited them in, management consulting firms have made themselves ever more attractive if not indispensable. Trade publications aimed at civil servants are filled with . advertising for management consulting firms. In Canada, KPMG has recently created the KPMG Centre for Government Foundation, which in turn has launched a joint venture with the Institute of Public Administration of Canada, the main professional body for academics and civil servants, to research 'Alternative Programme Delivery and Financing' (Lindquist and Sica, 1995). Former bureaucrats and others with public sector expertise have been hired by these firms to develop a rapport with civil servants and to sell the firms' many and varied services. The use of consultants' services has spread across and up different levels of government. Increasingly, members of the political executive make direct use of consultant reports in decision making, often in contentious areas. In Canada recently a special commission, appointed by the separatist Parti Quebecois government, contracted with Samson Belair/Deloitte Touche (the Quebec office of Deloitte Touche Tohmatsu International) to supply it with studies purporting to show only limited economic consequences should the province of Quebec separate from Canada. Clearly the intent was to use this information to help reassure citizens in the weeks leading up to the Quebec referendum on sovereignty in the autumn of 1995 that the breakdown of the Canadian state and the transition to a sovereign Quebec would be a relatively painless one.

Management consulting firms, in turn, are driven to search out government work for a number of reasons, and the craving for power and influence is not necessarily foremost among them. Nor, for that matter, is working for government *per se*. The interest in management issues arose in the evolution of the accounting profession itself. Major firms, such as Andersen Consulting, have had management advisory services since the 1920s. The consultancy part of their business began to grow in the 1950s and 1960s as issues such as corporate strategy development and information systems development began to grow in importance. As well, in the 1970s accountants increasingly began attaching comments to their auditing statements concerning management practices they had uncovered during the course of audits that they felt could be improved. Clients, in turn, found this information useful and soon this practice expanded into the provision of full-scale management advisory services, which led these accounting firms to acquire further capacity and specialized skills in these areas. It was in the 1980s that growth in the consultancy sector exploded. In Britain, for example, the number of member firms in the Management Consultancies Association (MCA — the main UK trade association) grew from 25 to 33 and the number of consultants employed and clients served grew fourfold from 1980 to 1990. Income over this period grew nine times at constant prices (HMSO, 1994).

This development began in the private sector, but soon extended to the public sector as well. In Canada, for example, the Auditor General in the late 1970s and early 1980s began to expand his focus from simply auditing to making statements about value for money and the well-performing organization. Management consulting firms too began making inroads in the public sector.

In the UK, for example, MCA members' annual consultancy income from all government work (including local government and bodies such as the National Health Service) grew from £35 million in 1985 to £209 million in 1993. This increase was in step with the general increase in consultancy work although the proportion of consulting revenues derived from government work did increase from about 24.5 per cent in 1985 to 28 per cent in 1993 (HMSO, 1994). Data prior to 1985 are not available, but one suspects that in the mid-1970s the comparable figure would be less than 15 per cent. In any event, 28 per cent is not an insignificant amount and represents a lucrative and growing part of management consulting firms' income.

This growth in government work came about both because there was a demand for specialized expertise to help with designing and implementing management information systems and the like and because many of the traditional areas of accounting were beginning to shrink. The original professional body for accountancy, the Institute of Chartered Accountants in Commonwealth countries, in which the big six have their basic roots, began to be undercut by competing professional bodies in areas such as industrial accountancy. The arrival of personal computers and accounting software meant that smaller firms could now handle their accounting needs internally. More recently the issue of liability for audited statements has made what was essentially the bread and butter of the accounting profession much less lucrative. All these reasons, therefore, have led accounting firms to pursue other sources of work much more aggresively. Furthermore, the forces that have led to increasing integration, mergers and the like in the private sector generally have also affected the accounting practice. More so than ever before, the capacity to deliver an array of specialized services through one firm and in an integrated package is something that clients, in both private and public sectors, find attractive. There are still several niches for smaller, highly specialized firms, but by and large at the intermediate level the trend has been for increasing concentration as local, regional and national firms have merged with one or other of the big six. And in terms of recruitment, the majority of new hirings are not traditional chartered accountants but individuals with expertise in data management and security, professional credentials in public sector management and the like. Thus, more so than the other outside advisory bodies discussed so far, management consulting firms appear to be best positioned to influence the making of public policy and perhaps most likely to usurp some of the core functions of the executive.

It should be stressed that many such firms, as well as the politicians making direct use of them, would deny that they wield unusual influence or are arrogating core executive functions. The view is that the basic decisions on what to do are left to political leaders; consulting firms only provide advice on how to implement the goals formulated by leaders. In one sense this is quite true. There are two qualifications. First, when discussing the matter of policy choices, in the present era there is simply little room left for developing and implementing new policies. The current agenda is preoccupied chiefly by what policies and programmes should be ratcheted back or even abandoned and how existing programmes can be delivered more efficiently and at lower cost. Management consultants have made themselves particularly useful in managing cuts. Even at the level of efficiency and cost reduction, policy choices are often embedded in recommendations ostensibly concerning managerial issues, the extent of public sector involvement in service delivery, for example. At broader levels, whether or not to privatize is in many ways fundamentally a policy issue.

Second, management consulting firms often have distinct views on what is good or bad public policy, albeit cast in the language of managerialism. It is extremely rare, for example, to find among current management consultants recommendations that run counter to market-driven, client-centred solutions. Management consultants bring an implicit, and at times explicit, policy perspective to the task of advising governments. Combined with the eagerness with which many core executives make use of their services, the trend confirms the hollowing out thesis. There are a couple of points worth noting, before reaching such a conclusion. First, the current influence of management consulting firms is largely a matter of timing.

While these firms are now perhaps more anxious to press their services on government than before, the use made of their services is nothing new. For example, the Canadian Royal Commission on Financial Management and Accountability (the Lambert Commission) of the 1970s relied almost exclusively on management consulting firms for its background studies and in formulating specific advice. It is just now, given the preoccupation with privatization, cost cutting and deficit reduction, that these firms have become particularly important because they are well equipped to deal with these issues. In other words, should circumstances change, governments may decide that they need to crank up spending again and the influence of management consultants could wane.

Second, management consultants are, essentially, hired guns. They are above all adaptable; that is, susceptible to changing not only the services they offer but also their views, in keeping with fresh demands that governments may wish to have addressed, such as new ways of spending money. So, management consulting firms can be seen not necessarily as contributing to the hollowing out of the state but as instruments that executives can use to help implement their agendas. To be sure, management consultants can be, indeed certainly have been, used by the bureaucracy to gain influence over the political executive, to provide the bureaucracy with incontrovertible evidence about the appropriateness of the course of action it recommends to the executive. Yet the potential is there for executives to use management consulting firms as resources to gain advantage over other actors, including the bureaucracy, in setting and implementing its agenda.

Political Staff

Variously labelled as 'minders', (Australia), 'special' or 'policy' advisers (Britain) and 'exempt staff' (Canada), these people are recruited directly into a prime minister's or minister's office. They serve the minister directly, their primary loyalty is to the minister and they are not seen as part of the regular bureaucracy. Like many of the concepts used to describe informal political processes and structures, it is a little fuzzy around the edges. A minister's political staff may well include one, two or more departmental assistants, as they are called in Canada, drawn from the bureaucracy, whose role is often to liaise between the minister and the line department. In Australia some members of the minister's staff will be seconded from the bureaucracy with the understanding that they will be fully under the control of the minister's office (Walter, 1986: 53). Political staff draw their salaries directly from the government and in most cases ministers are given specific budgets for such staff. However, they are by and large chosen and remain under the control of the minister rather than the public service.

Following Walter (1986), a minister's political staff tends to encompass three main functions: advising, administering and communicating. The last is usually performed by a press officer while administration includes matters such as scheduling and liaison with the parliamentary caucus and political party. It is the advising function in which we are most closely interested, but obviously administration of a minister's office can be crucial in supporting this function and is best done with full awareness of the political nuances associated with different courses of action. A press officer also frequently acts in an advisory capacity and as the main communications arm of the minister plays an important role in disseminating proposed programmes.

The three systems operating under the Westminster model — Australia, Canada and Britain — are characterized by weak political staff. The bureaucracy tends to have the upper hand in tendering advice and ultimately in policy formulation. There are some important differences between the three Westminster systems and, in these differences, certain ironies as well.

Britain has had numerically the smallest political staff, which is the case even now despite expansion of the political staff role under Thatcher. Traditionally the minister's private secretary and limited support staff have been supplied directly by the bureaucracy. Yet historically Britain also provides examples of ministers creating their own almost parallel bureaucracies to direct and second guess the normal line bureaucracies, the first being Lloyd George, who

> is said to have been the only minister of modern times who could defeat the obstinacy even of Treasury officials. Usually, however, he preferred to circumvent them. He carried his private secretaries with him from one department to another . . ., culminating, when he was prime minister, in the creation of a duplicate civil service dependent on himself, the 'Garden Suburb' (A. J. P. Taylor, quoted in Mallory, 1967: 32, n. 14).

Winston Churchill was a close competitor, however. Where Lloyd George had his 'Garden Suburb' located in temporary quarters in the back of 10 Downing Street, Churchill had his S Branch. In both cases these personal bureaus were headed by powerful figures, adjuncts to the prime minister, who while not unfamiliar with bureaucracy tended to be critical of it. At the same time, it was the exigencies of wartime that allowed these personal advisers and their support staff to have such critical influence; in both postwar periods, political–bureaucratic relations reverted to normal Westminster style where ministers depended mainly on civil servants, the permanent undersecretary in particular, for guidance (Plowden, 1991). Since then, individual prime ministers have all brought their own small coterie of press officers and advisers to No. 10; and beginning in 1974 under Harold Wilson the Prime Minister's Policy Unit institutionalized and strengthened the role of such staff. The main innovation wrought by Thatcher was to abolish in 1983 the Central Policy Review Staff (CPRS), the agency supporting cabinet, and essentially to make the No. 10 Policy Unit not only its successor but also to restrict its responsibility to advising only the prime minister (Willetts, 1987). Furthermore, the Policy Unit has placed much more emphasis on tactics as distinct from strategic issues. Nothing comparable transpired with respect to individual ministers' offices, except that with the demise of the CPRS the initiative for new policies was lodged much more clearly in the departments themselves. Ministers no longer had the CPRS looking over their shoulders; but at the same time they also had less access to resources outside the department to be used to counteract the influence of their own officials.

The Canadian system provides a contrasting example of an executive having much more extensive but arguably less effective political staff. The Liberal government elected in 1993 deliberately restricted the number of exempt staff each minister could have and set a budgetary ceiling for their office, largely in order to distinguish themselves from their alleged more profligate predecessors. None the less, even under the new restrictions the size of ministerial staff is greater than that found in the other four countries. And, using the 1980–84 Liberal and 1984–93 Conservative governments as points of comparison, ministerial staff size in Canada has at times exceeded that of the typical French cabinet. Through the creative use of consulting contracts and secondment of public officials to the minister's office, a minister could easily triple or quadruple his or her normal allotment of staff at his or her direct disposal. Yet the irony is that as sources of policy advice political staff in Canada probably rank among the weakest. By and large a typical minister's office tends to be unduly preoccupied with *picayune* political matters. In 1984 the new Progressive Conservative government introduced a more rigorous design with a chief-of-staff in charge of an expanded staff in each minister's office. The initial calculation was that the chief-of-staff would be from outside the bureaucracy, have substantive policy expertise and be paid accordingly. The system did not fulfil the expectations that the architects of the system had for it: despite the better pay, few of the people hired as chiefs-of-staff could be deemed experts. Most came up through the partisan ranks and most saw their task as being the day-to-day management of the demands placed on their minister. While they saw their primary role as that of advising the minister, little of this advice appeared to be of a long-term strategic nature (Plasse, 1994). In emphasizing the short-term political dimension of the role played by political staff one should note that in many respects this simply reflects the predilections of ministers themselves. As Donald Savoie (1990) has noted, few ministers have a strong policy orientation. Most tend to be 'process participants': 'They rarely question policy or the policy process itself. Their purpose is to make deals for a designated clientele. They usually understand how parliament works, enjoy parliamentary jostling, get along well with their colleagues and take particular delight in striking deals' (Savoie, 1990: 193).

Under the current Liberal regime, the number and pay of exempt staff has been severely restricted, which would appear to limit even further the capacity of ministers to draw on external policy advice or to second guess the bureaucracy. Part of this downsizing stems from the overall effort of the prime minister, Jean Chrétien, to project an image of a lean and more pragmatic government. But it may also represent an effort by the prime minister and his office to exert greater control, and strengthen collectivity. While the Prime Minister's Office (PMO) has also been downsized, it is still substantial and contains a policy secretariat responsible for monitoring government programmes in relation to the party's 1993 election programme. The PMO is also staffed by the prime minister's key operatives, personnel who have been close to the PM for some time and who were principal members of his transition team. As well, one of his key advisers was appointed to the Privy Council Office, with the responsibility of coordinating a major review of government programmes. With individual ministers having more limited staff, this gives them less in the way of resources to question directives from the PMO or to chart their own political courses of action.

Until the early 1970s the bureaucracy held full sway in Australia. It was in 1972 with the election of the reform-minded Labor government under Gough Whitlam that attention turned to altering the influence of the bureaucracy and to 'the first systematic institutionalization of personal advisers' (Walter, 1986: 48). The number of ministerial staff was increased and the Prime Minister's Office strengthened. Initially, the intent was to adopt something akin to the French cabinet system with a group of competent partisans placed between the minister and the bureaucracy and with the permanent head being politically appointed. The Whitlam government backed away from the full implementation of this scheme but an understanding was reached with the bureaucracy whereby each minister would have in his office a limited number of ministerial advisers recruited on a partisan basis. Significantly, it appears that under Whitlam approximately half such ministerial staff consisted of public servants on secondment.

The Whitlam period proved controversial in several respects (and not just in relation to ministerial staff), and in battles between outside advisers and civil servants the former seem to have been the losers in most instances. None the less the basic pattern was set. Malcom Fraser did not appreciably alter the paradigm and Bob Hawke continued to build on it (Weller, 1987). Over time the number of ministerial staff has grown with current estimates placing it at around 350 (Oliver, 1993). Yet it is not clear if the functions these partisan individuals play are appreciably different from those in Canada, that is, a focus on short-term political objectives. At the same time, the parties appear to have well-developed networks that allow them to tap into the expertise of university-based academics and consulting firms. The Coalition's (Liberal–National) *Fightback!* manifesto of 1991, in many respects a far more detailed document than the Canadian Liberals' *Red Book*, and the somewhat less detailed 1992 *One Nation* statement of the Labor party are evidence of the parties' capacity to develop coherent, detailed and reasonably plausible plans for governance.

Most important, perhaps, the executive and the highest echelons of the bureaucracy were able to develop a *modus vivendi* on basic policy issues. Without necessarily accepting the entirety of Michael Pusey's (1991) controversial analysis of changes in policy making during the 1980s, during the Hawke period the group of key ministers, advisers and bureaucrats centred around the Expenditure Review Committee of cabinet were largely of a single mind, forming a distinct and coherent entity (Campbell and Halligan, 1993).

Certainly, in comparing the Hawke era with the Mulroney period in Canada, the Australian 'economic rationalists' were able to set about tackling the problems of economic and government reform, and deficit reduction, in a relatively systematic and effective fashion (Aucoin and Bakvis, 1993). The Hawke executive appears to fit into the 'collegial' quadrant but at the same time does borrow some elements from the 'collective' quadrant. While the intellectual impetus may lie outside the immediate cabinet–bureaucratic arena, many of the key figures in the 'economic rationalist' circle are bureaucrats or ex-bureaucrats (Weller, 1989a). What may also be important, however, is that the political leadership itself has played a key role in deciding who among the bureaucrats would play the advisory role. For example, in the transition from Hawke to Paul Keating, the latter replaced a number of senior officials, suggesting that it is not simply a matter of bureaucratic dominance but more one of selective engagement and disengagement of bureaucratic talent on the part of the politicians.

Of the five systems, it appears that political staff are least important in Germany and the Netherlands. Andeweg (1991), for example, notes that in the Netherlands such staff are small and play only a limited role. Yet, as in the case of think tanks, it may be wise to look for functional equivalents. In this instance, the functional equivalent may be found in the politicization of the upper reaches of the bureaucracy. As noted by Aberbach *et al.*'s

(1981) cross-national study, bureaucrats in Germany were rather more likely to fit into the Image III and even Image IV categories, that is, as partisans of particular policies if not of political leaders or parties. Second, it does appear that civil servants and politicians in Germany are more likely to come from the same milieu or share similar characteristics compared to other countries. Third, in Germany techniques such as 'external recruitment' and 'early political retirement' for top bureaucratic positions are available that allow the executive to have much more control over the composition and direction of the bureaucracy (Derlien, 1988). The term 'early political retirement' is a bit of a misnomer since it entails shuffling unwanted civil servants into alternative positions rather than retiring them outright; but it does represent an important clue about how the political executive is able to obtain more partisan advice without necessarily having to go outside the confines of the bureaucracy. Essentially, there is a class of 'political civil servants', comprising some 25 secretaries of state and 100 division heads. When a minister or the whole executive changes (e.g. as in 1969 and 1982) these political civil servants can be temporarily 'retired' and replaced with those more congenial to the new executive. The number involved and the actual turnover is limited, but still enough to provide an incoming minister or chancellor with an opportunity to staff at least some key positions with those known to be sympathetic to the party. In addition, the reservoir can be enlarged through the recruitment of sympathetic experts from the *Länder* governments (Murswieck, 1993).

The bureaucracy in the Netherlands also appears to be more attuned in a partisan sense. Daalder (1989: 8) notes that 'there is not a strong demarcation between politicians and career officials'. Ministers and junior ministers are not infrequently recruited directly from the bureaucracy and in turn members of parliament are often appointed to civil service positions. There is also a certain amount of external recruitment for top positions, and in general an effort is made to ensure that the distribution of party loyalties of civil servants is roughly in proportion to that of the political parties (Andeweg and Irwin, 1993). In the event, a bureaucracy that is more likely to be sympathetic to the government or specific ministers, or at least is easier to engage selectively, will to a large extent remove the need for a sizeable political staff to counterbalance the power of the bureaucracy. This is not the whole story, however, for in both countries there is an extensive and continuing reliance by leaders on the political party for advice and there is evidence that this reliance is increasing rather than decreasing.

Mayntz (1987: 15) points out that Helmut Kohl has relied less on the Chancellor's Office than his predecessors, has 'particularly close links with the party organization', and 'is said to consult regularly with the other members of the CDU's executive organ before major decisions'. In the Netherlands, both premier and ministers consult regularly with their political parties and, according to Andeweg and Irwin (1993: 129–32), within cabinet ministers have increasingly been following the political position of the parties they represent rather than their own judgement. To varying degrees, the previously mentioned party foundations are plugged into these consultative networks.

Political staff fill many of the needs for advice of core executives. First, they play some role in developing a party's proposed mandate and those closest to the party leader will have been involved in drafting party strategy and campaign proposals. While in opposition, however, the size and depth of a party's expertise is limited, especially in Westminster systems. Perforce more reliance must be placed on contacts with experts outside the immediate party (or shadow cabinet).

Second, political staff are clearly more important in the transition phase, taking the party's platform and seeking the cooperation of, or otherwise mobilizing, the bureaucracy in translating lofty goals into reality. However, the political staff of a newly elected government may be inexperienced thereby limiting the ability of a new government to implement its mandate.

Third, partisan tasks are the primary *raison d'être* of political staff. Preoccupation with the minutiae of political administration, however, could well come at the expense of broader policy objectives. In particular, it could harm the capacity of staff to deal with the fourth need, that is, to offer countervailing advice to ministers on proposals from the bureaucracy. On a day-to-day basis political staff are in the best position to respond to, and keep on top of, such proposals, but unfortunately the sheer weight of numbers and expertise is on the side of the bureaucracy.

Political staffs are crucial in providing legitimation and mobilization to ministers who attempt to break new ground or innovate. It is the minister and his or her press secretary among others who must cultivate support in important constituencies such as cabinet, the party and ultimately public opinion. In effect no one else can do these tasks. Mobilization means in part mobilizing public opinion but also and perhaps more critically mobilizing the bureaucracy. There are many ways of so doing but they boil down to engaging those elements of the bureaucracy that are sympathetic to the minister's agenda and disengaging those who are not. Across-the-board attacks on the bureaucracy will not help the cause of introducing new programmes. The mobilization process will involve conflict and co-operation. Case studies of successful policy innovation in Canada suggest that alliances around specific proposals will cut across the political–administrative divide (Bakvis, 1991; Johnson, 1981).

Finally, a minister's political staff will not be able to meet the need for reflection and rejuvenation, given their continual preoccupation with pressing political matters. A new staffer, particularly a fairly senior or knowledgeable individual, may be able to inject a fresh perspective into a minister's office. The pressure cooker atmosphere of the minister's office, however, will likely result in the new staffer having limited impact as well as being drawn into the maelstrom.

Before moving to the topic of kitchen cabinets it is worth stressing that a well-functioning and effective political staff, while perhaps not in a position to reflect on longer term strategic considerations, none the less acts as a primary node in a network or more likely a number of networks of specialist advisers and contacts, channelling critical information to the key decision maker, the minister.

Kitchen Cabinets

The term 'kitchen cabinet' has its origins in the presidency of Andrew Jackson. He apparently failed to meet with his official cabinet during the first two years of his term, relying instead on 'old friends' (Pfiffner, 1994: 110). The term therefore is often seen as synonymous with cronyism. I prefer to equate it with 'close personal advisers', the circle with whom the prime minister or minister interacts most closely on a regular basis and draws on for advice. It can be seen in part as a subset of the first two structures, think tanks and political staff, but it is not restricted to those two structures. The circle can include a close family friend; it can also contain key bureaucrats; and it will contain one of the high priests or priestesses in political augury, the professional pollster. By virtue of its informal nature, it is difficult to describe kitchen cabinets in structural or organizational terms as one might do with political staff, for example. Furthermore, the extent to which a kitchen cabinet meets the core executive's needs for advice will vary considerably with the type and number of people who are part of this inner circle.

What can be said is that some political leaders may rely much more on their kitchen cabinet than on more formally organized structures for political advice, both bureaucratic and political, while others are less dependent. Second, some may depend on one or two close advisers while others depend on a rather larger and perhaps more fluid circle. Third, some leaders may use their kitchen cabinet as a means of testing ideas or as an opportunity to let their hair down (i.e. for purposes of reflection or rejuvenation), while others use it as a crucial arena for hammering out final choices.

The extent to which a kitchen cabinet is a function of personal style and, further, coincides with formal structures can be illustrated by the German case. Helmut Schmidt used the apparatus of the Chancellor's Office extensively to manage the policy-making process and as sources of advice, including the different 'mirror-image' sections for each of the ministries. In contrast, Helmut Kohl has never fully trusted or utilized the Chancellor's Office. The device of 'early retirement' notwithstanding, he apparently felt that the office was organized too much in the image of his predecessor. Instead he relies more on a limited circle of close advisers, the core of which includes the heads of the press office and the Chancellor's Office and a state minister attached to the office. The circle extends outside of the Chancellor's Office to include, as noted earlier, high-level functionaries in the CDU. He also has a proclivity to consulting over the phone with prominent experts, high-level functionaries in banking and industry and contacts in the other parties. Since Kohl sees himself as a consensus builder rather than master policy maker (Mayntz, 1987), his reliance on a much less formal kitchen cabinet is not unexpected. His style is also consistent with fragmented decision making, where the responsibility for policy initiatives is left mainly to the line ministries.

Another figure who has relied extensively on the telephone as a means of tapping into different sources of advice is Brian Mulroney, Conservative prime minister of Canada from 1984 to 1993. From the late 1960s onward, efforts to provide assessments to ministers of proposals emanating from line departments submitted to cabinet have been primarily the responsibility of non-political officials in the PCO (Campbell, 1983). The PMO, despite its expansion over time, has never figured prominently in this process, and over the years some of the people who have been closest to the prime minister have been key bureaucrats, the Clerk of the PCO in particular. Brian Mulroney, however, was elected on a platform stating that a new Conservative government would set the agenda and ensure control over the bureaucracy, and do so by recruiting outside of the career civil service.

Ironically, after well-publicized organizational problems in his office, he recruited a career civil servant as his chief-of-staff, and ultimately his closest adviser proved to be the Clerk of the PCO, Paul Tellier. Most of the inner circle with whom he began in 1984, many of them cronies from his university days, were gone within two years. While the Mulroney government did put considerable pressure on the bureaucracy, and subjected it to a number of reviews and renewals, these have been fairly mild by international standards. Furthermore, the top levels of the bureaucracy and the executive were more or less in harmony on key issues. To the extent that there was a single unit or agency driving overall policy it was probably the Department of Finance, largely because of the relatively long stewardship by the Minister of Finance, a coincidence of views between the minister and his officials and because of an absence of direction from other ministers.

The Mulroney example reflects weaknesses both in Mulroney's leadership and the Conservative party's capacity to bring knowledge of substantive policy and the workings of government to bear on the problems of developing and implementing a mandate. It also reflects a more general weakness in Canadian political parties in this respect (Chandler and Siaroff, 1991). Prior to the 1993 election the Liberal party under Jean Chrétien appeared to make virtue out of the necessity, promising that it would rely more explicitly on civil servants than the Conservatives, to force ministers to depend much more directly on departmental officials than political staff for policy advice. Yet significantly, the Liberals did produce a party platform, their *Red Book*, which was far more detailed than is the norm for Canadian parties. Much of the research was produced by the Liberal party's parliamentary research office while in opposition. Some of the key figures responsible for it are now located in the PMO. The intent, at least, is to monitor the progress made by line departments in implementing the *Red Book* proposals. Some of the other people close to the prime minister, his chief-of-staff and his personal adviser, have been with him for several years. They are also staff on whom the PM has placed close reliance. In brief, the Liberal government has probably been better prepared for the transition than most governments; indeed they may yet end up demonstrating a stronger capacity for influencing the activities and policies of the state apparatus than their predecessors. Furthermore, in relying on a smaller yet more sophisticated and experienced coterie of advisers, the Chrétien government helps confirm the lesson of Thatcher's Policy Unit, the locus of her kitchen cabinet, that larger is not necessarily better.

While there will be considerable variation from leader to leader, a kitchen cabinet can play an important role in ensuring that there is substance in the core. This role is vital to develop and implement the mandate (including matters such as selecting political staff). Since the focus of a kitchen cabinet would be on broad strategies, on the one hand, and highly visible political issues, on the other, it would have rather less direct involvement in the handling of partisan tasks and the evaluation of specific proposals from the bureaucracy. With respect to legitimation and mobilization a kitchen cabinet would have more of a role; advice from pollsters, for example, will influence how leaders deport themselves for the presentation if not the contents of the message being conveyed to relevant constituencies and publics. On the reflection–rejuvenation dimension, a kitchen cabinet will fulfil this role for a leader in opposition, particularly after a recent defeat when there is a distinct need to reflect on the state of the party, the need for change and the long haul of getting back into power. While in power, there is much less opportunity (although the need is probably still there) to engage in reflection by both the leader and the kitchen cabinet. The exception would be those leaders who have regular contact with old friends in a previous political (or other) life, perhaps back in the leader's home town, with whom they can ruminate about their current dilemmas and what to do about them. As the case of Brian Mulroney illustrates, however, there is a distinct danger in relying on old cronies as a basis for constructing a permanent kitchen cabinet. To the extent that the leader moves away from those familiar with the inner workings of government, he or she needs to be extremely careful in selecting the inner circle.

Summary

The 'court politics' of yesteryear, in the form of whispered advice and the careful husbanding of critical information, are still alive and well in the modern state, though now the 'court' is no longer situated in the Crown (hollow or otherwise) but in the offices of ministers and prime ministers and, some would argue, in the offices of think tanks and management consultants. Four informal advisory structures — think tanks, management consulting firms, political staff and kitchen cabinets — were singled out for analysis and evaluated in terms of seven categories of executive 'needs', ranging from developing a government's mandate to reflection and rejuvenation. Table 5.1 summarizes the results of this evaluation, noting the strengths and weaknesses of each body in each need category. It is based on experiences in all five political systems; it does not imply that any one form of advisory structure is strong or weak in each and every system.

Table 5.1 *Strengths and weaknesses of non-bureaucratic advisory structures*

		Think tanks	Management consultants	Political staff	Kitchen cabinets
1.	Mandate	moderate	moderate	weak	moderate
2.	Implementation /Transition	moderate	moderate	strong	strong
3.	Partisan tasks	moderate	weak	strong	moderate
4.	Evaluation	moderate	moderate	moderate	moderate
5.	Legitimation	strong	weak	strong	moderate
6.	Mobilization	moderate	weak	strong	moderate
7.	Reflection /Rejuvenation	strong	moderate	weak	moderate

It is also important to note that the need for external advice varies across the five countries. The three Westminster systems — Australia, Britain and Canada — are characterized by relatively weak parties and relatively more independent bureaucracies resistant to political direction, a setting where the need for external advice would appear to be strong but where suitable alternative advisory structures are not always available. In Canada links between the executive and think tanks are minimal and political staff, despite their substantially greater number, are not really up to the task of providing either tactical advice or more detailed technical advice, although the current Liberal prime minister, in contrast to his Conservative predecessor, does appear to have a more experienced and skilled circle of personal advisers with strong partisan connections.

In Britain think tanks and key personal advisers in the Prime Minister's Policy Unit have played an important role in supporting Thatcher's command style of decision making. The Thatcher example also illustrates that under the Westminster system with single-party government and executive control of the legislature, outside advice can have the greatest impact in structuring the executive's mandate and agenda. In Australia, a circle of key personal advisers and bureaucrats, with input from think tanks and political parties, have supported a well-developed and highly integrated collegial decision-making style on the part of cabinet.

In Germany and the Netherlands political parties are much stronger, encompassing in-house think tanks and well-developed networks of policy expertise, and the bureaucracy is more politicized. Here it is important to remind ourselves that in both countries cabinets are invariably based on a coalition of parties. Particularly in the Netherlands, where four or five parties can be represented in any given coalition, political heterogeneity within the executive tends to be high (Andeweg, 1988). This fact produces a collective decision-making style, that is, a decentralized system with relatively independent ministries. This is most pronounced in the Netherlands where prime ministers have much less influence over their cabinet colleagues than elsewhere and traditions of departmental autonomy are well entrenched (Andeweg, 1991).

Andeweg, it should be stressed, characterizes the Dutch cabinet as collective, which means essentially that ministers are allowed to go their own way with little or no interference from their colleagues. This is rather different from what are labelled collegial practices in Westminster systems where, under the rubric of collegiality, not only general issues but also many departmental matters will be decided upon by cabinet on the basis of a common consensus. In Germany, a collectivity and fragmentation coexist. More so than in the Netherlands there is also a corporate dimension in evidence. In both countries, however, the reliance by the executive on networks based within the parties, the careful selection of personal advisers and the selective engagement and disengagement of key bureaucrats have evolved to mesh with, and indeed support, the exigencies of this kind of decentralized decision making.

Concluding Comments

Within the hollow core there is an important role for outside advisers and advisers inside but separate from the state bureaucracy. The question remains, though, whether this role represents a significant contribution to the hollowing out of the central core, to wit the central executive and its support agencies. By turning to think tanks and management consultants and relying on them for ideas and specific proposals on the conduct of the business of the state, this would suggest that the core executive has effectively abdicated part of its mandate to entities that are neither elected nor directly accountable in any way. The fact that many of the ideas and specific proposals have their origins outside not only the core executive but also the borders of the nation state must also be troublesome to those who worry about influence leaching away from the state. Simply from the perspective of democratic theory, where the concern is with the capacity of the electorate to hold governments accountable, the distinct possibility that the definitive advice on what to do with government-owned industries or utilities is provided by a multinational management consulting firm is disturbing. As a 1994 report by the British Cabinet Office Efficiency Unit makes clear, typically controls and checks on how management consulting contracts are evaluated and utilized by government departments and by the executive tend to be weak (HMSO, 1994).

On the other hand, it can be argued that while the state, broadly defined, may have lost a number of its functions, the actors at the core of the state still have considerable capacity for autonomous action. Indeed, according to Saward (Chapter 2), this capacity is increasing. It has been suggested here that less formal, more flexible advisory mechanisms such as outside think tanks and political staff can play an important role in sustaining this capacity, both in providing substance for the government's mandate and in managing its agenda. As Desveaux, Lindquist and Toner (1994) argue, bureaucracies on their own are neither innovators nor have the capability to adapt government policies and organizational regimes to changing circumstances. The forces unleashed in recent years as a result of an increasingly globalized economy may limit the capacity of the state to act in what hitherto were uncontested domains, whether it be agriculture, transportation or telecommunications, but nevertheless they are a fact of life. In these circumstances outside advice may well be necessary to help political leaders to persuade, cajole or shock bureaucracies to adapt and innovate. The impact of such cajoling and external shocks is evident in some instances. The role of the Centre of Policy Studies in shaping Margaret Thatcher's political agenda is one example. In other instances the impact of such advice appears more ambivalent or perhaps even counterproductive. Nevertheless, regardless of the outcome one can also argue that outsiders can help increase transparency and accountability. Even if outside advisers have only limited influence in terms of specific policy decisions *vis-à-vis* the bureaucracy they can still play a positive role. Thus Walter (1986: 57) notes in the case of Australia 'To the extent that the "smooth" functioning of government . . . was disrupted, the inner workings of the public service were opened up to ministerial scrutiny and challenge. The public service was gingered-up, forced to argue for and justify its case in an unprecedented way.'

In conclusion, non-bureaucratic advisers may well contribute to a hollowing out of the core executive. The issues of accountability and the role of money in politics (to the extent that non-bureaucratic advisers are financed by interests external to the state) are particular concerns that arise in this context, as is the real possibility that critical ideas arise less from within the domestic polity than from a narrow international community whose values are not necessarily shared by the electorate. The influence of non-bureaucratic advice may be particularly pronounced when the elected executive is both distrustful of the bureaucracy and uncertain as to what policies to pursue. In other words, such advisers may simply fill a vacuum left by a less than competent political executive. Yet this last point also suggests that, if the executive is clear as to what it would like to achieve, non-bureaucratic advice can be enormously useful (and quite possibly necessary) to overcome bureaucratic inertia and breathe new life into the civil service. So, non-bureaucratic advisers can reinforce the capacity of the core executive to impart direction to the affairs of state.

6 Executive Coordination Mechanisms

Glyn Davis

The desire to influence events, to make a difference, remains strong among executives. Few people seek high office in order to be ineffectual; the crown, once grasped, is supposed to stand for something. Executives develop elaborate central coordination systems because they believe governance will be given substance if structures and rules can bind the activities of the state to the will of its elected leadership. Their coordination efforts reflect in miniature the difficulties of governing — how to bend public agencies to those activities chosen by the executive, and how to sequence initiatives so that government is not simply circular movement, with each new measure cancelling another. Such coordination is inherently political in nature, since the objective is for governments to be and appear in control, yet it relies on policy and administrative systems which may be beyond the immediate direction, or understanding, of the executive.

Governments invest in coordination systems because they wish to shape what happens within the state. Without such mechanisms there is little to encourage coherence, so even a quick glance across nations such as Australia, Britain, Canada, Germany and the Netherlands reveals apparently similar central agencies and coordination machinery. One expects the drive for coordination to be shared across parliamentary systems, even if the means differ to reflect local preferences and history.

Yet a closer inspection suggests differences in the value placed on coordination. Those variations in turn reflect the diverse state traditions to be found in any sample of nations. State traditions, following Dyson (1980), influence the authority and configuration of government and the relative importance of consistency. Dyson distinguishes between what he terms 'state societies' and 'stateless societies'; others characterize nations with liberal, often fragmented state customs as falling within an Anglo-Saxon tradition, in contrast to the emphasis on unity of administration which characterizes a continental tradition of state philosophy. For Dyson, as for writers such as Peters (1994), Germany is the pre-eminent state in the continental tradition of state philosophy. Germanic practices stress the permanent nature of the state, and so the transient character of any particular government. This organic model of state and society implies that 'despite the inevitable division of government into a number of departments and agencies, the authority of the state is not really considered divisible or bargainable' (Peters, 1994: 7). What gives the state its distinctive and enduring character is not a dominant political executive but the rule of law. The state is above all a legal entity, an authoritative moral and public agent 'acting to protect and defend civil society' (Kvistad, 1988: 97).

With government a visitor in a permanent legal structure, the realm of politics is confined to expressly partisan offices such as the Chancellery and the parliament. Policy and administration operate at some remove from the political process. German public servants are not simply instruments of the government but represent, even personify, the long-term responsibilities and legal obligations of the state. As Kvistad (1988: 109) notes, this identification of bureaucrats with the state, in their public and private lives, 'is clearly problematic from an Anglo-American liberal political perspective'.

Dyson's 'stateless societies', those in the Anglo-Saxon tradition, emerge from different habits about the state and its role. Here a private world precedes the state, and delegates some of its authority to government. There is no organic relationship between state and society, since citizens always take priority, and so the boundaries between the public world and its private setting remain clear and distinct. In these societies the public service may be influential, 'but it is not assigned a constitutional role and tends to be subject to structural changes dependent on the government of the day' (Peters, 1994: 10). In societies within the Anglo-Saxon tradition the executive has more control over the shape and function of government; indeed in Britain, with its common law tradition and unwritten constitution, there is no meaningful distinction between government and state. Such traditions, based on liberal beliefs, provide no necessary sense of unity or identification between citizens and the state structure within which they live.

While the institutions and procedures adopted in societies shaped by Anglo-Saxon or continental tradition of state philosophies have much in common, it is likely the concept of coordination conveys a somewhat different meaning in each of these settings. In a society shaped by continental state traditions, coordination is an essential role of government, though its attainment can take different forms. In modern Germany, for example, there are factors such as federalism and the autonomy of federal ministers which apparently work against coherence. Yet the emphasis on the law and its accurate implementation, the influence of specialists rather than politicians in policy making and the role of a permanent, politically sensitive, bureaucracy ensure a high measure of integration. While attempts to create a central planning function in the Chancellor's Office have ebbed and waned, governmental procedures and the habits of consensus within cabinet continue to work toward unitary policies supported by shared administrative norms.

There is a wide variety of practices in societies within the Anglo-Saxon tradition, but generally integration of policy and administration is not so clearly built into state structures. On the contrary, the striving for consistency may be a difficult and unending battle as the forces of fragmentation frustrate imposition of shared objectives and norms. Some such societies, notably the USA, make a virtue of the relative powerlessness of their executives, seeking in the pattern of brokerage within government a reflection of their diverse and pluralistic constituencies. Others within the responsible government tradition place more emphasis on consistency, stressing the right of a politically elected executive to govern while it retains a parliamentary majority.

This chapter explores differences between understandings and practices of coordination across traditions of state philosophy. It argues that while three coordination dimensions — political, policy and administrative — characterize the coordination task, these are realized in subtly different ways. Five nations inform the study: Germany as a classic expression of a society in the continental tradition of state philosophy, and Australia, Britain and Canada as examples of societies in the Anglo-Saxon responsible government tradition. The Netherlands forms the final case study, a nation which combines the pluralism of Anglo-Saxon states with administrative traditions similar to German practice (if based on French models). In the Netherlands, we see most clearly a value judgement about the worth of coordination, with the drive for policy consistency tempered continually by the need to respect social and cultural differences.

Why Assume Coordination Matters?

Coordination arises as an issue because of the necessary compartmentalization of the state. Governing is made possible by specialization. Undifferentiated, the issues which flow through the state would be overwhelming. So ministers specialize, creating portfolios which deal specifically with transport or health or education. Advice is provided by functional agencies with responsibility for particular client groups and policy areas. This division of labour breaks government into defined and manageable tasks, allowing the application of expertise.[1] Once government becomes a series of separate entities, the question of coordination arises. How can each minister, each agency, be made to act in concert? As Martin Painter notes (1981: 266), there is a pressing need to 'reactivate some sense of government as a whole. Coordination is a problem arising as a secondary matter out of the prior need to subdivide and specialise'.

Ensuring decisions made in one portfolio did not contradict a choice settled in another would be complicated enough if units of government were logically structured entities, without overlap. Yet any division of functions in a government is necessarily arbitrary. Public agencies may be designed around policy concerns, around particular clienteles or for administrative convenience. It is likely several different principles of organizational arrangement will prevail at the same time, for there is no intrinsically rational way to carve up the tasks of the state even if tradition pushes structures toward familiar functional groupings — portfolios of Primary Industries, Health, Justice and so on. Nor are there necessarily optimal ways to organize responsibilities within agencies. As March and Olsen (1983: 291) conclude, 'hopes for a firm theoretical basis for institutional design have been mostly unfulfilled; and prescriptions tend to be contradictory. No matter what principles of organisation are followed, it seems to be inevitable that administrative problems will persist'.

The coordination task then is not one of finding agreement between units which share a common foundation or goals. On the contrary, governments are likely to be riven by conflict between agencies, as two or more assert jurisdiction over a particular policy area or clientele. Indeed in the Netherlands commentators joke about the 'fourteen legal families' since agencies do not even share a common legislative tradition (Andeweg, 1988: 132). Specialization in national governments also causes gaps if no agency is assigned, or asserts, responsibility, and governments risk incoherence when pressure groups lobby successfully to establish still further agencies, devoted to a particular policy agenda and granted legislative autonomy.

Reporting findings of the Bielfield Project on guidance and control, Rhodes (1988b: 123) notes the state has developed not just more bureaucracies but also more networks across those agencies. The state must now be understood as essentially fragmented, comprising 'a large number of specialised networks'. The work of the state is 'decomposed into manageable "bits"' so that policy problems are dealt with by designated agencies. As a consequence coordination becomes more difficult, since the logic of central control is undermined by the tendency to specialization. The central question becomes one of how the executive deals with this fragmentation of the state. Does it too break up into discrete units, without common purpose, or can the executive hold together despite the tendency everywhere around it to disaggregate into specializations?

If administrative functions are difficult to coordinate, then the policy challenges confronting the executive simply compound the coordination task. Recent political science literature stresses the potential for the state to become a loose confederation of separate policy domains or subsystems, each dominated by local economic and political interests. Jordan (1990) notes the importance of subsystems, defined earlier by Freeman (1965: 11) as 'the pattern of interactions of participants, or actors, involved in making decisions in a special area of public policy'. This sometimes is labelled an 'iron triangle', suggesting a relationship of symbiotic convenience encompassing the legislature, regulatory agencies and the relevant industry, to the exclusion of those critical of present policy (Peters, 1986). Olson (1982) talks of 'distributional coalitions', cartels of manufacturers or farmers who band together to control a market and protect themselves through government regulation. These studies share a common sense of 'policy closure' around vested interests and government agencies. The policy domain, and the networks it generates, are dominated by elites; the unorganized such as consumers or voters have little voice in policy choices.

The idea of policy communities (Jordan, 1990; Rhodes and Marsh, 1992) presents a variation on the theme of subgovernments forming around particular policy domains. Policy communities do not always share an iron triangle's unity of objective. Indeed the policy community can incorporate two or more opposing coalitions contending for influence, and may not generate a network of interested actors (Wright, 1988). Yet policy communities, linked in what Sabatier (1988) calls a policy subsystem, may include industry association representatives and environmentalists, regulators and consumer groups. Differing positions become well known within the subsystem, but so does shared information about the available policy options and, often, agreement on process. A policy community, therefore, provides a less closed system, with opportunities for networks to form and exchange information. Those in the policy network are incorporated into the policy process through consultative committees, placement on the boards of statutory authorities and regulators, and through regular interchange of personnel.

Policy communities connote long-term relationships, gradual accumulation of information about a policy problem and some agreement on appropriate rules of the game. Heclo (1978) takes issue with the relative stability implied by the 'sectorization' of policy making into separate domains, each with its own policy community. He instead suggests that a rapid growth in interest groups has fragmented the policy process, allowing entry to multiple policy players. The dynamics of Washington encourage 'the development of specialised subcultures composed of highly knowledgeable policy-watchers' (Heclo, 1978: 99). These experts, located both in government and in think tanks and lobbyist organizations around town, link as webs or 'issue networks' within a policy domain. Their participation produces disjointed policy making, with unstable coalitions and ever-shifting agendas. Issue networks influence politicians and bureaucrats by providing detailed information; in so doing they make policy making less able to close around a settled policy, more open to dispute. Where the networks of policy communities are long term, issue networks are *ad hoc* and tenuous.

Whether the more solid world of policy communities or the fluidity of issue networks characterizes policy making, there are clear implications for coordination. The literature describes states in which decision making is specialized and segmented, structured around policy areas and dominated by coalitions of interests which span the public and private sectors. These subsystems may disagree on substance but will share agreement on process and a resistance to 'interference' by central agencies and uninformed ministers. In this setting it is not easy for the executive to impose coherence across government; clustered around each activity of the state are networked communities with an interest in maintaining their influence, able to mobilize against unacceptable government decisions. Their task is made easier by forces which may encourage a hollowing out of the state, as privatization limits the range of public intervention, national governments devolve responsibilities, international agreements shape policy and public servants become managers, responsible for efficient delivery of particular services regardless of overall consequences for coherence (Rhodes, 1994: 138–9).

An elected executive confronted with a state which simultaneously encompasses internal conflicts, competing external imperatives, contested boundaries, unclear jurisdictions, policy lacunae and interest capture is likely to desire some form of coordination. Traditional solutions include cabinet systems, to bring all interests together, and strong central agencies tasked with ensuring consistency. Campbell (1988b: 57), for example, argues that central agency reorganization is a favoured political tool when states must address 'global problems originating from fundamental economic, political and governance problems'. Yet he finds in the Canadian example that creation of 'central agencies to address sectoral issues ran the danger of simply mirroring fragmentation in line departments' (Campbell, 1988b: 72).

Some societies within the Anglo-Saxon tradition of state philosophy have suggested a quest for coherence is not worth the price. American writers such as Donald Chisholm (1989) celebrate redundancy, duplication and overlap in public services (see Craswell and Davis, 1993; Wilson, 1989: 274). Complex systems such as government can be directed from the centre, but only with significant transaction costs. From the perspective of clients a carefully regulated system which avoids redundancies may offer less flexibility than the opportunities available within apparent chaos.

This redundancy school of thought stresses that coordination is a value rather than a necessity in government, and one with significant opportunity costs. Lindblom (1990: 250–1) counsels that coordination is only 'one among competing values and can be overdone'. The possibilities for discovery under chaos may be more valuable than the gains from strong central control, for 'it is often the defect of central coordination that it seeks coordination and nothing else'. The choice we must often make, suggests Lindblom, is between 'intellectual and administrative tidiness, on the one hand, and flexibility for innovation on the other'.

If coordination is a value rather than a necessity in government, its worth should vary across state traditions. For societies in the continental tradition of state philosophy, coherence is an imperative, particularly in laws which govern policy. State authority is legitimate in large part because it is seen as rational, that is, consistent, structured and without ambiguities. The option of embracing a pluralism of policy and structure is not open to such nations. Elsewhere diversity is a more plausible approach, and sometimes realized in practice, but even among Anglo-Saxon-style societies the American outlook is something of an extreme position. In parliamentary systems the logic of adversarial debate does not allow a government to embrace too much incoherence. A government apparently unable to impose policy on public agencies would quickly lose the confidence of the legislature, and office soon after. Coordination is not just a policy or management virtue but has an overt political dimension. Most executives will not long endure accusations that programmes are inconsistent, ministers divided or initiatives dissipated because one policy undermines another. The Opposition is always searching for evidence of governmental failure, and examples of apparent duplication and resulting inefficiency are prized. Political survival requires a government to appear coherent and united, in control and able to account for the resources in its care. The interests of the government therefore require a series of coordinating mechanisms if the executive is to project a sense that the ministry is in command of the state, that the Crown still stands for something. Coordination may be a value rather than a necessity, but it remains the consistent choice among even the most fragmented of societies.

This stress on the virtues of coordination is expressed in political language and embodied in public institutions. Wildavsky (1973: 142) suggests that coordination 'is one of the golden words of our time . . . Policies should be coordinated; they should not run every which-way. No one wishes their children to be described as uncoordinated. Many of the world's ills are attributed to lack of coordination in government'. A preference for coordination informs much policy analysis, so that a discussion of services for the chronic mentally ill can begin by asserting that 'improved coordination via centralized control and other means represents a reasonable, indeed obvious, approach for improving the performance of the mental health system' (Dill and Rochefort, 1989: 145–6). Whenever policy outcomes are unsatisfactory, we look to the internal operations of the state, and blame commonly identified barriers to implementation such as 'vested interests, structural complexity, divergent professional and organisational cultures' (Webb, 1991: 231).

The Coordination Principle

Though a shared virtue, coordination is sought through varying means. Its influence over the structures and operations of executives fluctuates, though in all modern states the sheer size and complexity of government and the relatively modest scale of the central agencies restrict the capacity for control of those at the centre. As Painter (1987: 9) observes, 'it is now commonplace to think of modern government structures as "multi-organisational" networks or "loosely coupled" organisational systems rather than hierarchies of command and control. Coordination in this context involves the management of differences and the accommodation of diversity'. To coordinate means setting out the rules of the game and ensuring their adherence. The objective is guaranteeing a process by which policy conflict within government is recognized, played out and a decision reached. Painter (1981) calls this focus on procedure rather than policy content 'the coordination principle'. Coordination is a political value, pursued by procedural means within government.

But what exactly is being coordinated? If the state is understood as being subject to fragmentation because policy communities cluster around agencies and pursue sectional interests, then at least three distinct coordination tasks confront the executive:

1. *political* — the need for government to appear in control with common objectives and agreed procedures, and to set an agenda for public policy debate;
2. *policy* — the need to achieve objectives, and to prevent contradictory policies in which one choice undermines others;
3. *administrative* — the need to ensure the public sector is working efficiently and effectively toward goals set by cabinet.

These coordination tasks broadly correlate with the primary public institutions found in each of the states in question — a legislature as a forum for political debate, an executive with responsibility for policy formulation and a bureaucracy which delivers those policy initiatives. Yet just as the relations between these institutions vary across states, so do coordination arrangements. A society such as Germany in the continental tradition of state philosophy imposes constraints on the actions of the executive which are less sharply defined in Anglo-Saxon counterparts. The emphasis on law in a continental-style state binds the three dimensions of coordination more tightly than elsewhere, so that

> ... the fragmentation of policy-making which is inevitable in a network of highly specialised and separated organisations is counteracted to a substantial extent by the need to maintain coherence in public law which is itself a major facet of German legalism. The separate parts of the federal administration *cannot* go their own ways or establish their own idiosyncratic methods and procedures. The legal environment and constitutional requirements forbid this, imposing instead common conditions and to some extent common values (Johnson, 1983: 111).

Anglo-Saxon approaches to state philosophy, in contrast, tend to keep the three domains separate, with each developing its own institutions, processes and actors. Idiosyncratic methods and procedures are possible, and perhaps inevitable, reinforcing social and political cleavages within the executive. Yet some measure of coherence is found in the ultimate claims of political coordination over the others; the government has a right to modify policy settings and administrative structures in pursuit of its objectives. In the case of Britain the Constitution can be rewritten by a parliamentary majority if the executive so desires. Because the state is less fixed and solid in character, coordination mechanisms are not so obviously built into public institutions and must be imposed continuously.

A survey of each coordination task highlights divergence in the way the coordination principle is evoked. In political, policy and administrative matters the Netherlands tends to stand out as the interesting exception, an attempt to balance the separation of politics and the state found in the Germanic state with the need for pluralist, permeable structures associated with Anglo-Saxon societies. Holland is a meeting point for two apparently incommensurable models of the state. In places the Dutch executive deals with coordination by abandoning the field, as in the traditional if diminishing reliance on corporatist arrangements in some economic sectors (Wolinetz, 1990a: 417), while in others the state has been able to fashion a consensus across different social pillars. The Netherlands is the test case for any distinction between coordination practices in states in the Anglo-Saxon and continental traditions of state philosophy.

Political Coordination

Politics can be everything, a term too broad for real meaning. Yet in the five nations under study, politics is assigned a clear and narrow character: it is the electoral contest to decide who will form the executive. Political coordination in turn becomes the task of keeping together a team once in government, projecting an image of coherence and achievement and ensuring the executive does not fall through disunity.

The need to practise such political coordination varies across state traditions, despite their shared parliamentary heritage. In continental traditions of state philosophy societies, political coherence is perhaps less expected than elsewhere, reflecting political and structural characteristics. Politically Germany and the Netherlands both rely on coalition governments, and such arrangements inevitably constrain the unity possible within the executive. Indeed in the Netherlands the prime minister can neither appoint nor dismiss members of cabinet selected by coalition partners, and must concentrate on establishing consensus among ministers. As a consequence the 'Dutch prime minister plays a limited and largely reactive role over policy' (Andeweg, 1991: 117), while in Germany the principle of ministerial autonomy is reinforced by section 65 of the Basic Law which requires ministers to make decisions in their own name. A minister cannot be given orders within their own domain, 'not even by the Chancellor' (Mayntz, 1987: 143).

Yet in such societies ministers remain politicians. While German ministers are selected for their substantive policy expertise, they also usually hold leadership positions within their party and the *Bundestag*, and are often former *Länder* representatives (Johnson, 1983: 99). Sensitive to the electoral fortunes of the government, they view policy proposals from both a technical and an electoral perspective and listen to political arguments from the Chancellor. Even so, there remains little solidarity among the executive; 'German ministers seem to be loners who have to fight on all fronts: against at least some of their officials, of their colleagues, and of the factions within the party' (Mayntz, 1987: 153). Indeed in West Germany's SPD–FDP coalition government some ministers maintained special staff specifically to 'shadow one or more departments led by a minister from the other party' (Andeweg, 1988: 130).

To attain coherence, Chancellors must stress discussion and agreement within the government, seeking a consensual style at the inevitable cost of a slow-moving decision making process (Smith, G., 1991: 55). Political coordination relies on the good judgement of the coalition leadership, the influence of the parties and the moral and persuasive authority of the Chancellor. Interestingly all this is achieved without recourse to the private advisers and political staff so prominent in stateless societies. While the *Kanzleramt*, or Office of the Chancellor, has several hundred staff these are predominantly bureaucrats. Dutch prime ministers only intermittently hire personal staff, generally relying on a dozen senior officials employed by the Department of General Affairs (Andeweg, 1991: 118).

Westminster-style government nations such as Australia, Britain and Canada present a contrast. Political coordination is vital, for without unity in parliament the government will fall. Ministers are therefore bound by strong expectations of solidarity, and unambiguously owe their loyalty to the government, if not always to the leader. In such majoritarian parliamentary systems the capacity to govern depends on maintaining a cohesive executive and supportive backbench. Ministers must spend significant time in consultation with colleagues, often through the medium of cabinet committees, and work with large and influential political private offices.

These political staff cast an electoral eye over all major policy decisions falling before government. While in less hectic days 'ministers were their own political advisers', according to former British Prime Minister Harold Wilson (Rose, 1980a: 28), such political confidants are now essential links to the party at large, the parliamentary party, cabinet colleagues and the media. Yet the role of such staff is not without controversy. Rose (1980a: 29) notes that within No. 10 Downing Street friction occurs 'between the short-term political appointees who have no job security, an ill-defined role, and only nominal responsibilities, and civil servants who reckon to know exactly what the PM is expected to do'. Canadian advisers too may find themselves at odds with the expertise embedded in the larger, permanent Privy Council Office. In Australia an accommodation has developed between bureaucrats and ministerial 'minders', to use the term favoured by Walter (1986), but the inevitable overlap between politics and policy threatens jurisdiction confusion. The pattern of influence is, to a significant extent, decided by the relative weight prime ministers assign to their own staff and advice from the Department of Prime Minister and Cabinet.

The use of private advisers in Westminister-style government societies reflects a long-standing tradition about the realm of politics. In such nations it is still largely taboo to 'politicize' the bureaucracy, that is, to appoint too many ostentatious supporters of the government to senior administrative posts. The public sector is expected to retain a non-partisan stance, with appointments and promotions outside the reach of governments. Consequently, political activity is kept separate from policy and management advice. While in practice all senior administrators understand the political context of a government and frame their advice accordingly, constitutional theory demands they not become involved in electoral considerations. Political coordination must therefore be confined to the world of parliamentarians and their staff, sealed hermetically from public administration. That ideas and people regularly breach the closure reflects the practical realities of working closely together rather than the formal distribution of authority under the Westminster-derived model.

In a society shaped by continental traditions of state philosophy, by contrast, 'ministers name all the leading civil servants in their departments' (Mayntz, 1987: 143), choosing senior advisers 'in whom they have personal confidence' (Johnson, 1983: 189). With ministers exercising authority in their own right, rather than on delegation from the cabinet, they have no need for a layer of private staff who can communicate with colleagues and the party. Thus the distinction between partisan and public administration duties found in Australia, Britain and Canada would serve little purpose in a system in which there is no sharp line between ministers and officials in policy making. Officials 'are accustomed to act in political matters on behalf of ministers and this is accepted as perfectly normal in German political life' (Johnson, 1983: 204).

The Netherlands offers a counter example to both state traditions. As a nation of coalition governments, political coordination is immediately constrained by the contending interests of different parties. This limited sphere for coordination is accentuated by corporatist arrangements in some policy spheres, meaning the relevant constituency for a minister is interest groups rather than cabinet. However, the Dutch also choose to separate politics and administration even more sharply than majoritarian nations, by insisting that ministers not be members of parliament. Cabinet is a mixture of technocrats and seasoned politicians. Ministers can be questioned during parliamentary debate, but the executive is expected to exhibit a 'non-partisan character' (Andeweg, 1988: 131). Ministers then are no longer directly part of the political game. They have only a few or no private staff, and are expected to concentrate primarily on their own, narrow, departmental interests. To maintain its consociational political life, in which accommodations must be found across different ethnic and religious cultures, the Netherlands has developed a doctrine of 'government above politics' (Andeweg, 1988: 134). With some restraint Gladdish (1991: 107) describes the Dutch separation of cabinet and government as a 'striking departure from the stereotype of responsible democratic government'.

Political coordination thus takes on a different character according to prevailing state traditions. In Germany political coordination is not a central imperative for government. Diverse views within a coalition are expected and ministerial autonomy is protected; political coordination may be sacrificed if it threatens coalition arrangements. The role of the Chancellor, supported by party leaders and politically attuned bureaucrats, is to forge a consensus about policy and presentation. Political co-ordination is integrated with the policy process rather than forming a distinct and separate realm; indeed in the Netherlands it is hard to see any role at all for political coordination, with government and politics considered separate pursuits. By contrast, in Anglo-Saxon-style societies the executive cannot fall back onto strong legal traditions or consensual forms of policy making to forge a coherent political identity and programme. Political coordination is more central to governmental survival, and requires a cadre of visible and experienced advisers, collegial ministers and strong expectations of unity and cooperation to ensure the executive can withstand assault in parliament and the media.

Policy Coordination

If political coordination is optional, few societies appreciate uncoordinated policy initiatives. Policy coordination, the search for consistent and coherent governmental action, attracts strong interest, and similar institutions, across parliamentary nations. The resulting policy domains bring together representatives at senior levels in each agency to maintain the flow and congruity of government business.

Policy coordination systems tend to look the same because most nations use a cabinet as the decision-making forum in which programmes are presented, discussed and given legitimacy. Cabinets are a shared mode of coordination, though operations vary across nations. The most commonly cited example, the cabinet of the United Kingdom, developed as a solution to the 'perennial power struggle between sovereign and Parliament' (Hennessy, 1986: 2). Ministers were members of the Privy Council who could command the support of both the monarch and the parliament. Faced with an issue, ministers would withdraw from the monarch's presence to a convenient nearby 'cabinet room' and consider their advice. Over time real authority shifted from the monarch to the cabinet room, and the basic model of ministers meeting regularly, debating proposals, and then uniting behind an agreed position has become the norm for parliamentary governments, whether in republics such as Germany or in the constitutional monarchies of Australia, Canada, the Netherlands and the UK.

Cabinets vary in structure and decision rules, from the technocratic style of Netherlands government to the overlay of political and policy concerns which characterize Westminster-style cabinets. In nations which follow the responsible government model, cabinet ministers are drawn solely from parliament, though in Canada this principle may apply retrospectively, with potential ministers found a riding by the governing party. Dutch cabinets are presided over by that nation's non-elected prime minister, while in Germany the chiefs of the Chancellor's Office and Press Office join ministers at the cabinet table. Westminster-style cabinets tend to be deliberative, with outcomes rarely certain before all interested voices have been heard, while in the Netherlands and Germany it is considered inappropriate for a minister to speak on issues outside their own portfolio. Indeed most business coming before the German cabinet has been decided in advance, and cabinet offers formal endorsement of proposals already worked out between agencies. It is the fact of a cabinet as a necessary hurdle before proposals can go to the *Bundestag*, rather than the actual operations of the meeting, which matters.

Yet through these variations cabinet remains the central coordinating mechanism which draws together political and institutional interests in search of coordination. As Mayntz (1987: 153) notes of Germany, in a description which holds true for most parliamentary nations, cabinet's role is to

> . . . coordinate and integrate departmental policies and to resolve conflicts between ministers. The Cabinet should also evaluate policy proposals from different departments in terms of a common frame of reference. If this does not happen collectively, the policy process will be fragmented, disjointed and bear the seeds of conflict, which will emerge only later when programs with discordant effects are implemented.

To support this coordinating role, cabinets and their chairs rely on the support of bureaucratic advisers. These central agencies draw together the policy capacity of departments and ministries, police the routines of cabinet procedures and, in particular, ensure the leader is briefed on all issues before the government. Such agencies have become increasingly prominent as government has become more complex; executives now require 'a more sophisticated set of support mechanisms than was needed when the only real question about a policy proposal was "How will it sell in Moose Jaw?"' (Van Loon and Whittington, 1981: 486).

In Canada the Privy Council Office is the central body for policy coordination; it is matched by the Department of the Prime Minister and Cabinet in Australia, and the Cabinet Office in the UK. The core coordination staff are small in number (200 officers in the UK, less in Australia and Canada) and comprise senior public servants who specialize in policy development, evaluation and coordination. In these offices cabinet agendas are prepared, briefing papers drafted and cabinet decisions recorded. Often the coordinating bodies work closely with the prime minister's political staff, but the divide between the domains remains in Westminster-style systems, with the prime minister's private office guarding its separate, political role.

The German central agency devotes rather more resources to policy coordination. With around 500 staff the Federal Chancellery has a structure which mirrors the ministry, so providing the Chancellor with detailed advice on every activity of government. Despite the potential fragmentation of a coalition government with autonomous ministers, the *Kanzleramt* achieves a high degree of policy coordination. It does so partly through responsibility for planning cycles within government (Johnson, 1983: 110) and partly by supplying detailed assessments to assist the

Chancellor in maintaining a consensus within cabinet. A skilled and professional *Kanzleramt* enables the Chancellor to fashion his or her own 'policy preferences and priorities without exclusively having to rely on his ministers and their departments' (Smith, G., 1991: 50). Interestingly though, the *Kanzleramt* is not described as a 'central agency' within Germany, because patterns of interdependence and a stress on coordination are shared strongly and equally across government.

As always, the Netherlands stands outside the pattern of strong central agencies. Faced with ministers loyal to their coalition parties, and only a small staff within the Department of General Affairs, the Dutch prime minister is bound by the tradition of collegial government. A handful of ministerial advisers, all public servants, advise the prime minister directly, while administrative support is provided through the semi-autonomous Office of the Cabinet Secretary (OECD, 1992: 198). In cabinet the prime minister cannot compel. In other nations, though, the authority of the prime minister over policy matters is not guaranteed by large and imposing institutions. The varying capacities of leaders is an endless source of political commentary, so that even when structures remain constant, observers perceive substantive differences of influence between a Margaret Thatcher and a John Major. In a detailed study of successive Canadian prime ministers Aucoin (1986: 90) argues that new leaders rearrange the machinery of central government to match their 'personal philosophies of leadership, management styles, and political objectives'. Aucoin compares the 'rational management' approach of Trudeau with the 'brokerage politics' style of Mulroney, while for Germany Johnson (1983: 115) suggests that 'the effective co-ordination of the Federal Government's work does depend heavily on the style, methods and capability of the Chancellor'.

Beyond agencies directly supporting the leader, most nations have other mechanisms to encourage policy coordination. Alongside the central agencies, ministerial committees keep a watching brief over aspects of government performance. These can be both standing and *ad hoc*, as in the cabinet committees of ministers found in Australia, Britain and Canada. German cabinet committees have an explicit coordination role, and may be led by public servants rather than politicians. The committee created in January 1991 to coordinate unification policy, for example, was chaired by the head of the *Kanzleramt* (OECD, 1992: 122). In the Netherlands each cabinet committee works with an allied committee of civil servants, known as the *voorportalen*, which may itself become very influential on policy matters (R. Andeweg, personal communication).

Federal nations often create additional coordinating structures to manage relations between national and regional governments. In Australia this is the Council of Australian Governments, in Canada a host of intergovernmental officials' meetings and the First Ministers Conference. Germany employs a range of councils to coordinate particular sectoral policies, such as the Financial Planning Council which includes representatives of the federal, *Länder* and local governments and the German Federal Bank. Consultative bodies reinforce these intergovernmental links in a number of nations, but usually as policy advisers rather than as agents of coordination.

Structures are important for shaping policy coordination, but the day-to-day work of the policy domain occurs through systems and routines. Established and maintained by the centre, these routines create recognized channels for decision making, and detailed rules for consideration of policy proposals by government. Such rules may be set out in departmental procedure manuals or, as in most Westminster-style nations, detailed in a cabinet handbook. Regular process provides a predictable, orderly flow of government business. It ensures the executive has only to deal with proposals written to a formula, supported by adequate financial and consultation data, and subjected to rigorous bureaucratic scrutiny before coming forward for political decision. Such routines bring stability and predicability to choices. As 'well-defined procedures that precede decisions', coordination routines serve to standardize processes and focus executive attention on a limited number of considerations (Sharkansky 1970: 3).

The political domain works with the intangibles of politics — personal contacts between cabinet ministers, and between the leader's office and ministerial advisers, common responses to the crises of office, an innate understanding of a government's political priorities and strategies. Few procedures need to be documented in a domain which relies on old hands for its continuity and operations. Policy routines, in contrast, are the province of bureaucrats. Knowledge about procedures must be widespread and easily accessible. This standardized process requires rule books, training and an agency with responsibility for enforcing standards. Behind the cabinet, therefore, must stand a central policy agency as the bureaucratic expression of executive authority, the tie which binds together policy work across the government. Such agencies are rarely popular with line departments, since they appear interfering and ill-informed, always imposing demands for information or briefing against otherwise sound policy submissions. Yet from the executive's point of view, these central policy agencies are essential for policy control and consistency. They make the policy domain manageable, and coordination possible.

Administration

Ministers contest office to implement policies but find themselves in charge of large organizations which require constant managerial attention. Much of their time is taken up with administration — both to give expression to their policy and, more pragmatically, to prevent the political damage which accompanies exposure of a poorly run or incompetent government agency. The executive thus has political and policy reasons for coordinating its management of the public sector. Typically it coordinates through three key instruments — design of the structure of government, control of the budget and establishment of consistent personnel procedures.

The capacity of governments to structure and restructure their operations varies considerably. In Anglo-Saxon-style societies the chief minister can generally order a reorganization of functions, though the considerable freedom enjoyed by an Australian or a British prime minister is tempered in Canada by the need to support administrative changes with enabling legislation. Yet the practice remains of periodic rearrangements of the state machinery around priorities, available cabinet talent and party or regional considerations. In 1987, for example, Prime Minister Hawke initiated an unprecedented recasting of the Australian federal government without consulting cabinet or parliament. During her brief prime ministership, Kim Campbell also began structural reform in Canada, and her successor has followed Australia's example in consolidating many ministerial agencies. More radically, Prime Minister Thatcher in the UK used the 1988 *Next Steps* report to begin substantial structural change to the civil service. Her division of agencies into policy and delivery organizations is one factor cited by Rhodes (1994) as hollowing out the British state.

In Germany, as in Holland, coalition political considerations constrain structural change. Given the authority of individual ministers, major reorganization is only possible at the start of a government, since once ministers are appointed any substantive alteration of the architecture also reopens coalition negotiations. In Germany close links between federal policy ministries and the *Länder* which implement initiatives may also restrict too regular shuffling of functions. In the Netherlands the prime minister has no power over the structure of government, and does not even assign portfolios. Such decisions are made within the coalition, following extensive negotiation.

If state traditions differ on fluidity of structures, they share enduring financial control systems. Governments rely on their treasury or finance ministry to monitor and restrain expenditure. Budget controls may be built into the decision-making process so that in Germany the Minister of Finance can lodge an objection to any government decision, and require fresh cabinet consideration. In all systems the chief financial minister is a powerful player in policy decisions and, by extension, in coordination since the budget process usually also serves as the annual survey of policy activity and programme evaluation.

The introduction of 'managerialist' financial management improvement programmes in Australia and Britain has tightened this scrutiny role, making the budget a decision about whether particular expenditure still meets government objectives. In Australia the Department of Finance, and in Britain the Treasury, encouraged a move away from separate accounting of dollars and people in the public sector; henceforth programmes would have budgets and objectives, and could manage the former to achieve the latter without detailed intervention by central agencies. None the less Australia retained its Public Service Commission and Britain the Office of Public Service to maintain some consistency in public sector human resource management. Canada followed a similar pattern, combining all forms of public sector resource management under the Treasury Board Secretariat, though also retaining a Department of Finance and a Public Service Commission.

While financial devolution is a recent trend in Westminster-derived countries, German administration has long been decentralized with each ministry setting its own pattern of expenditure and employment. Although not acting as central coordinating agents in the sense found in Australia, Canada and the UK, the German Federal Ministries of Finance and the Interior do set overall policy guidelines for public service budgeting and employment. The Netherlands is characterized by even greater devolution. Its Directorate General for the State Budget within the Ministry of Finance and the Directorate Generale for Management and Personnel Policy within the Ministry of Home Affairs are primarily concerned with coordination of management policies rather than controlling transactions within the public sector. Ministries in the Netherlands value their sovereignty, and this tradition of independent action restrains the executive from imposing too exacting prescriptions on agency management. As Andeweg and Irwin (1993: 176) note, the 'most striking characteristic of the Dutch civil service is that as such it does not exist; each department is largely autonomous'.

At first glance its seems curious that a nation which embodies the importance of the state, such as Germany, and one at least influenced by this continental tradition of state philosophy, the Netherlands, should display less concern for administrative coordination than the so-called 'stateless societies' of Anglo-Saxon nations. Neither Germany nor Holland seeks the standardization of public service conditions and operations which characterizes Australia, Britain and Canada. As Andeweg (1991: 120) reports, in the Netherlands there is 'no general civil service and departments are relatively autonomous in recruiting personnel or in preferring particular types of policies'.

Unity of administrative action in such nations must have another source, or be missing altogether. The Netherlands suggests an absence; the system of 'consociational democracy' stresses relative autonomy for pillarized organizations, seeing in decentralization and a weak central state the essential character of the Dutch compromise. Recent initiatives to improve coordination, including coordinating ministers for women's emancipation, immigration and minorities, and the use of project ministers, reflect change in a society which appears to be moving away from its 'pillar' system and from corporatist economic arrangements. Yet more ambitious attempts at coordination processes, such as mega-ministries and 'overlord' ministers, have failed in a nation which still values a decentralized state.

In Germany, by contrast, elaborate management coordination procedures are made less relevant by the shared attachment to legal definition of actions and relations. Johnson (1983: 110) talks of 'the preference in German government for the formalisation of procedures and relationships and the precise definition of powers, conditions which have been reinforced by the Basic Law itself'. For Dyson (1980: 8) this pattern of integration through underlying shared values embodies the difference between traditions. German practice emphasizes a

> . . . normative concern with the nature of public authority and the terms on which it is to be exercised, its rationalist preoccupation with the creative role of institutions and with giving its constituent ideas institutional expression as a way of 'fixing' certain meanings within public life. The state tradition reflects a series of intellectual preoccupations which have not been as strongly represented in the Anglo-American tradition.

Anglo-Saxon tradition societies have no such overriding mechanism to secure administrative coordination. Lacking integration through other means they must rely on conscious effort, detailed procedures and regular reworking of structures. It is their fragmented state, and liberal state philosophy, which makes coordination such a preoccupation.

Conclusion: Executives and Coordination

Parliamentary systems display an imperative toward coordination. The American celebration of a compound republic, built around fragmentation and overlap, does not sell well with the electorates of Australia, Canada, Germany, the Netherlands or the UK. Few ministers in these nations would stand before parliament or its committees and support incoherence, duplication and redundancy in government structures and policies. Coordination then is a primary political virtue, espoused by executives and practised through a complex array of agencies and routines.

As Figure 6.1 suggests, there are similarities across parliamentary nations in the major agencies used to pursue coordination. Faced with the same problem — how to impose coherence across the state — executives reach for like institutions.

Yet though coordination systems attract sustained and detailed effort, they are not valued equally. Strategies vary, and the idea of state traditions provides a useful heuristic for understanding these differences. In a society such as Germany, firmly in the continental tradition of state philosophy, political coordination is built into the policy and administrative process, while Australia, Britain and Canada all operate with a more clear distinction between realms. In this study the Netherlands remains outside either tradition. Holland has many characteristics of Anglo-Saxon-style states, but also political and administrative procedures which recall the closer integration of state and society in Germany. It is a reminder that ideal types are always unsatisfactory when used to classify complex, unique and evolving entities such as governments and societies.

Rhodes (1994) raises a provocative issue about all such state traditions: that the capacity of even the most coherent and integrated of states may be undermined by pressures toward 'hollowing out'. Rhodes draws evidence from Britain, where it can be argued the reach of government is being eaten away by international obligations and by new forms of management which stress efficiency over political direction. The capacity of the centre is diminished until those elected to office can no longer achieve their aims, and must be content with empty statements and echoing halls.

If Britain presents a possible example of hollowing out, an even stronger case can be mounted for the Netherlands. Here decision making is either exercised below, in relatively autonomous communities, or above, through regulation imposed by the European Union. Industry sectors shape relevant government policy, leaving an apparently ineffectual or at least irrelevant centre. As the nation under study most subject to international trade, Holland may represent simply the most advanced case of 'globalization' — the eclipse of nation states as the principle political unit, foreshadowed by a society already accustomed to moving between local, regional and international identities.

Yet Holland and Britain both also contain countervailing trends. Membership of the European Community has indeed shifted some decision-making power to a supra-national forum, yet compliance with European Union dictates has required an increasing centralization of authority within the state. Consequently, argues Rhodes (personal

Political Domain	Australia	Canada	United Kingdom	Germany	Netherlands
Decision making	• Cabinet	• Cabinet	• Cabinet	• Chancellor/Cabinet	• Cabinet
Political advice	• Prime minister's private office • Ministerial advisers • Governing party/ies	• Prime minister's private office • Ministerial advisers • Governing party/ies	• Prime minister's private office • Ministerial Advisers • Governing party	• Coalition colleagues • Senior public servants	• Coalition colleagues • Senior public servants

Policy Domain	Australia	Canada	United Kingdom	Germany	Netherlands
Decision making	• Cabinet	• Cabinet	• Cabinet	• Chancellor/Cabinet	• Cabinet
Cabinet committees and memberships	• Seven standing committees • Ministers	• Ad hoc and standing committees • Ministers	• Four standing and numerous ad hoc committees • Ministers	• Ad hoc and standing committees • Ministers • Senior officials	• 14 standing committees • Ministers • Secretaries of state • Senior officials
Central coordinating body	• Department of Prime Minister & Cabinet	• Office of the Privy Council	• Cabinet Office	• Federal Chancellery	• Prime Minister's Office within the Ministry of General Affairs
Intergovernmental coordination	• Council of Australian Governments	• First Ministers Conference • Privy Council Office	—	• Sectoral policy committees (e.g. Financial Planning Council)	—

Administrative Domain	Australia	Canada	United Kingdom	Germany	Netherlands
Control over machinery of government	• Prime minister	• Prime minister	• Prime minister	• Chancellor and coalition	• Coalition and prime minister
Control over government expenditure	• Minister for Finance • Department of Finance	• Treasurer • Treasury Board • Department of Finance	• Chancellor of the Exchequer • Treasury	• Minister for Finance • Ministry of Finance	• Minister for Finance • Directorate General for the State Budget, Ministry of Finance
Policy for Public Sector Employment	• Public Service Commission • Industrial Relations • Finance	• Public Service Commission • Treasury Board	• Cabinet Office • Treasury	• Ministry of the Interior	• Directorate Generale for Management and Personnel Policy, Ministry of Home Affairs

Figure 6.1 *Lead agencies for co-ordination mechanisms*

communication), 'the European Union both strengthens and weakens co-ordination simultaneously' (see also Rhodes, 1996). Similarly, the Netherlands demonstrates the continuing importance of processes contained within the nation state. In 1989 the government fell over an environmental plan presented to cabinet, emphasizing the need for continuing informal coordination and bargaining between ministers and agencies. A recent analysis by Andeweg and Bakema (1994: 66) suggests developments with the Dutch government have 'strengthened collective decision making at the expense of individual ministerial autonomy', reinforcing the role of cabinet government in making binding decisions.

So movement toward a hollow state, toward national governments no longer carrying real authority, is at best only one of several contradictory trends shaping alike Anglo-Saxon and continental states. If the state is being hollowed out, then the ideas and programmes being marshalled through coordination routines may no longer be important. Anglo-Saxon societies perhaps provide the strongest evidence for such hollowing out, in particular with the emerging preference for markets over hierarchy as a coordinating mechanism. Yet even in Britain and Holland other factors stress the need for greater, rather than diminished, coordination systems. Rhodes (1996) uses the evocative expression 'more control over less'. Policy complexity, interrelations and European Union dynamics require even decentralized nations to develop national responses to policy issues. The pressure toward globalization is felt too outside Europe, as international treaty obligations require coherent responses to economic, environmental and legal obligations.

That coordination may become less relevant because the state is hollowing out would perhaps come as a surprise to those executives which still invest so heavily in coordination, and to the numerous officials who spend professional lives pursuing the coordination principle. For them, state capacity remains real and tangible, to be achieved through systems which entrench government priorities, and channel all fundamental choices to the chief minister and cabinet for resolution. If the state is hollow they have not noticed, so demanding is the task of governance, so strong the belief that executives can still make a difference.

Note

1. This discussion of the characteristics of coordination draws on Davis (1996), *A Government of Routines: Executive Coordination in an Australian State*, Melbourne: Macmillan.

7 Managing Budgets

John Wanna

Responsibility for the public purse in parliamentary democracies lies with parliament, which enjoys constitutional or conventional control over revenue and expenditure (Savoie, 1990; Lessmann, 1987). Realistically, however, responsibility for budgets and resource management falls to the core executive (Thain and Wright, 1995). To the extent that they provide a political programme and a framework for resource allocation, budgets are proposed and implemented by the executive. Budgets are the executive's framing and implementing capacity, although not necessarily its steering capacity. It is the executive, not parliament, that establishes fiscal limits, proposes revenue policy and finds the size of the public purse a constraint to ambition. While parliaments authorize and legitimize budget allocations, the legislature has but marginal involvement in determining resources. Annual budgets are virtually complete before they are presented to parliament and in one case, Germany, draft budgets are presented to the public and interest groups before the *Bundestag* (Sturm, 1985).

The political executive does not determine the budget or indeed orchestrate the budgetary process unconstrained. External economic considerations and international financial markets limit options and set parameters, especially for key indicators such as debt levels or expenditure ratios. The political core executive is often frustrated at the lack of responsiveness of the budgetary process to its preferred intentions. Budgets appear unfathomable and clouded in mystique (cf. Weber, 1978; Wildavsky, 1975). A multiplicity of institutions and players are involved, and sequential processes or incremental cycles prevail. Inherited patterns of resource allocation are stubborn (some protected by constitutional provision), and many areas of public expenditure or revenue arrangements are not subject to change by simple executive order. The political executive may declare fiscal strategies and pin their accountability and credibility on achieving publicly announced targets, but they are also aware they often cannot control the factors that determine the outcomes. Hence, the executive's actual capacity to influence budgets may apply to relatively few instruments within the budgetary process.

Responding to global and national macroeconomic pressures and the seeming intransigence of budgets, the core political executive and central administrative agencies have shown keen interest in reform. Over the past two decades, executives have demonstrated a desire to control budgets, limit aggregate expenditure and gain greater influence over the principles of resource allocation. Their agendas for change have embraced not only expenditure restraint but also the processes of resource allocation and financial management. The announced intention of many reforms was to promote accountability and the transparency of resource allocation to legislatures (Zifcak, 1994; Aucoin and Savoie, 1994; Forster and Wanna, 1990). But empirical evidence suggests most budgetary and financial reforms have been introduced by the executive to *control more by doing things differently and spending the same or less*. Reforms have been promulgated with nominal concern about accountability to the legislature, and a far more explicit agenda about budget restraint, fighting deficits, greater efficiency and improved resource management. The main consideration in budgetary reform has been the capacity to allow modern executives to control more (agencies, programmes, activities) within tightening resource limits. Reforms have been implemented principally to assist the executive, to increase their levers and options for control, and make the process of resource allocation more responsive to political concerns.

The emerging literature on these reforms provides extensive detail on the range of reforms attempted (Aucoin 1991b). Studies have related the progression of reform phases, the endeavours to achieve fiscal restraint, the specific types of reform initiatives adopted, the institutions involved and the dimensions of public sector restructuring. As ideas and practices find resonance in other countries some even stress the internationalization of reform (Aucoin, 1991b; Aucoin and Savoie, 1994; but see Hood, 1995). While some policy analysts talk of the problems associated with 'perfect' implementation, many practitioners are prepared to assert that greater political control and responsiveness has already occurred (see OECD, 1995; Keating and Holmes, 1990; Bestebreur, 1993). Generally only selective proof is offered. It is often presented as incontrovertible that budgetary reforms allow greater scope for political priorities. Yet, there has been relatively little research undertaken on the extent to which budgetary and financial management reforms have enhanced the capacity of the core executive to drive policy and impose their policy preferences.

This chapter explores the processes of budget allocation and resource management and assesses the ability of the core executive to use the budgetary system as a means to achieve its declared intentions. While considerable activity has occurred in reforming resource systems, the core executive has simultaneously experienced some erosion of influence over the wider public sector. Although there is far more information, monitoring and control over resource usage across the public sector, much state activity has moved beyond the immediate or effective power of the executive.

Paradoxically, two countervailing trends are occurring simultaneously, and to describe this the 'hollowing out' metaphor has enjoyed currency in recent years (Heinz *et al.*, 1990). 'Hollow state' theories have posited a transference of power from the central agencies of the nation state to other loci within and outside the territorial state (Rhodes, 1994). Budgets are an important tool in this process of centralizing control while 'hollowing out' takes place. Government fixation with expenditure management and reducing budgetary dependency are clearly consistent with the intention of controlling more by doing less. Yet at the same time, analysis should not lose sight of the fact that demands on governments, their collective responsibilities and political preferences have not abated. This means that overall public expenditure has continued to increase (in real terms and as a ratio of GDP) for most OECD nations (OECD, 1995). Within these expenditure patterns, however, some states have experimented with structural and organizational changes, and following some private sector practice moved away from large, hierarchic, multi-divisional corporate organizations to contractual, flexible agencies (Dunleavy, 1989; Fox and Miller, 1995). In the process core executives have variously separated policy functions from operational and delivery functions, while clarifying objectives, establishing indicators, monitoring service standards and allowing greater devolved autonomy within subordinate agencies.

The Main Themes of Budgetary Reform: Providing Executive Discretion in Restraint

Faced with fiscal stringency, most OECD nations have undertaken major budgetary and financial reforms in recent decades. Substantial public sector reform initiatives were also attempted especially over the 1980s and 1990s, varying from managerialism to corporatization, devolution to citizen charters. Both Shand (1996) and Hood (1995), however, warn of the dangers in overgeneralizing about such initiatives. But, by examining the nature of broader public sector reforms and describing the main issues addressed, it is possible to gain a clearer picture of the complexity of budgetary processes across the five cases and provide a context within which to identify forms of executive influence.

Across the five countries, there was no single logic, format or sequence behind budgetary and financial reforms. To be precise, budget reform has not generally been a subset of New Public Management — even though some common threads can be identified. Within individual countries, reform scenarios tended to respond to different problems or forces, and to emerge incrementally often from compartmentalized sources. Diverse rationales and competing logics arose, some of which proved contradictory

— such as service quality with expenditure cutbacks (Hood, 1995). Some reform initiatives were driven by different objectives; some were intended to improve agency responsiveness to executive preferences (contributing to the executive's steering capacity); others were designed bluntly to cut spending; others of a more technical nature were intended to improve efficiency (and transfer devolved authority to programme managers). Budget restraint was often used as a surrogate for public policy making — 'policy' was often the residue left after budgets had been cut or spread more thinly.

With the benefit of hindsight, some writers find it possible to fit diverse reforms into a common pattern even though the interrelationship between specific reforms was not initially explicit and changes often occurred as part of an iterative process. Thus, some may perceive the agenda of budgetary reform as part of a wider neo-liberal managerial revolution informed by economic rationalism (Boston, Martin and Walsh, 1991; Pusey, 1991). Yet in Germany and Holland no overall philosophy of budgetary reform was articulated, while in Australia, Canada and the UK philosophies and the objects of reform changed over time. Consolidated reforms appeared as a coalescence of piecemeal emergent strategies, to use Mintzberg's (1988) terms, which sometimes were subsequently rationalised by practitioners and commentators. Moreover, when major reforms were undertaken the implementation problems (and the eventual behavioural consequences) were not always recognized (as with Canada's introduction in 1979 of the Policy and Expenditure Management System (PEMS), Britain's Financial Management Initiative (FMI) in 1982, or Australia's Financial Management Improvement Program (FMIP) in 1984). Thus, core executive strategies to modify resource management behaviour produced some perverse outcomes; in Canada the PEMS experiment, according to one source, created 'immense problems of coordination' and excited 'competition among the various central agencies involved' rather than coherence (Jackson and Jackson, 1994: 402). Ultimately, the PEMS reforms were discredited (and more or less abandoned by 1986) and replaced in the 1990s with a system of expenditure reductions based on top-down 'financing by reallocation' (Canada, 1995b: 2).

But not all reform initiatives addressed the concerns of the core executive. Internal political concerns of politicians or executive agencies, therefore, were not necessarily the principal initiators behind such reforms. External market forces were often the main catalysts of budgetary reform: protracted economic recession, inflation, currency devaluation, central bank policies, or international agreements such as the European Union or NAFTA. Hence, it is difficult to assess the extent to which such reforms contributed to executive capacity when some were not intended to do so from the outset. Reforms designed to 'align' fiscal strategies with macroeconomic conditions were not inevitably intended to augment executive influence, and may indeed have limited the scope for political decision making. This point has been repeatedly made by serving finance ministers (see Zijstra, Andriessen and Ruding, in Clerx, van Griensuen and Stevens, 1993; Kok, 1994; Walsh, 1995; Pimlott, 1993). There is also a tension between budgetary mechanisms designed to improve coordination and guard against the executive centre being 'hollowed out', and other structural reforms which promoted managerial criteria for decision making and transferred authority to devolved levels within agencies or lower levels of government.

Fiscal restraint became a prime objective of governments from the early 1970s essentially because of macroeconomic pressures, concerns over the size of public expenditure, political difficulties in accepting responsibility for revenue raising, and desires to accommodate new priorities within existing budgets. Budgets were conceived as economic tools with particular sensitivity toward expenditure or debt levels. Central agencies responsible for economic policy like Finance or Treasury became the major initiators of such reforms. Top-down aggregate expenditure controls were defined by a variety of targets and invested with overt political commitment. Expenditure restraint focused on aggregate budgeting targets and various schemes to impose limits on expenditure. Dutch cabinets imposed 2 per cent cuts in staff numbers between 1983 and 1986 (but exempted about half the service), then committed itself to reduce employment by 26 000 'person years' over the four years 1987 to 1990 (in the *afslankingoperatie* involving 10 000 person years transferred by privatization and 16 000 lost by retrenchment — Breunese and Roborgh, 1992). In other cases, central cash ceilings or cash limits on expenditure were imposed (in Britain in 1976, Australia 1976–77, Canada after 1979). Also the budgetary cycle and submission process were improved and made forward-looking, and various estimate arrangements and programme structures were intended as controlling frameworks (Caiden, 1992). Actual cuts or measures to reduce expenditure were often manifest through arbitrary cuts to total, portfolio or programme outlays. Expenditure control initiatives were, therefore, principally top-down or 'global' impositions which made dubious improvements to the routine behaviour of budget-dependent organizations. Despite recurring frustrations with aggregate controls, macroeconomic concerns have remained at the forefront of budgetary reform since the 1970s. Indeed, concerns over the ratio of public debt to GDP or size of the public sector generally have survived even to the mid-1990s, and according to surveys were still seen by OECD nations as the most important issue still facing the public sector (Shand, 1996).

Supplementing aggregate expenditure controls, financial and resource management reforms were aimed at institutional practices, patterns of resource usage and internal incentive structures. These reforms addressed the problems of managerial and organizational behaviour (under the umbrella of New Public Management) while making resource allocations and reporting more transparent to the executive (and sometimes to parliament). Ostensibly, financial reforms were intended to provide freedoms, allowing managers enhanced discretion and flexibility to manage programmes and focus on results. Often resource management initiatives dispensed with the need for earlier crude controls (e.g. cash limits on departments, central pay factors, or central limits on staff numbers — although in Canada expenditure management systems coincided with politically declared targets for expenditure and staff cuts until 1993). Modified forms of accrual accounting were increasingly adopted, providing both central agencies and operational managers with information on total costs, revenue flows, asset maintenance, accounting for capital outlays and long-term liabilities. Such accounting systems provided central government with greater capacity to implement commercialization (or the possible privatization) of public undertakings, and facilitated partnership or contractual arrangements with private sector contractors. Together, these financial management techniques have largely been instigated by central finance agencies less concerned about budgets as economic policy instruments and far more about internal resource management and the 'bang for the buck'.

Hence, across parliamentary systems a wide variety of instruments of internal resource management systems evolved from the late 1960s. Countries moved with different orientations and speeds but also drew on comparative experience. Some separated key functions of top-down budgetary policy to give a specialized focus or provide additional clout. For instance, in Canada, which reformed early, responsibility for programme allocations and management was institutionally separated from the responsibility for overall fiscal budget in 1966 when a specialized Treasury Board Secretariat was carved out of the Department of Finance (Savoie, 1990). Later Canada's introduction of PEMS included both aggregate envelope limits on related portfolio areas (in eight envelopes — meaning broad related policy areas or supra-portfolios) together with an emphasis on internal management systems. Canada subsequently introduced a cabinet-level Program Review process (1994) which assessed agencies and programmes against a declared series of criteria designed to cut back on programmes and expenditures (including tests for the public interest, the role of government, federalism, partnership, efficiency and affordability). In Australia the Finance Department was created in 1976 to fulfil bookkeeping and managerial functions and provide advice separate from the economic ministry of Treasury. In Britain, Germany and the Netherlands the principal budgetary agency remained unified, usually devoting specialist divisions to expenditure and financial management policy. As will be evident below, many of the budgetary and financial reforms adopted in one parliamentary system were influential in another with some even borrowing similar agendas (e.g. financial management improvement plans, the identification of operating or running costs, carryover provisions and efficiency measures).

Notwithstanding country-specific differences, five main areas of concern can be distinguished in budgetary and financial management reforms. These categorize the various types of reformist concerns paid to budgetary and resource management processes by key players in the core executive. While no common pattern emerges, these areas of concern provide a necessary context from which to evaluate the degree to which the different components of the core executive were *involved* in resource decision making, pursued ostensible *priorities*, or achieved *success* or effectiveness with their attempts.

1. *Macroeconomic considerations.* These considerations took three forms. Fiscal strategies began to define budgets (especially expenditure levels and deficit or debt levels) as economic instruments. Rates of economic growth (GDP) were used as measures against which to assess public sector growth. Treasury or finance ministries and some central banks (e.g. the *Bundesbank*) relaxed Keynesian interventions and began 'market guiding' (through taxation, economic policy adjustments, fiscal budgets, inflation policies). Moreover, macroeconomic predictions on such factors as economic growth rates, inflation, interest rates, or trade balances became crucial determinants of budgetary parameters. Agents of internationalization (such as financial markets or credit rating agencies as well as organizations like the OECD) were important in transferring international pressures for fiscal reform to specific countries.

2. *Policy coordination dimensions* refer to broad initiatives by central policy or finance departments/ministries in which budgets were increasingly seen as convenient instruments of policy coordination. Central agencies placed greater reliance on demonstrated accountability and on financial management data for performance evaluation, and in some cases coordinated strategies also involved improved funds management by central financing agencies.

3. *Political executive participation* refers to a greater reliance on ministers to set budgetary parameters, approve fiscal strategies or impose spending cuts. Examples of such political participation include: the emergence of ministerial expenditure committees with express programme review functions; portfolio ministers gaining greater control over bottom line fiscal targets; the use of specialist cabinet

committees, ministerial councils or intergovernmental executive institutions at different stages of the budgetary process; and the development of key relationships between senior ministers such as prime ministers/chancellors and finance ministers/treasurers over budgetary decision making.

4. *Portfolio budgeting, organizational redesign, programme management and administrative systems.* Here reforms have focused on devolution and discretion within budgetary control frameworks including: forward estimates, running costs allocations, administrative/programme carryovers, productivity clawbacks or efficiency dividends and revenue-sharing schemes. Generally these reforms have been most pronounced under formal programme management systems such as FMI, FMIP or PEMS and Program Review.

5. *Accounting techniques and information systems.* Governments have pursued reforms to accounting and reporting systems. Some have adopted accrual accounting systems, improved cash and risk management practices and given attention to property and asset valuation/ management. Many of these technical reforms were well established in public enterprises (GBEs) and have increasingly been applied to operational departments.

None of these areas of concern are mutually exclusive but intersect and feed into each other. Specific reforms within these categories have not necessarily been coherently developed or coordinated in parallel, or even developed in a linear, evolutionary manner. Inherited budgetary systems cannot change too abruptly from year to year. Consequently some initiatives were little more than temporary mechanisms, in other cases experiments have been made and then U-turns or revisions announced. The most noticeable case occurred in Canada after 1989 when the Mulroney, Campbell and Chrétien governments retreated from ministerial control over resource envelopes because such political involvement made the process more convoluted, was not conducive to other objectives such as expenditure control, and had become ineffective if not counterproductive. Canada's Expenditure Review Committee was abolished because the atomization of the budgetary process made expenditure control unworkable.

So, while comparatively speaking core executives have considered budgetary and resource management issues as intractable problems, they have demonstrated a willingness to address seriously and systematically these problems. However, particular reform initiatives have diverged and more accurately reflected compartmentalized agendas. The more technical reforms emphasized different criteria from those adopted to increase political oversight. While the first three of the above areas can be seen as attempts to augment the involvement of the political core executive, the latter two suggest that the executive's involvement is peripheral once resource parameters are established. Indeed, technical and managerial reforms were often commissioned precisely to save the core executive from detailed control, to allow them (although not require them) to focus on strategic agendas or substantive policy issues.

Executive Involvement in Budgetary and Resource Allocation Processes

Core executives have different levels of involvement in budgetary preparation, and comparatively there is no uniform pattern characterizing parliamentary systems. While central governments are confronted with the imperatives of sound financial management, the precise meaning of this term and the mechanics through which it is attempted differ from one parliamentary system to another. Budgetary stress has translated itself into deficit reduction strategies for central governments in Germany and Australia, whereas Canada during the 1980s and 1990s attempted both deficit reduction strategies simultaneously with absolute cuts to total expenditure. Britain has been more obsessed with reducing the ratio of the public sector to GDP over the medium term and since 1992 with reducing the public sector borrowing requirement. The Netherlands has adopted a series of deficit targets to contain public sector expenditure in selected areas. Often the Dutch government's tactics involved devolving financial responsibilities to local government, in effect hiving-off responsibility for cutbacks to lower levels and disguising central government strategies. Canadian and Australian governments have also imposed financial discipline on governments at other levels mainly through restricting transfers to provinces and states. The scope for executive involvement is reviewed under a series of headings compartmentalizing budgetary and resource management within the central state (revenue systems, expenditure allocations and off-budget items).

Revenue Regimes

While central governments may disguise their responsibility for expenditure control within consolidated budgets and fluctuating parameters, they find it difficult to evade direct electoral accountability for revenue raising. Thus far there has been great political reluctance to announce planned revenue requirements ahead of time (through revenue estimates or predicted revenue load). For instance, Britain only linked detailed revenue and expenditure statements in the budget from 1993, while Australia published revenue estimates for the first time in 1993–94. Revenue requirements may appear in multi-year planning strategies or medium-term projections (Britain, Canada, the Netherlands and Germany), but as with inflation forecasts there is a strong political logic for announcing conservative predictions. Some nations, however, attempted to use revenue receipts as a means of disciplining expenditure; in the early 1980s the Thatcher government tried to insist that 'revenue determines expenditure' but this precept failed to work effectively in limiting public expenditure (Thain and Wright, 1992a, 1992b, 1995). Governments have also been reluctant to incorporate revenue recognition into accounting systems (particularly important if accrual accounting is used to gauge tax obligations). Nevertheless, substantial changes to the mix of revenue sources have still occurred (principally towards broadening tax bases — VAT in Britain in the 1960s, GST in Canada in the early 1990s and the incremental drift to broader taxation in Australia after 1985 despite the rejection of a GST). But such changes are fraught with political dangers best exemplified by the rout of the Canadian Conservatives in 1993. Imposing revenue adjustments seems destined to remain an *ad hoc*, expedient process, with adjustments on the margins. Within this context, however, the scope for political decision making remains because adjustments to change tax rates usually involve legislative changes (via budget statements or specific tax bills) and must, therefore, if not emanate from the political executive, have the consent of the cabinet. Executive discretion is assured because it has an institutional monopoly to protect its capacity in this respect. But this does not mean that all executive proposals survive the legislature. Upper houses in particular tend to extract concessions, especially the *Bundesrat* in Germany which can amend tax measures but not, ultimately, the federal budget, and the Senate in Australia which can veto taxation bills but is constitutionally prevented from amending 'money bills'. Paradoxically, the area of budgetary discretion most able to be influenced directly by the political executive is one that is generally found unpleasant and most visible to the electorate.

Revenue arrangements necessarily involve interjurisdictional or intergovernmental politics which are routinely formalized in federations, but still significant in unitary systems. Arrangements involving constitutionally guaranteed formulae proved politically attractive in Germany to the federal government, the *Länder* and *Gemeinde* or *Kreise* (local authorities). Fixed shares of income and corporation taxes are written into the Constitution (but not in the case of value added taxes which are set by biannual agreements) indicating a high acceptance of the legitimate requirements of each level (Leonardy, 1994). The other federations approach revenue arrangements from a more overtly political stance with looser, negotiable arrangements. Canada opted for policy-specific funding arrangements usually involving long-term commitments which are either conditional (health, social welfare, child care) or unconditional (post-secondary education) (Savoie, 1990). Australia preferred annual negotiations for general and tied grants but sometimes involving commitments beyond one year. The division of policy responsibilities and the proportions of tax collected by different governments appear to be the major factors in determining financial relationships between central and regional governments (OECD, 1987: 14). Moreover, for the individual European countries the European Union contributions based on 'own resources' (around 1.2 per cent of the GDP of member states) constitute a capped revenue transfer to countries raised across the European Union from four sources of economic activity (Nugent, 1992). Again political discretion has been pronounced in the levels and areas of revenue extraction (customs, agricultural levies, VAT, and GDP national contributions).

Budgetary Processes and Expenditure Allocation

Generally budgets take the form of legislative proposals presented to parliament on an annual basis (in all five countries). The intensive preparation time for a particular budget varies from six to nine months with early planning, forecasting and survey preparations spanning over three years (OECD, 1987: 27). Budget proposals tend to be broad aggregates of expenditure with little actual detail of spending (the exception is Germany which according to the budget law of 1967 formulates a bottom-up budget across 8000 items and appends these as a 'budget plan' to the bill containing general provisions). The annual presentation of budgets in programme format with functional 'policy area' allocations often disguises expenditure commitments and provides less detailed information than traditional line-item presentations. In many ways programme budgeting preserves the opacity of the budget not only to the legislature, but also to other parts of the executive (including other cabinet ministers). Central executives have been reluctant to change this mode of presentation for annual appropriations perhaps because of the political advantages to them or the behavioural expectations of administrative elements. Only the Dutch parliament uses the programme as the unit of appropriation; in Germany appropriation is on a line-item basis aggregated to ministries, while in the UK, Australia and Canada portfolio/ministerial structures are funded (where programmes can be between but are largely within portfolios). The length of time allowed for parliamentary deliberation averages around four months but the level of discussion may vary; in Germany item appropriations are discussed in detail while in parts of the budget in Britain 'taking note' occurs.

The degree of consultation with departments or line agencies depends on custom and precedent. In Australia the Department of Finance negotiates separately with line departments at both portfolio and administrative (running costs) levels. Ministers may only be brought into the process where officials from the respective agencies disagree (Campbell and Halligan, 1993). In Canada department submissions are discussed at a cabinet level (and with key institutions such as the Treasury Board Secretariat) with ministers actively involved on multiple cabinet committees. Since 1993 the Treasury Board has set programme limits and expected departments to absorb some policy initiatives within proposed limits by identifying equivalent savings elsewhere. In Germany submissions are discussed at three levels involving officials, budget directors and ministers. In the UK, after total planned expenditure has been approved (and departmental baselines established), individual departments submit bids for the whole of their programmes which are collated by Treasury's General Expenditure Policy Division. After preliminary negotiations, the Chief Secretary produces 'agenda letters' and the 'shadow boxing' begins. Some agreements can be settled without ministers, but otherwise the Chief Secretary conducts the bilateral negotiations (with the Chancellor rarely involved — except in informal discussions) (Thain and Wright, 1995). In the Netherlands, the Minister of Finance presents a budget framework or memorandum of expenditure limits *(Kaderbrief)* before allocating resources across eight policy sectors along with proposals for cutbacks (Andeweg, 1989b; Brinks and Witteveen, 1994). Dutch Finance officials then commence a ritualistic series of bilateral negotiations *(hangpunten)* with departments to ensure that agencies adjust to these overall ceilings. As ministries still assemble their own estimates (subject to inspection by Finance) some do not fit well with overall constrains and ministerial level negotiations are required (OECD, 1987, 1995).

While finance ministries are crucial in setting and guiding the budget agenda, cabinets or the wider ministry tend to come in only if there is substantial disagreement over a programme or item. Generally the involvement of cabinet ministers occurs over unresolved conflicts or additional spending initiatives. But even in these circumstances conflicts may be disposed of without involving the whole of cabinet. In Britain conflicts once went to the Star Chamber, consisting of a council of senior ministers, but it was abolished and replaced by a specialialist expenditure review cabinet committee (EDX) chaired by the Chancellor. In Australia, disputes remaining after the preliminary meetings of the Officials Committee on Expenditure (consisting of senior federal budgetary officers) go to the Expenditure Review Committee rather than the whole of cabinet.

Unlike the Canadian Expenditure Review Committee, the Australian version has been an effective mechanism for imposing expenditure restraint.

Traditionally, therefore, cabinet as a whole has rarely been a major player in the formulation of central budgets. Negotiations occur elsewhere, principally between the operational departments and the central finance agency, and in federations with other levels of governments. Such 'bottom-up' budgeting generally requires final endorsement from cabinet but not always. In the Netherlands, budgets are largely the political province of the finance minister and/or prime minister, and may be drawn up (as in 1994 by Wim Kok, the previous finance minister and later prime minister) between governments, after elections and usually before a new cabinet has been formed. In Germany, the finance minister draws together a disparate set of budget bids, negotiates separately with ministries and higher level authorities, most of which have a high degree of institutional autonomy *(Ressortprinzip)*. The German cabinet is less cohesive as a political entity than Westminster cabinets (Mayntz, 1980; Schmidt, 1985) and financial decision making is concentrated in the finance minister who has the power alone to veto spending proposals (and with the Chancellor's support cannot be overruled by other ministers). German budgetary decisions are also constrained by the Constitution (e.g. Article 115) and budget law *(Haushaltsrecht des Bundes)*, and by federal court rulings limiting public sector borrowing requirements. Equally, in some Australian states budgets have been known to be presented to parliament by the treasurer or premier without cabinet involvement. The Department of Finance in Canada would also occasionally 'spring the budget on the cabinet at the last possible moment before budget day' (Jackson and Jackson, 1994: 399). Such practices have reputedly disappeared, but they serve as a reminder of the marginal role cabinets once played (or need to play) in budget preparations and deliberations. The process could work well without cabinet; it is not an indispensable part of the process.

Constructing the annual budget via self-perpetuating routines entrenches a conservative bias in the preparation of expenditure plans and forward estimates. Although there are changes to levels of funding from year to year, the finance ministries inevitably rely heavily on previous allocations and some countries have built on these routines as a formal part of the process (possibly justified on the grounds that such routines reduce the 'politics' in determining expenditure allocations). But, as Wildavsky (1975) suggested, governments also lack the time, resources and intellectual capacity to begin the budget afresh each year. The British, German and Dutch budgets, for example, explicitly adopt a 'baseline' model within current policy settings as a basis for planning — sometimes up to five years ahead as required by law in Germany. Canada's operational plans allocate nominal resources to planning elements by costing the components of service delivery, thereby producing a 'reference level' against which any proposed changes can be made. This divides the expenditure budget between an 'A base' for ongoing programmes and a 'X budget' for 'new money' policy initiatives (not expected to be absorbed in existing appropriations). Such measures, while administratively convenient, provide finance agencies with a privileged position and in effect mean that substantial parts of the budgetary process do not rely on the active involvement of the political executive.

Off-Budget Items: Public Enterprises and Other Agencies

Given recent trends to commercialize the operations (and in some cases dispense with ownership) of public enterprises, parts of the state once within political control have moved further away from the reach of ministers. Some nations have privatized extensively (UK, New Zealand and France), placing agencies outside the state (except for regulatory frameworks and in New Zealand these are often left to market forces). Sales of assets were generally incorporated into recurrent budgets and not used to retire debt (OECD/UK, 1993). Others, like the Netherlands, have few public enterprises dependent on the central government but have privatized or outsourced government services, while Australia and Canada retain substantial public investment in infrastructure, transport, communications and economic services. Mostly these agencies or separate authorities are 'off budget' and subject only to relatively infrequent (though at times strategic) ministerial direction. But, even if ministerial authority is preserved over public enterprises, the conditions under which those bodies operate or the market expectations to which they are subject may make this authority purely symbolic. It has become increasingly difficult to reconcile commercial or corporatized forms of public provision and allow scope for detailed political interference. This is further recognized with the appointment of business boards often without community or overt political appointments, and laterally recruited managerial executives. While such bodies have formally been separated from political involvement (i.e. close ministerial discretion) government policies and regulatory provisions maintain a semblance of public influence over their operations. In some cases ministers can exert indirect influence through government-appointed regulators charged with establishing prices monitoring service or enhancing competition.

Priority Setting by the Core Executive

Recently the core political executive has become more involved throughout the budgetary process. In tight fiscal times, cabinet solidarity has been relied upon to initiate or ratify intended aggregate expenditure targets or broader fiscal strategies as a formal part of the budgetary process. Although cabinets do not necessarily set fiscal targets themselves, they tend to debate and approve proposed targets presented by the treasurer, finance minister or other senior ministers. Once approved, though, these aggregate targets impose a necessary discipline over cabinet as a whole and over individual ministers and their departments. In Australia and the Netherlands cabinet collectively approves outlay targets and in some cases portfolio/department limits. In Canada during the 1980s, the prime minister and the (then) influential Priorities and Planning Committee of cabinet established total spending limits (on an annual and multi-year basis presenting them to cabinet between April and July) before then recommending envelope limits (which cabinet discussed in December). This committee was eventually abolished by the Campbell government (and replaced by more focused committees), nevertheless the intent was to impose cabinet priorities even if the mechanics proved frustrating. The British Treasury currently proposes aggregate expenditure levels to cabinet in July for approval. By November or December the UK cabinet receives recommendations concerning ministerial allocations from the powerful cabinet expenditure committee (EDX) consistent with the broad aggregate target previously approved. The alliance between the British prime minister and Chancellor plays a crucial role in this process as a guardian against other spending interests. The German Minister of Finance initiates the commencement of the budgetary process in November by announcing broad guidelines for overall expenditure to the federal ministry for approval. While departments formulate specific requests, the Minister of Finance imposes overall control in line with planned guidelines (although after unification this control was eroded substantially by spending obligations to former eastern *Länder*).

Cabinets not only signal their intentions through aggregate limits, but variously exercise influence by declaring priorities over particular policies, determining growth or cuts to sensitive outlays, and by resolving any remaining issues arising during the preparation phase. In the most pronounced case, the Dutch cabinet usually plays a key role in ensuring that the priorities agreed in the cabinet formation process are implemented. Coalition agreements can cover expenditure limits or deficit targets, or centrally imposed increases or cuts to selected policy areas. This feature means that 'perpetual budgeting' remains a near-permanent item on cabinet agendas (Andeweg, 1989b). Despite changing coalitions, Dutch fiscal targets have remained remarkably consistent over time. The role played by the Dutch prime minister and finance minister is often paramount in negotiating the details of resource outlays sufficient to sustain a fragile consensus. By contrast, Dutch cabinet committees do not generally play a role in the budgetary process.

The Westminster-derived systems of Australia, Canada and Britain place cabinet in a stronger position *vis-à-vis* caucus or parliament; and on budget matters Westminster cabinets are far more tied to convention than strict legislative or constitutional principles. But while this strong political executive model may enhance the impression of collective purpose, it also tends to make cabinet a less active player in the details of budgetary allocations. This feature may partly explain why these systems have gravitated towards New Public Management where direct detailed influence by the political executive is regarded as unnecessary (and perhaps unwelcome) once parameters are set. After aggregate priorities are approved Westminster-style cabinets tend to be influential only if required to undertake programme review or scrutinize particular items. Hence, in reaction against its marginal budgetary role, cabinet's review function has been enhanced in recent years with the refinement of powerful specialist cabinet committees (see below). Yet the point remains, Westminster cabinets as a collective entity have minimal decision-making influence during the formulation stages of the budgetary process; to the extent that they are able to impose their authority they do so through programme and expenditure review. Westminster systems have deliberately established a core inner executive which institutionalizes the shift of emphasis over budget decision making.

Least influential in the budgetary formulation process, the German cabinet tends to give formal approval at an early stage then hand over the process to the duumvirate of the Chancellor and finance minister. According to Sturm (1985) few budgetary decisions are taken at cabinet level, although Schmidt (1985) refers to party splits in the 1970s over broad directions. Moreover, while the Ministry of Finance establishes spending limits and regular consultative practices, the power of the finance minister is qualified because budgets have the status of law and 'legal norms restrain [the minister's] handling of the budget during the fiscal year' (Mayntz, 1980). As a consequence cabinet is not actively and regularly involved in detailed priority setting but rather assumes a more passive role in legitimating decisions (although this practice can vary depending on the personal style and preferences of the Chancellor). Germany's formalized relations between federal ministries, its financially 'weak' central government, and the constitutional relations between the central government and the *Länder*, all reduce the degree of discretion open to the central political executive.

By contrast, central finance agencies possess an institutional influence due to their many roles. While the budgetary process became more consultative and with potentially greater opportunity for ministerial input, the principal budget agency remains the dominant influence in the process. Finance ministries (including the Treasury Board Secretariat in Canada and Treasury in the UK) provide the institutional context within which the process takes place; they make the fundamental assumptions, select and weigh information, and prepare economic planning data so crucial to the remainder of the cycle. They propose the timetable, perform the book-keeping/housekeeping and eventually assemble the final budget. Most finance ministries (except the Dutch and German) now determine rigorous forward estimates to apply to other agencies and undertake preliminary work toward identifying aggregate expenditure targets (Dutch and German ministries of finance construct surrogate estimates against which to measure departmental bids). They mediate the processes of information exchange, and in collating responses from departments determine categories of acceptable outcomes (agreed bids, negotiated compromises or disputed items). Their substantive authority derives from holding purse strings and their control over the processes of negotiation.

Finance agencies largely set the ground rules for the process while becoming the principal mediator through which virtually all other players must interact. Finance agencies therefore develop extensive procedures, schedules, meetings, committee structures and formalized networks on annual cycles. The procedures governing bilateral negotiation between finance agencies and operating departments may operate according to combined interests or mutual convenience (often meaning adversarial self-interest) but the framework of negotiations is set by the finance agencies. On the other hand, a prosaic consequence of this procedural power and functional specialization is that finance ministries become isolated, technically oriented and develop insular cultures. However, this conduit, 'rules-making' role indicates that finance ministries are indispensable to the budgetary and expenditure control processes, although the degree to which their own preferences prevail is not simply a consequence of this procedural power. Thus, for Britain, Wright has referred to a 'confederacy of major spenders' which up to 1992 resisted Treasury and made it difficult for the Treasury both to determine levels of spending and enforce its decisions. Even though Treasury remained at the centre of the allocative process, it was not until 1992 when it gained the power to determine aggregates that its expenditure preferences were enhanced — although it may be too soon yet to tell whether Britain's fundamental expenditure review has been effective in limiting expenditure.

As a consequence of their positional influence, finance agencies have extended the scope of their responsibilities to encompass other priorities.

Particularly in the Westminster-derived systems, finance ministries have historically been at the forefront of budgetary and financial reform initiatives even if in conjunction with other core executive players (and in Canada and Australia separate institutional agencies were created precisely to enhance a managerial focus). System-wide reforms (many influenced by neo-liberal or public choice orientations) have been proposed and implemented which were designed to change the resource relationships between budget-dispensing and budget-dependent agencies. Although some reforms have devolved decision-making authority, many have also tightened central controls over operational activities because finance agencies are able to codify and impose performance expectations (indicators) and require greater levels of reporting on performance (prompting comments in Britain that the FMI offers 'a little bit of freedom and a lot of grief'; see Gray and Jenkins, 1992).

Some more tentative managerialist initiatives have emanated from the Dutch Finance Ministry, although the wider public sector, like the German, retains a stronger tradition of functional autonomy for agencies (Bestebreur, 1993). Measures to improve managerial practices across the public service were implemented in 1993 for senior staffing and over 1991–95 for financial discipline, preventing departmental 'overshoots' and containing administrative costs. Although incremental modifications in resource management have occurred in Germany, little by way of an orchestrated managerialist agenda has emerged from the Finance Ministry. The highly formalized and incrementalist nature of federal resource allocation in Germany has meant that little interest has been shown in managerialist strictures. Instead, greater reliance is placed on aligning federal budgets to macroeconomic conditions (including the use of regular supplementary budgets for economic stability) and this gives the budgetary process a reactive character (Sturm, 1985).

Executive Strategies to Contain Running Costs and Manage Expenditure

Across the five parliamentary systems marked similarities emerged over strategies to control administrative expenditure or manage the costs of programme implementation in the public sector. On the containment of operating costs a strong convergence of interests exists between the core political executive and central agencies. Because administrative systems usually attract 'technical' and procedural solutions, central agencies have shown greater willingness to borrow efficiency measures from each other, and this interaction is sustained by regular international communication, managerial exchanges and visitations.

Canada's adoption of PEMS in 1979 placed growing emphasis on internal management systems and operating costs, but these tended to be overshadowed by ministerial difficulties with the envelope arrangements. When the PEMS system was dropped in 1989 to be replaced by a more managerialist Expenditure Management System (EMS, in 1994) the government specifically introduced one-line operating budgets at the programme level effective from 1993. Two specialist cabinet committees (served by the Privy Council Office and Finance) segregated budgetary decision making between macroeconomic inputs (Economic Policy Committee) and programme cutbacks (Program Review Committee). The management systems introduced in Britain (FMI) and Australia (FMIP) progressively allowed Treasury and Finance to separate programme from administrative running costs (1986 in the UK and 1987 in Australia — but with different definitions of what was included; see Zifcak, 1994). Subsequently the identification of distinct departmental running costs (or operating costs) allowed the executive to extract 'efficiency dividends' (usually set at fixed, across-the-board percentages) from designated administrative areas. In the Netherlands a systematic programme review was adopted (the 'Reconsiderations Procedure') which could include up to 20 per cent funding reductions within line article or cash allocations (although some provision for carryovers was introduced at .25 per cent of departmental budgets or up to Gld 2 million). The Dutch also made 1–2 per cent efficiency cuts but these reductions were varied by ministry, and by 1994 had begun to identify running costs, adopting an 'integrated approach' which contained increasing efficiency measures or cuts to 1998 — although many administrative and accommodation costs still remained with common service agencies. And in Germany, without formally separating programme and administration costs, resources can be transferred for specified purposes provided equivalent savings can be found elsewhere, and limited carryover provisions apply.

Britain's elaborate Public Expenditure Survey (PES) conducted annually by Treasury since 1963 has produced a detailed survey of programme expenditure to facilitate the formulation of forthcoming budgets (OECD, 1987; Thain and Wright, 1992a, 1995). Other intentions behind the survey were to control expenditure, review programme priorities and identify areas for reduced allocation. As an instrument of expenditure management the survey provided Treasury with detailed knowledge of programmes, allowing improved central monitoring of current and forthcoming spending. As Thain and Wright (1992a) recount, the original imperatives driving the survey changed dramatically as it became more oriented toward cost reduction. However, given Treasury's own objectives (to 'deliver the planning totals decided by cabinet' — Thain and Wright 1992b: 218), the survey allows for longer term expenditure controls and tighter discipline to be imposed and total expenditure limits to be set, but is ineffective in evaluating competing priorities between individual departments or programmes.

In addition, administrative costs have been contained as governments have opted more for selective interventions: the Dutch government created 'savings' to the central government of Gld 500 million in 1992–93 by decentralizing financial responsibilities to local and municipal governments. Transfering selected functions (housing, roads and welfare), the central government imposed a 10 per cent cut on local government, but the strategy was compromised by deficiencies in services and by some supposedly transferred staff remaining on departmental budgets. As part of a deficit reduction strategy, these cuts were designed to impose operating efficiencies on lower levels of administration.

Administrative costs are also contained by regular central monitoring. Australia, Canada and the Netherlands collect departmental accounts on a fortnightly or monthly basis and departments are 'expected' to remain within approved appropriations.

Not all of these measures have been warmly received. Canada has faced public sector strikes from 1991 after the central government's wage restraint policy and further cuts to public employees pay occurred at the provincial level. Provinces have also been hit by cuts to their funding from the federal government during the 1980s and 1990s, and because they are centrally imposed on another separate jurisdiction some reductions have been maintained. Australian state governments after 1987 faced similar general and programme cuts from the federal government, and in response have sought (so far unsuccessfully) a redistribution of taxing powers or guaranteed sharing formula (along the lines of the German system). The Netherlands operates under its Rules of Stringent Budget Policy which, like Treasurer's Instructions, codify aberrations or unusual transactions for the current year (overruns, shortfalls), and any changes to approved items can only be made with the prior consent of the Minister of Finance. These impositions have been contentious in departments and in municipalities.

Specific Reforms to Enhance Political Executive Influence

Specific initiatives to enhance the core executive's political input and influence over the budgetary process and expenditure outlays have been undertaken in each of the five countries. These initiatives tend to be somewhat arbitrary and idiosyncratic, with local political considerations taken into account (although some borrowing of ideas has occurred as with the replication of standing cabinet committees for expenditure review). Specialist cabinet committees have indeed proved the most noticeable formal mechanism for political influence in Westminster-derived systems, with formal involvement structured throughout the annual budgetary timetable. In Canada the role of cabinet committees has been separated by function with three (partly overlapping) committees addressing different stages or aspects of the budgetary cycle: Priorities and Planning for formulation and expenditure planning; Treasury Board for estimates and managing the expenditure budget; and Expenditure Review for expenditure reduction. Australia also retains a standing Expenditure Review Committee (of senior economic ministers) which combines various functions but principally engages in expenditure planning and limits. In the past specific committees or non-cabinet task forces have undertaken additional exercises in 'razor gang' expenditure reduction. Britain, which has been less open about its cabinet committee system, has now formed a specialist Expenditure Committee and other resource-related *ad hoc* committees have been formed as the need arose (including the Star Chamber). The Netherlands does not rely on standing cabinet committees but where strategic issues emerge the whole cabinet may undertake expenditure review where necessary. In Germany a standing Finance Cabinet Committee may be called upon to resolve disputes over programme expenditures but does not involve itself in general expenditure review.

Within their portfolios ministers have also acquired greater say over bottomline targets, but such influence has often been at the expense of direct influence in how activities are performed or discretion at the margins. Ministerial influence over budgets can be defined either as the latitude to introduce new initiatives (their capacity to act), or the achievement of disciplined deficit reduction (their capacity to manage). As in Canada during the past decade, the relative significance of these two types of influence may change as governments progress through their electoral terms. Ministers also enter the fray to resolve disputes and negotiate 'bilaterals' if they feel strongly about an issue or consider their department hard done by. In Britain where perhaps the most convoluted procedures exist, department ministers may only be involved in significant disputes (after staff have agreed on the 'undergrowth', identified contentious issues and separated the significant from the peripheral) (Thain and Wright, 1995). The Chief Secretary as minister responsible is charged with resolving these bilaterals through formal or informal discussions (with both ministers and officials having combined interests in reaching agreement rather than appealing to higher levels — the Star Chamber, prime minister or cabinet). Most individual ministers may, therefore, only have input into the budgetary process if called to bat for their portfolio. The exceptions are of course finance ministers, prime ministers and those ministers selected for cabinet committees with budget responsibilities.

The Success of Executive Intentions

Thus far, two dimensions of the capacities of core executives have been discussed: the patterns of involvement of core executives in the budgetary process; and the degree to which executive influence is apparent, especially the ability to impose controls over expenditure and input priorities. From this input-intention analysis only certain aspects of the core executive's capacity to shape budgetary frameworks or drive policy preferences are revealed; to complement the analysis an evaluation of outcomes is required. Consequently, discussion now turns to gauging how successful executive intentions have been in practice.

Gauging the success of political, governmental and administrative intentions is difficult. Governments often cannot control the factors that determine success. Some announced goals are not meant to be judged on a statistical basis; they are made for heuristic purposes, perhaps to emphasize an agenda, or educate the electorate, or to illustrate the seriousness of a particular leadership. Judging success by quantitative measures (e.g. figures for expenditure growth) reduces the evaluation to limited types of evidence and may neglect qualitative changes (to management systems and resource usage). Governments may also find ways to sidestep, hide or restructure such that evidence for specific commitments is disguised especially when little real achievement is apparent. If priorities are intended to signal an overall approach but come down to one or two specific targets (such as over the size of cuts, deficits, ratios of growth or expenditure levels), any achievement may be disputed if non-targeted measures 'blow out' or are used to syphon resources. Moreover, intentions are rarely simple, and may be multifaceted within the core executive itself. Hidden agendas may be as important as public declarations. On the other hand, governments have continued to announce specific intentions against which they invite their performance to be measured.

At a broad level the core executive has contributed to a major change in the culture of governance. Generally today's governments are far more focused on neo-liberal agendas and being 'fiscally responsible' than in the immediate postwar decades. While pressures have often emanated from outside government, the medium-term commitment, persistence and ideology of the executive is not irrelevant to engineering cultural change. There is now a greater stress on the economic role of budgets and the importance of financial planning. Budgetary practices have become less accepting of automatic adjustments based on inherited relativities. There is major emphasis on value for money and performance reporting across the public sector. Instrumental goals addressing resource management through frameworks such as PEMS, FMI or FMIP have displayed qualified success although over time inertia and some counterproductive tendencies have arisen. The political executives in both Britain and Canada have announced major departures in central budgetary practice to reinvigorate formulation processes and circumvent cumbersome procedures (but also changing internal power relations). Australia, Germany and Holland have tended to adopt incrementalist changes on a trial basis.

Alternatively, measuring the effectiveness of expenditure limits imposed by the executive produces some evidence of executive capacities, but the evidence is only partly convincing. Quantitative assessment indicates that the effectiveness of executive strategies is at best patchy, often only temporary in duration, and highly susceptible to business and electoral cycles. Even after establishing their own goals, core executives are prone to goal displacement and goal redefinition as they face changing circumstances. But it is also important to note that the core executive encompasses both guardians and spenders — hence a structural tension is built into both the institutional makeup of the executive and the processes of compiling budgets.

In assessing more than a decade of Canadian expenditure targets and spending cuts under Trudeau and Mulroney, Savoie concluded that from 1975 to the early 1980s it is 'not possible to determine precisely if the cuts led to permanent decreases in departmental budgets' (Savoie, 1990: 162). Some expenditure targets were achieved between 1975 and 1979 but not between 1980 and 1984. In the latter half of the 1980s, the Mulroney government was unsuccessful in meeting its targets and annual outlays 'started to shoot up' as expenditure increased in real terms and spending departments began to 'win some major battles with the guardians' (namely Finance and the Treasury Board Secretariat — Savoie, 1990: 171). Total public debt grew from 26 per cent of GDP in the early 1980s to around 60 per cent by the early 1990s. But this did not mean that cuts were not made, nor that expenditure limits were not important (Aucoin, 1991b). Savoie also indicated that while political executives and key central agencies were tempted to announce objectives, they often neglected implementation plans and were forced to rely on other line institutions ('spenders') who did not necessarily share the objective (Savoie, 1990: 171). Federal cabinets were also conscious of not appearing to discriminate against Quebec by advocating expenditure restraint which targeted the French-speaking province. Other expenditure programmes were proposed which may have been less than optimal simply to demonstrate that Quebec was receiving its fair share of central outlays. In short, the political fault line in Canada prevented the central political executive from being as disciplined as they might otherwise have been.

Dutch governments have focused systematically on deficit reduction strategies (often quantified in coalition agreements) resulting in strict expenditure controls. The central government deficit grew each year from

1977 to 1983 rising from 4 per cent to 10 per cent of national income, but since then has steadily declined (with 1987 the one exception) to levels of around 3.5 per cent. The declining deficit ostensibly appears successful, but total debt continues to rise, and debt refinancing has extended maturities (thereby reducing interest costs but transferring debt liability to the longer term). The second Lubbers cabinet (1986–89) met its targets for reducing the numbers of government employees, if often by abolishing vacant positions or privatizing services. However, achieving staff reductions became increasingly more difficult and in 1993 as part of a wider managerial restructuring, middle to upper levels of department staff were transferred to central government in order to underscore central discipline. The third Lubbers cabinet (1989–94) continued the strict deficit targets and was successful in containing deficit levels relative to national income. Maintaining the Dutch tradition of consensual, collegial government, the Kok cabinet (Labour–Liberal) in 1994 extended the annual deficit targets to 1998 (aiming to lower the deficit by 1998 to 2.9 per cent of GDP). Public debt, however, has tended to increase most years since 1986 and is forecast to increase until 1997 (rising to 8 per cent of GDP — see Miljoennota, 1995: 22).

Assessing the effectiveness of German fiscal policy is complicated by reunification (for an earlier assessment see Schmidt, 1985). During the 1980s the West German total public sector translated a small annual deficit in 1982 (3.3 per cent of GDP) to a small net lending position in 1989. Government expenditures had declined as a proportion of GDP and total public debt was low by international standards (43 per cent). Since unification, federal expenditure has blown out and doubled between 1989 and 1995; the federal deficit has grown to around DM 560 billion per year (or 2.2 per cent of GDP), and the total public deficit to DM 1200 billion in 1995 (4 per cent of GDP) (OECD/G, 1993). Transfers to the new *Länder* caused much of the expenditure surge (with the federal government meeting 60 per cent of the transfers), but expenditure overruns also occurred in administration and unemployment payments. Hence, according to the OECD, the 'gains achieved during eight years of budgetary restraint since 1982 were wiped out within two years after unification' — essentially a political decision (OECD/G, 1993: 79). Moreover, because budgetary discipline was exercised on the expenditure side during the 1980s, revenue levels were left unchanged (and even fell slightly); since unification the federal government has increased revenue by a series of *ad hoc* measures.

British Conservative governments have been particularly prone to setting targets and indicators. Indicators included balancing budgets, reducing the ratio of public sector expenditure to GDP over the medium term, and reducing the public sector borrowing requirement (PSBR). British cabinets required specific limits on expenditure when in practice

Treasury was initially ill-equipped or lacking sufficient power to determine spending levels and then impose necessary discipline. While total expenditure rose to 45 per cent of GDP in 1984, and fell to 38 per cent in 1988–89, it had climbed back to 1984 levels by 1994. Government debt as a percentage of GDP fell from 48 per cent in 1984 to 30 per cent in 1990 but again rose to around 45 per cent by 1994 (OECD/UK, 1993: 43–9). More pertinently, planned PSBR for 1991–92 was announced as £7.9 billion but doubled to £13.7 billion (or 2.5 per cent of GDP — despite proceeds from privatization being £2.4 billion above estimates). In 1992–93 the government was forced to admit that the PSBR would approach £28 billion or 4.5 per cent of GDP (with an underlying deficit of £36.1 billion). These ballooning deficits were blamed on the recession and a drop in taxation returns, and increased expenditure in basic services around the 1992 general election. The returned Major government then announced changes to the budget process in 1992. These included stricter enforcement of limits, global expenditure limits declared by cabinet as binding, bilateral discussions between Treasury and departments to concern only allocations within totals, not totals themselves, and the presentation of a consolidated revenue and expenditure statement to parliament in November.

Australian federal governments managed to declare and deliver budget surpluses in the late 1980s as a result of sustained fiscal discipline and an incremental broadening of the tax base. The PSBR dropped from 7 per cent of GDP to a surplus of 1.6 per cent of GDP in 1988–89. The budget position deteriorated in the 1990–92 recession (combined with electoral pressures and discretionary changes such as bail outs for state banks) as outlays rose and revenue stabilized. General government debt also rose from 13.5 per cent of GDP in 1990 to 18.5 per cent in 1993. However, while the federal government has taken credit for budget surpluses and attributed deficits to cyclical factors, much of the central government's control of outlays (and reductions in the 1980s) were the result not only of fiscal policy but also of cuts in central expenditure to other levels of government. These cuts were effective because they involved political decisions which were binding from the revenue-rich Commonwealth jurisdiction to the dependent state jurisdictions which possess relatively limited revenue capacities of their own.

Conclusions: Institutional Capacity and Executive Influence

Like the struggle to secure the 'hollow crown', core executives in parliamentary systems have long committed themselves to implementing budgetary and financial discipline across the public sector. Driven by fiscal problems, core executives and central agencies have invested considerable political energy in devising controls over both expenditure levels and budgetary systems. Debt and deficit levels provide executives with the justification to attempt to gain greater control over the policy process. But ultimately the quest for greater 'control' may simultaneously be an overriding imperative beyond political choice, and a consuming effort of dubious political worth. The process is continually frustrating and politically tortuous. There are few votes in fiscal discipline and executives committed to sustained reform often become locked in bitter struggles with line departments or consumed by conflicts with subgovernments. And if procedural innovations lose their effectiveness, cabinets may resort to old ways and cruder controls. Frustrations may also arise over privatization or other organizational reforms to public bodies (managerialism and devolution) which may erode policy capacity and make political control more difficult over traditional public sector activities. Paradoxically, therefore, fiscal and managerial disciplines may compromise the core executive's capacities and make the state more difficult to steer.

Yet governments throughout parliamentary systems have shown a propensity to set objectives — perhaps as a way of declaring their seriousness or intentions to steer the state. Some objectives are carried into government (as initially with Thatcher, Hawke or Mulroney), but most are determined after the event when the responsibilities of office sink in. Such priority setting tends to produce identifiable targets, which are often narrowly defined, contextual in nature and symbolic of wider intentions. But targets are frequently beyond the effective control of the core executive; and success in achieving targets depends upon a vast range of contingencies. Nevertheless, cabinets across parliamentary systems have increased their input into resource management, influenced budgetary frameworks and imposed disciplines over expenditure allocation. If central budgets are not totally controlled by central executives, they are far from being out of control.

Budgeting is not an end in itself. The intense interest in reforming budgetary processes indicates that core executives realize that budgetary discipline is necessary to the achievement of other purposes, and that such discipline remains to be exerted. The fact that reform agendas have been pursued indicates an admission of weakness in previous institutional structures, a weakness the core executive was anxious to rectify. Budgets have been instrumental in allowing governments the scope to control more by doing less while keeping a tight rein on spending. Rather than allowing a 'hollow core' to be eaten away by other forces, core executives have consolidated the institutional structures that guide and produce budgetary decision making. The formal role of core political institutions (such as cabinet, prime minister, finance minister and specialist review committees) has increased with many exercising veto rights. Central finance or budgetary institutions (such as treasury, finance, planning councils, efficiency units) have tended to become more specialized and the processes more compartmentalized. If together core executives are more influential (as some evidence suggests), then such influence has been directed toward aggregate targets (which have met with mixed success), decision-making frameworks and procedures, and monitoring or review. The detailed line controls so much in vogue in the 1960s have largely been replaced by more resilient expenditure controls. While no common, consistent pattern of budgetary management emerges from these cases, political leaders have attempted to constrain the multiplicity of institutions that affect decisions within budgetary processes. Overwhelmingly, expenditure limits and deficit controls have been the principal weapons by which the political executive has attempted to impose its will. The state may be fiscally constrained but not 'hollow', and a variety of influential players dominate selected components of the budgetary process. The budgetary centre of modern government, therefore, consists of overlapping executive institutions which are polycentric and functionally discrete; there is a political investment in the 'core' to counter trends toward looser more fragile networks in other policy areas (Heinz *et al.*, 1990).

The main differences characterizing budgetary systems in parliamentary democracies stem from the nature of collective solidarity in cabinet together with the degree of separation or fusion among key institutions. For instance, Westminster systems tend to generate cohesive cabinets, strong party discipline and are characterized by an institutional fusion between the executive and legislature. Within cabinets the existence of expenditure review committees tends to fuse guardian and spender perspectives and allow scope for greater budgetary discipline. Functional responsibilities within executive institutions may also be fused. In Britain the functions of economic policy and financial management are combined in one institution — Treasury. Political commitment has been strong and budgetary processes centralized. From a similar tradition Australia and Canada retain cohesive cabinets but display greater institutional separation (through institutions of federalism, stronger upper houses, and the separation of macroeconomic policy from financial management). The political structure of these federations has fragmented fiscal and budgetary processes and provided potentially greater scope for political input (perhaps best demonstrated in Canada's cabinet committee structure). Greater political input, however, can compromise expenditure restraint or relax collective undertakings to limit spending and borrowing; hence with many similar controls in place Australia has generally enforced discipline whereas Canada has struggled. This indicates not only that Canada had less political commitment but that different political decisions were incorporated by a comparatively weaker central government (weak in both the federalist sense and in its inability to make targets stick). In other words, fiscal rectitude may not be absolute especially if it means that governments may have to trade off an assumed latitude for political discretion to secure other outcomes. Political executives may not be prepared to surrender traditional decision making purely to achieve fiscal objectives.

Cabinet coherence may be less in non-Westminster parliamentary systems. Fragmentation occurs through coalition structures, ministers not holding positions in the legislature, powerful upper houses and a separately elected chancellor. Both Germany and the Netherlands have retained finance ministries which combine macroeconomic and financial management functions. Generally these nations have shown more interest in expenditure management and have been less preoccupied than the Westminster-derived systems with financial management systems. Budget formulation tends to be more fragmented but tightly controlled by the finance ministry. Thus, political fragmentation has been compensated for by institutional consolidation.

Finally, the countervailing trends affecting modern government mean that attempts to centralize policy controls have occurred in conjunction with devolution and divestment. Thus 'hollow state' theories should be qualified when analysing parliamentary systems. Reforms to budgetary and financial systems have consolidated core executive framework controls and public expenditures have generally continued to increase or plateau. Core institutions have reformed themselves, strengthened their capacities and attempted to introduce greater consistency and transparency into budgetary processes. While overall objectives to control public expenditure are fairly similar, strategies to deliver these goals differ markedly, and differ in their effectiveness over time. The single most noticeable theme running through budgetary reform strategies is the requirement that the public sector be more responsive to central executive priorities. Presumably core executives seem motivated by focusing control strategies, and doing more with less or with the same level of public expenditure.

8 Decentralization and Public Management Reform

Peter Aucoin

A major theme of government reforms across the industrialized democracies over the past decade has been the decentralization of authority, responsibility and accountability in public management (OECD, 1990, 1993). While decentralization has meant different things in different political systems, in part because different political regimes have different starting points from which to decentralize authority, responsibility and accountability (or, for that matter, to centralize the same), the overriding assumption has been that it is a necessary, if not sufficient, condition to enhance the performance of government.

Both as a response to the exigencies of the contemporary context of governance and as an attempt to introduce a new paradigm of public management, efforts to decentralize authority, responsibility and accountability have sought to go beyond the normal incremental adjustments to changing circumstances, where swings of the centralization–decentralization pendulum are to be expected. Of the political systems considered in this volume, Australia, Britain, Canada and the Netherlands have each pursued major management reforms in which increased decentralization has been a central or prominent feature. Only in Germany has there been no comprehensive programme of public management reform at the federal level of government (OECD, 1990: 9–17, 1993: 9–19).

The implications of decentralization for the management of the state in the political systems considered here, as elsewhere, are at least twofold. First, increased decentralization necessarily entails greater delegation of authority to public service managers in the line operations of government, where services are provided and regulations enforced. In some instances the consequence is an increased deployment of 'indirect public administration' to manage public affairs, that is, by using organizations one or more steps removed from the 'core' executive apparatus of government (Modeen and Rosas, 1988). There is the obvious fragmentation of central executive authority that results from these designs, especially where they entail some separation of responsibilities for policy and operations respectively. Second, the centre's ability to 'steer the state', to provide strategic policy direction and to ensure its adherence depends upon the development of a capacity to steer without there being extensive intervention in policy implementation at the operational level. The challenges presented by greater decentralization in the state apparatus cannot but lead to concerns about the 'hollowing out' of the core executive structures of government.

In the following four sections of this chapter, I will seek to provide an account of the general foci of decentralization in contemporary public management; to outline the principal forms that decentralization has taken; to highlight variations across these systems and the principal reasons for them; and, finally, to consider the prospects for decentralization as political executives seek to enhance their capacities to redefine the roles and responsibilities of the state.

The Multiple Dimensions of Decentralization

In the organizational designs and practices of government, authority is always more or less centralized or decentralized, reflecting the fact that authority is relational, involving the different parts of government, and subject to change over time, either formally or informally. No complex organization can be either completely centralized or decentralized. This reality is what makes the question of centralization–decentralization 'the most complex of all the [organizational] design parameters' (Mintzberg, 1979: 182). Moreover, decision-making authority will invariably be centralized for certain purposes; decentralized for others.

Complicating the equation is the fact that organizations can move responsibility for specific functions to lower levels in the organization, or away from the 'centre', without delegating authority. In this sense, we can speak of decentralization as 'deconcentration' (Aucoin and Bakvis, 1988: 10–12), or, as the Australian vocabulary would express it, 'decentralization without devolution [of authority]' (Wanna, O'Faircheallaigh and Weller, 1992: 115). When responsibilities are decentralized without a delegation of appropriate authority, accountability often become problematic. The same occurs, but for a different set of reasons, when 'discretion' is increased without an accompanying specification and clarification of accountabilities.

Decentralization of authority in organizational design and practice is complex because it consists of a number of different, but related, elements. In public management, it affects, at a minimum, the following sets of relationships: (i) collective cabinet and individual ministers; (ii) central agencies and line departments; and (iii) the corporate policy and management authorities at the centre of ministerial portfolios/departments and a portfolio's/department's operational divisions and/or agencies. Decentralization has been a criticial dimension of public management reform over the past two decades in so far as reformers have promoted organizational designs and practices that seek to: (i) enhance the capacity of individual ministers to exercise greater authority over their respective portfolios; (ii) streamline administrative controls by central agencies over line departments and thereby increase the authority of the latter to manage their financial and personnel resources; and (iii) enable ministers and departments to delegate authority to those on the front lines in the delivery of public services, including regulatory enforcement. In addition to these developments, decentralization has been accompanied by more extensive contracting out to the private sector for the provision of goods and services used by government or for the direct provision of public services themselves.

On a separate, but related, front decentralization has also been applied to relations between different levels of government within political systems. In addition to constitutional changes which redistribute constitutional jurisdiction between levels of government, in the case of decentralization to lower orders of government, decentralization in intergovernmental relations also affects the degree to which central governments provide increased autonomy to state and/or local governments in their management of those public services prescribed and/or funded by the central government. This form of decentralization is especially germane to political systems which rely extensively on lower orders of government to deliver 'national' public services.

While the multifaceted concept of decentralization has many meanings across, and even within, political systems, as a broad generalization one can say that there has been a move to decentralize authority across almost all political systems over the past decade or so, at least for certain purposes. In each case this policy has been pursued in response to the perceived shortcomings and limitations of the increased attempts at centralized coordination that progessively characterized most political systems since the end of the Second World War, as governments sought, first, to manage an expansion of the state during a period of economic growth, rising expectations and increased confidence in the role of government and, then, to manage its contraction during a period of relative economic stagnation, budgetary restraint and diminished confidence in government. While there were the swings of the centralization–decentralization pendulum over the past four decades, what has distinguished more recent developments is the extent to which the current move to decentralization for certain purposes has been accompanied by even greater centralization for others, especially strategic policy change and enhanced expenditure discipline (Aucoin, 1990; OECD, 1993).

Rationales for Decentralization

Decentralization in public management has been pursued for several reasons. At the central apex of power, it has been viewed as a requirement to reduce the overload on cabinets, and cabinet committees, as decision-making bodies that resulted from efforts to ensure that ministers retained authority over public policy. Decentralizing schemes have sought to give individual portfolio ministers greater responsibility for making decisions on behalf of government within the overall policy priorities and strategic plans of the cabinet. According to this script, cabinet is thereby better able to focus its attention, and limited time, on its priorities and plans, rather than on the 'dross' which can all too easily absorb too much of its time when authority is not decentralized to portfolio ministers (Keating, 1993).

In the three Westminster cabinet systems, there has been a formal or *de facto* streamlining of cabinet systems or cabinet committee systems to give effect to such decentralization. This trend has been accompanied in Australia and Canada by major changes to portfolio structures, by consolidating portfolios through departmental mergers and by establishing a clearer demarcation between the roles of senior portfolio and junior ministers. These machinery of government reforms assumed that enhanced authority for portfolio ministers would strengthen ministerial control over the decision-making process. It would do so by consolidating more authority within individual portfolios, thereby diminishing the influence of both specialized departments and the organized interests which invariably flourish in a fragmented state structures. The paradox here is that decentralization of authority is viewed as a prerequisite to a more effective use of authority, by cabinet on the one hand and individual ministers on the other, in order to 'engage the state apparatus', as Campbell (1988b) succinctly puts it, and thus to counter the interests embedded in the several parts of this apparatus.

At the same time, the exigencies of fiscal restraint have made affordability a major objective of government reforms. As a consequence, centrally imposed expenditure restraint measures have been deployed in all five systems. These measures have further centralized authority at the level of treasury and finance departments, supported in some cases by strengthened expenditure budget committees of cabinet. None the less, it has also been recognized that there are limits to what can be achieved in this way. In order to achieve greater efficiencies with limited budgetary resources, while at the same time paying attention to the effectiveness of programmes, it has been deemed necessary to alter the incentive systems operative within public management.

Aside from the hyperbole associated with much management reform, particularly in regard to enhancing 'value for money', it has been increasingly acknowledged that a prerequisite to economy and efficiency is not merely 'to let managers manage', but 'to make managers manage'. Managers must be accountable for the performance and productivity of their organizations, beyond simple compliance with the law, policy and budgetary appropriations. But if managers are to be accountable for 'results' beyond such compliance, a new bargain is required between central management agencies and line departments and operating agencies. Implicit in this bargain is a greater capacity for operating departments and agencies to exercise authority in the use of the resources provided for the implementation of public services, in exchange for greater specificity in objectives, performance targets and measures, and thus increased accountability for results.

For the individual ministers who head the line departments of government, this new bargain means that they and their officials are afforded increased flexibility to manage what the Australian model refers to as 'portfolio budgets' (Keating and Holmes, 1990). Within their appropriations, they should be able to reallocate resources among programmes within their portfolios in ways that respect general government plans and priorities but without the requirement to seek cabinet or central department approval for all reallocations. If ministers and their departments are to respond to changing circumstances without clogging up the central decision-making processes, increased ministerial authority is required. But, where ministers and their departments wish to be able to respond to demands and yet resources are tight and tightly controlled, they must be more rigorous and explicit in establishing portfolio priorities and reallocating resources: new resources for proposed new initiatives cannot be assumed.

Under such a regime, it is assumed that ministers and their departmental executives have an incentive to ensure that existing resources are managed with the greatest degree of economy and efficiency possible, given that failure to do so will restrict their capacity to fund new initiatives from their own budgets. This approach assumes, of course, that the centre will not confiscate the resources made available as a result of management-driven economies and efficiencies. If savings from economies and efficiencies revert to general government revenues, there is little incentive for ministers or their staff to seek them out. On the other hand, if savings resulting from departmental initiatives, or mandated efficiencies, are retained, in whole or in part, within the organizations which secure them, there are incentives for being economical and efficient.

It has also been assumed that decentralization is necessary to enhance performance in the management of the financial and personnel resources of government. The assumption here is that highly uniform and standardized administrative systems and practices across government have not been sufficiently responsive to the particular circumstances that characterize the great diversity of operations found in the modern public sector. In one sense there is nothing new here. Each of the political systems considered here, some more so than others, is characterized by a public sector that extends well beyond what is encompassed by ministerial departments and the public service bureaucracy. In adddition to traditional distinctions between the military and civil services, the modern public sector extends to a wide variety of state agencies, statutory authorities and public bodies at arm's length from at least direct government direction, control and accountability. The diversity here is such that attempts even to define the public sector are incredibly difficult tasks (Modeen and Rosas, 1988).

Even within what is considered the core of government and thus the defined public service, efforts to promote and monitor standardized administrative practices could not but lead to a continual expansion in the central policy and management agency apparatus of government, as the centre sought to elaborate new rules and regulations to cope with the capacity of those managing operations to find ways to evade or escape central controls. Decentralization is, in this sense, an admission that highly centralized management regimes not only do not work as intended in all respects, but often have perverse effects which impede good management. With increased demands from a new generation of public servants demanding empowerment in the workplace, highly standardized regimes imposed by the centre have lost much of their former appeal.

Finally, decentralization has also been the result of increased demands from citizens for improved quality in public services. In all Western democracies, a better educated and informed citizenry has fuelled a more explicit consciousness of citizen rights. These developments have been intertwined with greater public exposure of government and public administration shortcomings by more aggressive mass media, parliamentary review and audit agencies, and the proliferation of specialized interest groups. Increased public access to government information, as a consequence of both new laws requiring such access and new information technologies, has fostered levels of scepticism and criticism of government that go beyond traditional partisan politics.

Demands for improved quality in public services have been stimulated by public perceptions that services in the public sector are less well managed than services in the private sector (Pollitt, 1990; Metcalfe and Richards, 1987), particularly in relation to the perceived responsiveness of public service organizations to citizens as 'customers' or 'consumers' of public services (Pierre, 1995). In some respects, this movement has entailed efforts to adopt a marketization of public services, especially as advanced by conservative governments; in other respects, however, it has been fostered by social movements on the left which seek to have public bureaucracies become more 'democratic' in their dealings with citizens as clients (Albo, Langille and Panitch, 1993).   In these respects, decentralization is deemed a necessary dimension of responsiveness.   In seeking to emulate what are considered the best practices in the private sector, public sector agencies are encouraged to decentralize authority in order that they might 'stay close to their customers' or enter into a mode of discourse that empowers citizens in relation to the agents of the state.

Intergovernmental decentralization has been sought for at least three reasons.   In some cases, central governments have been forced to decentralize authority to lower orders of government in certain fields of public policy, because they have insufficient financial resources with which to insist on state/local government compliance with centralized standards or directives.   In other instances, central governments are essentially 'off-loading' to lower orders of government those responsibilities they can no longer afford to undertake or finance.   In addition, public support for centralized governance and public management in certain fields has also diminished.   The recipients, or clients, of certain services perceive central government control over programmes as the chief reason for the bureaucratization of public services.   With less public tolerance for the latter, decentralized public services are regarded as offering increased responsiveness to citizens (Burns, Hambleton and Hoggett, 1994).

Forms of Management Devolution

In four of the five national governments considered here, that is, excepting Germany, new management regimes have sought to alter traditional relations between the central agencies which serve the cabinet as a corporate executive and the government's line departments and agencies in the direction of devolution.   The foci of these new management regimes have been threefold.

First, there has been a deregulation of centrally prescribed administrative policies covering financial and personnel resources and administrative practices broadly defined.   In respect to certain matters, standardized rules have disappeared altogether; in others, standards have been streamlined; while in still others, guidelines have replaced rules.   Second, there have been increased delegations of authority to departments and agencies to manage their financial and personnel resources and to institute their own management practices respecting such matters as the procurement of supplies and services.   These delegations have enabled managers to exercise greater authority over the deployment of resources to deliver public services and to mix the ways in which they use resources to achieve economies and efficiencies.   They also have enabled managers to contract out certain functions to the private sector on their own initiative and/or to undertake functions within their organizations that previously had to be secured from other 'common services' departments. Third, there has been increased decentralization down the organizational hierarchy, so that those in regional and/or local offices have greater authority to design and manage the actual delivery of programmes in ways that are more responsive to citizens, including the design of delivery systems that provide single points of access for citizens or business groups. In some instances, these single points of access integrate two or more parts of a department's or agency's specialized services; in other cases, they integrate the services of two or more departments and agencies in a single cluster of services (Seidle, 1995).

These changes had profound effects on central management, particularly in the area of personnel administration. While there remain important government-wide policies respecting personnel administration, in some cases established in legislation, decentralization has taken its toll on what were formerly powerful central personnel agencies. The Australian Public Service Board, for example, was replaced by a Public Service Commission with primarily a personnel policy advisory function, rather than an executive or regulatory management function (Halligan, 1991). With only a few exceptions, operational aspects of personnel administration have become the responsibility of departments. There were similar developments in Britain where the Civil Service Commission has been replaced by an Office of Civil Service Commissioners with policy responsibilities related to the maintenance of the merit principle in staffing, but with most operational aspects of personnel administration decentralized to departments and agencies (Wilson, 1991). In Canada, recent changes have been less significant. The Public Service Commission has for some time delegated many personnel functions to departments, and further authority has been given to public service managers under new legislation (Swimmer, Hicks and Milne, 1994). In general, none the less, there has been a greater unwillingness than elsewhere to tackle what is perceived to be a risky political issue, given the traditional independent role for the commission in implementing the merit principle in staffing. In the Netherlands, as in Germany, where there has not been a highly centralized personnel regime as found in the three Westminster systems, the Ministry of the Interior is in the process of losing its powers to negotiate conditions of public service employment. These powers are to be decentralized within the central government apparatus, as well as assigned to other government authorities and provincial and local governments.

In the area of financial administration, equally significant efforts at decentralization have occurred. The British Financial Management Initiative (FMI), the Australian Financial Management Improvement Program (FMIP), the Canadian Increased Ministerial Authority and Accountability programme (IMAA), and the Dutch Financial Accountability Operation

(FAO) had broadly similar objectives. Although there are differences in what is or was covered and what has been achieved in each case, the objectives of these schemes were the same, namely to enhance cost consciousness, improve financial management practices, financial management information systems and financial reporting systems, and rely on ministers and senior departmental officials to effect economies and efficiencies in exchange for reduced controls and interventions from the centre.

The combined effect of the above changes was to shift the focus of public management from centralized controls and standardized procedures over the use of inputs (budgets, staff and supplies and services) in the administration of public services to the management of these resources by those responsible for the management and delivery of services (Schick, 1990). Central powers were not entirely eliminated as a consequence. Rather, decentralization has been coupled with increased requirements to use performance targets, service standards, performance measures or indicators and, not the least, more stringent reporting requirements.

With a decentralization of authority and responsibility to operating departments, the capacity of ministers and public service executives to achieve economies and efficiencies was meant to be enhanced. At the same time, the capacity to achieve effectiveness in realizing policy objectives was also to be strengthened, given that greater control over the use of resources was to provide the flexibility needed to adapt to changing circumstances as well as to tailor management systems to varying situational requirements, especially at the front lines of service delivery. In these respects, accordingly, decentralization was to meet the twin challenges of coping with expenditure restraint and improving the quality of public services.

The effectiveness of these financial management programmes has varied across these systems, not only in the degree to which the intended measures were effected throughout government, but also in terms of the significance which reformers attached to their outcomes for public management reform generally. In Britain, for instance, it was decided that while the FMI advanced the cause of improved financial management in certain respects, a great deal more was required: hence the Next Steps initiative that instituted the 'executive agency' regime (Kemp, 1990). Under this regime, the government has sought to separate responsibilities for policy and operations respectively. While ministers remain constitutionally responsible for both policy and operations, a division of responsibilities has been effected between those who advise ministers on policy and those who manage operations. The link between the two is based on agreements which specify the volume and level of services to be provided by executive agencies, the resources and management authorities they require to achieve these agreed outputs, and the targets and measures necessary to assess their performance and to hold the chief executives of these agencies accountable.

The use of the model, it was assumed, would have several advantages over the traditional ministerial department. These agencies would be established with more clearly identified or discrete missions than is usually the case with departments (even where a single agency might provide all the services required by a minister/department). These missions, as detailed in agreements encompassing targeted outputs, service standards and performance measures, would be more specific and transparent than is usually the case with departmental plans. These agencies would be headed by a chief executive officer whose primary responsibility would be to manage the provision of specified services. Agencies would promote more productive management because chief executives would be given greater autonomy and flexibility in the management of agency resources than has been the case with departmental managers, including at times limited authority to generate their own revenues by adopting various commercial practices and to institute agency-specific performance rewards and sanctions for their personnel. Finally, given the above features, this model would enable ministers to establish a tighter accountability regime for agency chief executives than has been traditionally applied to the senior mandarins in government departments.

In the British case, almost two-thirds of central government public servants, once employed in line departments, are now located in executive agencies, even though most have retained their public servant status. Although there are still more candidates of departmental organizations to be transformed into executive agencies, the British government considers this approach to have been successfully implemented and achieving desired results. Its own evaluations of progress, as well as those of parliamentary committees, have called for further improvements, but there has been no major demand for a return to the previous model of ministerial departments (HMSO, 1994).

Both Canada and the Netherlands have borrowed this model in designing what the Canadian government calls 'special operating agencies' and the Dutch simply 'agencies'. The Canadian adoption of this model, also pursued in part because of the perceived limitations in its IMAA initiative, was initially introduced on a pilot basis in 1989. It differs from the British model in that the heads of special operating agencies remain subordinate to the deputy minister (the chief administrative officer) of the line department in which they are located. They do not report directly to their minister, as is the case in Britain. Moreover, the application of the model has remained modest: only 17 agencies have been created to date, employing less than 10 per cent of the federal public service proper. The Dutch adoption of this model was inspired by the same managerial ideas, but agencies were but one part of a more general scheme to 'autonomize' the administrative apparatus of the Dutch state (Kickert and Verhaat, 1995); other forms of administrative structures with an arm's-length relationship to government were also instituted.

Despite their differences, these agencies resemble, in several respects, the traditional non-departmental organizational designs used in all five systems for the purposes of what has been called 'indirect public administration' (Modeen and Rosas, 1988). In each system, government-owned corporations as well as numerous other types of public service and regulatory bodies with an arm's-length relationship to the central apparatus of government, continue to be found (Hogwood, 1995). Indeed, in some regimes, these non-departmental bodies outnumber traditional departmental organizations. These new agencies increase the variety, and diversity, of organizational designs, not the least because they themselves are not meant to be cast in a single mould, but rather are to be subject to different kinds of negotiated designs concerning their management structures, authorities and modes of financing.

What is common among these new agencies, along with their counterparts outside of the central apparatus of ministerial departments (what Hodgetts (1973) calls 'structural heretics'), is the extent to which authority, responsibility and accountability relationships between ministers and administrators have been transformed, at least in part, from the traditional hierarchical structures of public administration to contractual-type arrangements. Although ministers have not relinquished their statutory authority in either the British, Canadian or Dutch applications of the agency model powers, because in none of the cases have agencies been given an independent statutory basis, the assumption underlying the model is that ministers (and their departments) will forgo interventions in the ongoing management of these agencies. Where ministers want changes, these should be effected through changes in their 'contracts' with agency executives. In this respect, agencies are like government-owned corporations (and other statutory bodies with an arm's-length relationship to ministers), in so far as ministers who wish to effect new direction, priorities and practices must, in theory, provide formal policy directives when corporate strategies or business plans are being negotiated. The integrity of contractual arrangements, in theory, is maintained only to the extent that changes are effected through changes in contracts, and not through unilateral ministerial (or departmental) interventions which contravene existing contracts. In practice many politically sensitive agencies complain there is still operational interference in the administration; theory and practice do not fully coincide.

The intergovernmental dynamics of decentralization, especially where state/local governments provide national public services in lieu of direct public service delivery by central or federal governments, share some characteristics with the above developments. Where there is extensive centralization, as in Britain and the Netherlands (King, 1993; Andeweg and Irwin, 1993), the central government will have either the statutory authority or the budgetary resources to use state/local governments as essentially administrative arms of the central government. Decentralization, on the other hand, either will result in a deregulation of central government rules and interventions, and thus greater autonomy on the part of the lower orders of government, or, as in Germany especially, take the form of contractual agreements between governments, resulting in a form of intergovernmental public management characterized as 'co-government' (Lehmbruch, 1989).

In some cases, however, central governments, as in Britain and the Netherlands, for example, have sought to use the leverage they have over local governments to force, or cajole, the latter into instituting their own decentralization schemes, including measures to introduce greater competition and choice in the provision of public services. The paradox here is that centralized authority can be used, indeed may be necessary, to effect decentralization. In these instances, the driving force has been either ideological conviction, as in the case of Britain where competition and choice have loomed large on the Conservatives' agenda since the early 1980s (Mény and Knapp, 1993), or perceived public demands for more effective governmental responses to the socioeconomic dislocations caused by changing economic circumstances, as in the Netherlands (Hupe, 1990; Toonen, 1987). In Germany, the major thrust towards the implementation of a reform agenda that calls for greater competition and choice has occurred at the level of local governments.

Variations Across Political Systems

If decentralization has been pursued largely in an effort to force greater economy, efficiency and effectiveness in the management and delivery of public services, what factors account for variations across the political systems considered here? At least two major factors need to be considered: first, the extent to which political leaders have considered public management reforms central to reforms in governance and public policy broadly defined; and, second, the extent to which the prevailing designs of the state apparatus were perceived to hinder the pursuit of public management reforms.

Public management reforms have clearly been perceived as central to reforms in governance and public policy in Britain, Australia and the Netherlands. In Britain, the Conservatives, since 1979, but especially beginning in the mid-1980s, have sought to institute a radical change in

British public administration in order to force the state apparatus to become more cost conscious in the management of resources and to become more service conscious in its dealings with citizens. The political leadership, especially under Margaret Thatcher, held strong political convictions about what had to be done. In Australia, two successive Labor prime ministers since 1983 have been insistent that the state apparatus be reformed in order to produce better 'results' — in what the state does and how it manages resources to achieve its policy objectives. Policy and administrative changes have thus gone hand in hand; a comprehensive set of reforms has been implemented. In the Netherlands, comprehensive reforms encompassing decentralization in the central government as well as in intergovernmental relations have been linked to a major effort to contract the size and scope of the Dutch state (Wolinetz, 1989), although the political leadership took some time to secure the proposed organizational reforms (Wijngaarden, 1990; Andeweg and Irwin, 1993; Andeweg, 1989a).

Decentralization has been an important element in these efforts at reforms because political leaders have had to acknowledge that there are limits to what can be achieved by concentrating power at the centre for the purposes of strategic policy and expenditure discipline, imposing top-down economy measures or tight expenditure ceilings on public service managers, privatizing government undertakings, and contracting out public endeavours to the private sector. At some point, individual ministers must be charged with managing their portfolios (even if they cannot be transformed into 'ministers as managers' as the British sought to do under the FMI scheme) and public service managers must be given the authority necessary to manage their operations.

Decentralization, as with other elements of reform, was largely imposed on the traditional British mandarinate by a new breed of public managers supported by the British political leadership, especially Prime Minister Thatcher and her personal advisers. This thrust was continued by Prime Minister John Major in the implementing of his market-testing and Citizens' Charter initiatives, hence the progression of continuing 'steps' which has characterized reform measures in this system (Campbell and Wilson, 1995). Decentralization, especially as reflected in the use of executive agencies, was driven by the desire to diminish the power of the traditional senior civil service; hence the priority of recruiting outsiders as chief executives for the new agencies (and, more generally, making competition for senior executives open to external candidates), and changing the culture of the public service by enabling executive agencies to function in a more business-like fashion.

In Australia, vigorous political leadership was a driving force in reform, but it was coupled with a new bureaucratic leadership committed to 'managerialism'. Although there was no grand design at the outset, the unfolding of reforms has been more coherent and consistent, and, in this context, 'devolution', as the Australians have labelled what we have called decentralization, was viewed in a more positive light. Once ministers had assumed greater political control over the apparatus of the state, the structures were in place to devolve authority from central departments to departments and then down the line of departmental hierarchies. By establishing a partnership with the senior bureaucracy, the ministry generally trusted officials to pursue its reform agenda (Campbell and Halligan, 1993). The need to devolve authority further by using organizational forms such as agencies was seen not only as inappropriate but also as unnecessary (Australia, 1992). More recently, it has been acknowledged that devolution has not been achieved to the extent desired, and calls for changes that would introduce a greater emphasis on contract management, or output budgeting, along the lines of the British or New Zealand model (Boston, Martin and Walsh, 1991), have been advocated (Australia, 1995).

The Canadian experience is interesting for a different set of reasons. Public management reforms, especially in respect to organizational and managerial changes affecting decentralization, have been undertaken over the past decade along lines similar to other systems, but the political leadership has evinced little interest in them (Canada, Office of the Auditor General, 1993; Savoie, 1994). On the contrary, the first steps of the Conservative government which come to power in 1984 were to seek greater political control over the public service bureaucracy by enhancing the role and number of partisan-political staff in ministerial offices, including the Prime Minister's Office (Aucoin, 1986). Organizational and administrative reforms were not viewed as contributing to political control over the state apparatus. As a consequence, public management reforms and measures to effect expenditure restraint measures have been pursued on parallel tracks (Clark, 1994). Only the latter were perceived by political leaders as crucial to governance and public policy; the former were regarded as largely matters of internal 'plumbing' to be left to the bureaucracy itself. This dynamic changed somewhat with the restructuring of the cabinet, portfolio and departmental architecture in 1993, along the lines of the Australian changes in 1987 (Aucoin and Bakvis, 1993). The Liberal government elected in 1993, following almost a decade of Conservative rule, has professed an interest in what it calls 'public service renewal', but to date the chief focus has been on downsizing the state through a process of policy and programme reviews. Experiences elsewhere are of increased interest, however, and further changes to decentralize along the lines of the New Zealand or British models may well be forthcoming.

In Germany, there has been no formal programme of public management reform at the federal level, although there has been some increased attention given to management training and an expanded use of information technology. The highest priority respecting public management since the early 1990s, moreover, has been on improving public management in the five Eastern German *Länder*. The absence of a reform agenda similar to that pursued elsewhere is due to several factors. In comparison to the politically driven reforms in Australia and Britain, for instance, there has been a lack of major criticism of the responsiveness of the federal bureaucracy to the political executive, or, for that matter, of its competence. Among a number of reasons for this the chief ones are the provisions which enable the political executive to appoint party supporters to key bureaucratic positions, the fact that many ministers themselves have had bureaucratic careers, and the minimal need for 'managerial' competencies in what is essentially a policy oriented federal bureaucracy. As noted, however, changes have been introduced in local government.

The basic designs of the state apparatus have been a second reason for variations in the pursuit of devolution. The British move to executive agencies, for instance, was partly a result of the increasingly accepted view — a view that dates at least from the 1960s with the Fulton Committee (Drewry and Butcher, 1988) — that improved public management could not be achieved so long as there persisted adherence to the central, and centralizing, idea of a unified public service system. Uniformity and standardization in the management regime were thus explicitly identified as constraints to productive management. The practice of centralized controls and micro-management by the centre, especially on the part the Treasury, had to give way if major changes were to be realized.

In Australia, there was a similar concern, although here the emphasis was as much on changing the capacity of individual ministers to provide direction to their respective portfolio organizations as it was to unleash the managerial potential of the public service. Devolution, accordingly, had to start with a structure that enabled ministers to manage their portfolios as a condition of enabling greater devolution within departmental organizations themselves. A reorganization of the cabinet and the portfolio system was thus central to public management reforms, including the pursuit of devolution as an integral element in a new system of programme management and budgeting (Weller, Forster and Davis, 1993).

Significant organizational change to promote decentralization was eschewed at the outset of the Canadian Conservative government, following its 1984 election victory, notwithstanding the fact that it was widely recognized by then that the centralized, albeit fragmented, management regime imposed on departments could not but adversely affect productive management (Canada, Office of the Auditor General, 1983). In fact, the executive system was further fragmented with an expansion in the size of the cabinet and the creation of new ministerial portfolios. It was not until the end of the Conservative regime in 1993, and under a new Conservative prime minister, that a consolidation of cabinet portfolios was effected. Even within the bureaucracy, however, the operative assumption was that public management reform was primarily a matter of changing public service attitudes, especially in respect to service to the public and the management of 'people' within the public service. This approach was the underlying philosophy of the Public Service 2000 programme that prescribed little in the way of formal organizational change, even though its preached an 'empowerment' of public servants, especially on the front lines of service delivery. Following the massive 1993 restructuring which reduced the size of the cabinet to the low twenties with roughly the same number of ministerial departments, there has emerged a greater interest in new organizational models for delivering public services, but change continues to proceed, as in Australia, primarily in an incremental fashion and depends largely on the willingness of individual departments to take the required initiatives.

In the Netherlands, the excessive degree to which the governmental and public service system had been long characterized by a 'functional decentralization' (Andeweg and Irwin, 1993; Andeweg, 1988; Daalder, 1989) in regard to policy management by departments has been reduced by increased ministerial control (Gladdish, 1991). However, policy and operational responsibilities had begun to be decoupled by making the central government ministries more 'policy oriented' and by creating agencies 'as more independent parts of the civil service with greater managerial powers and responsibilities than 'normal' civil service departments' (OECD, 1993: 119; Kickert and Verhaat, 1995). At the same time, decentralization has been coupled with a new priority of developing a more unified senior public service to replace what has been highly departmentalized public service tradition. In order to promote greater responsiveness to corporate political strategies and priorities, a unified senior public service is seen as an alternative to a more politicized public service.

On the surface, Germany has been little affected by these kinds of developments for the simple reason that its basic structures are already highly decentralized in each of the several respects noted above. Along the several dimensions of devolution, the German system, for instance, has long been characterized by relatively autonomous ministerial departments, as well as a division of policy and operational responsibilities (Johnson, 1983; Mayntz and Scharpf, 1975). German line departments are essentially policy ministries; the management and delivery of public services, which have been the principal focus of public management in the Westminster systems especially, are undertaken either by a small number of relatively autonomous federal agencies or, for the most part, by lower orders of government in this highly decentralized federal system. In addition, and partly for this reason, there is little in the way of corporate management controls over the policy ministries or agencies of the federal government. Not only is there no central agency for personnel policy across the central government, the finance department, while powerful in regard to fiscal policy and the expenditure budget, has a relatively limited role to play in matters of financial administration across government. In any event, the bulk of federal spending is not managed directly by federal departments, but either by federal agencies with considerable autonomy over line operations, or, for the most part, by agencies under the control of the *Länder* or local governments. Indeed, the major efforts at reform over the past two to three decades have been to counter what have been perceived as the limitations or deficiencies in such a highly decentralized and fragmented public management system (Katzenstein, 1987; Benz, 1987; Klatt, 1989).

Prospects and Implications

Decentralization is but one element of public management reform. As amply illustrated in the aftermath of Canadian administrative reforms in the mid-1960s, letting managers manage, by itself, does not guarantee improved public management (Aucoin and Bakvis, 1988). At the same time, decentralization can be seen as a necessary prerequisite for improvements, that is, to reduce constraints on productive management. Decentralization, if well designed and managed, has the potential to enhance the clarity and precision of organizational missions, to make the management of operations and operational performance more responsive to the criteria of economy, efficiency and effectiveness, and to strengthen accountability mechanisms by improving the transparency of superior–subordinate (or principal–agent) relationships.

There is an acceptance that decentralization has occurred in the four countries formally moving in this direction, although stated intentions invariably exceed actual practice, and Germany may be achieving as much if not more in these regards without the fanfare of an official reform programme. Thus, for instance, while devolution was deemed a 'cornerstone' of Australian reforms, the Task Force on Management Improvement reported in its recent evaluation of a decade of reform that the record in respect to devolution had received a mixed assessment. Some officials felt devolution had not gone far enough and others were not certain it had secured the desired results. Equally interesting, however, it heard few calls from government officials for a recentralization of authority and many appeals for increased devolution, especially from central agencies and those on the front lines. The former view devolution as a means to extract greater performance from line managers; the latter want more authority devolved down the line by their departmental superiors (Australia, 1992: 89–112). Campbell and Halligan (1993: 227) concluded that 'the focus on the portfolio, while it has yet to be fully exploited, has produced greater effectiveness and possibly some efficiencies. The move to a decentralized public service — one focusing on the department rather than the central agency — has been an important systemic change'. As noted above, more recent evaluations have come to the conclusion that further organizational changes are required to effect greater devolution at the level of operations.

Recent Canadian changes, encompassing a new Expenditure Management System (Canada, 1995b), may also constitute the basis for a more explicit attempt to separate policy and operational responsibilities, to establish contract or output budgeting, and to couple these with a more rigorous performance management and accountability regime.

Jenkins and Gray conclude that the British move to executive agencies has 'succeeded as a management innovation', whereby at least some agencies have achieved 'real improvements in service delivery' and 'organizations have begun to relate to clients in a different way' (Jenkins and Gray, 1993: 93–4). While a number of academics, including Jenkins and Gray, would agree with Savoie that the 'jury is still out' on whether executive agencies can realize the objectives of autonomy and business-like management within the context of ministerial government (Savoie, 1994: 302), most admit that the central controls of the Treasury have been relaxed, although not as much as might be proclaimed (Savoie, 1994: 321). Whatever the academic evaluation, however, there appears both internal and external political support of the executive agency regime.

What is perhaps most telling about the moves to decentralization, however, as found in the Australian government's own evaluation, is that there is little support for a general recentralization of public management, at least as applied to the management of financial resources, staff and programmes at the level of operations. The answer to this dimension of the centralization–decentralization conundrum seems to have been settled for the time being. Making managers manage requires greater attention to outputs, service standards and performance in lieu of the micro-management from the centre of inputs, processes and procedures. There has, it appears, been a 'paradigm' shift in public management (Aucoin, 1990).

At the same time, greater decentralization of authority has brought with it a greater emphasis on accountability for results. For managers, the reduction in input controls by the centre has been replaced by new central demands for the demonstration of performance. Moreover, given the success of most governments in centrally restraining budgetary and/or staff resources, greater flexibility for line managers more often than not has meant doing the same, or more, with fewer resources. For many, this development appears to constitute a paradox: the trade-off for greater line management authority is less for line managers to manage. From the perspective of central agencies, of course, this development is hardly a paradox; it is the essential point about decentralization — which is merely the means to produce greater effectiveness while making organizations more economical and efficient. The fact that the greatest degree of economy and efficiency has been derived from centrally imposed restraints (or 'efficiency dividends' as the Australians call them) ought not to be surprising. Departments and agencies, especially those where is it possible to measure organizational outputs and performance, however approximate these measures may be, have demonstrated that they can do the same, or even more, with fewer resources, if they have greater authority over the use of those resources.

Similarly, it ought not to be surprising that central management agencies, especially finance or treasury departments, remain focused on inputs, that is, budgetary allocations to departments and agencies. They do so even where policy reviews or programme evaluations have recommended changes in policy or programme designs to enhance effectiveness while adhering to a commitment to expenditure restraint or reductions. Efficiency scrutinies in Britain and the 'reconsideration procedure' in the Netherlands, and selective policy reviews elsewhere, have been useful in these regards. Where a formal process of programme evaluation has been established, as in Australia and Canada, its intended effects on the allocation of budgetary resources on a regular basis has been less than hoped for, although Australia reports increased progress on this front.

There are three points that need to be addressed in response to these developments. First, decentralization may be viewed primarily, and simply, as a corrective to the increased centralization of public management which characterized at least three of these political systems during the 1960s to 1980s, namely Australia, Britain and Canada. By exacerbating the complexities inherent in the modern state, these centralized regimes not only had numerous perverse consequences for productive management but also failed to ensure compliance at the level expected (Campbell, 1983). Moreover, efforts at centralized policy planning, budgeting and evaluation failed to secure the desired coherence in governance, not merely because they encountered political as well as bureaucratic resistance, but, more importantly, because they sought to go beyond the limits of what applied social science could contribute to governance (Schick, 1986, 1988).

Second, the size and complexity of government operations produced organizational structures within which the linkages between policy, administrative and operational responsibilities became increasing differentiated (Carroll, 1990). The move to separate organizational responsibilities for policy and operations is in some respects merely a pragmatic response to this development, in much the same way that governments have traditionally resorted to non-departmental forms of government organization for a variety of undertakings. Executive agencies, for instance, are a continuation of this tradition. But even in Australia and Canada where the operative assumption has been that integrated departments are necessary to ensure the required 'feedback between implementers and policy-makers' (Australia, 1992: 525), it has been accepted that a significant delegation of administrative responsibilities for line operations, as well as a flattening of organizational hierarchies, is required.

Finally, greater coherence and coordination in managing the state apparatus, including intergovernmental relations, requires more than formal organizational design. It also requires competent political and public service leadership. The German experience, for instance, has long illustrated that even with a good deal of departmental autonomy at the centre, a policy–operations division of responsibilities, and a decentralized system of inter-governmental relations, a great deal can be achieved when there is adherence to a set of fundamental principles of governance, a shared set of beliefs about good management practices, and the use of explicit contractual-type arrangements for specifying authority, responsibility and accountability.

In these three respects, the paradox of centralization to achieve decentralization has also been present in changes to government organization and management within central governments. As noted, the driving force behind much of the public management reform programmes has been the intention 'to make managers manage', not merely 'to let managers manage'. As such, decentralization schemes have not had as their objective any diminution in the capacities of the centre to manage the state apparatus, or to 'hollow out the core'. Rather, they have constituted attempts to strengthen the strategic responsibilities of the core of the state (cabinet and individual ministers) by making bureaucracies more responsive to policy direction from political executives, citizens' demands for quality service, and the dictates of economy and efficiency.

The fact that these schemes are viewed in some quarters as essentially attempts by the centre to achieve in new ways what they could not realize by traditional methods is testimony to the continuing, indeed inherent, tensions between centralization and decentralization in government. Only to the degree that the various measures accompanying decentralization have failed to impose the required discipline, and therefore accountability, have the capacities of the core been diminished. This phenomenon is not new. Past failures to establish rigorous systems for the direction, control and accountability of state enterprises and other non-departmental public authorities, as well as poorly designed mechanisms for the intergovern-mental management of national public services, constitute lessons in these regards. In fact, other elements of public management reforms have centred precisely on these shortcomings, as governments have sought to strengthen their capacities in relation to their state enterprises (where they have not privatized them) and to exert greater control over a wide range of quasi-independent public bodies.

Conclusion

The New Public Management that has driven a good deal of the decentralization now found in four of these national governments (as well as in state and provincial governments in Australia and Canada respectively), and in local government in Germany, must be viewed in historical perspective. Many of the reasons for decentralization within the core executive–bureaucratic arenas are identical to the reasons for the extensive 'indirect public administration' found in each of these systems, namely an attempt to debureaucratize the administration of public affairs. In addition, in some cases the driving force was an attempt to depoliticize the administration of public affairs. In each of these respects, there is not much that is new in the new public administration.

What is new in the New Public Management is the assumption that decentralization within the core structures of the executive–bureaucratic arenas can secure, even enhance, strategic political direction and control, and thus maintain ministerial responsibility, while fostering improved management, both in the use of resources and in the delivery of public services. The separation of policy and operational responsibilities, the decentralization of management authority and the use of performance management systems, encompassing contract management rather than traditional hierarchical relationships, have assumed that the dictates of responsible government can be coupled with the principles of good government. In this sense, 'managerialism', viewed as increased bureaucratic discretion or autonomy along the lines of private sector management regimes, does not sufficiently capture the full range of dynamics at play here (Aucoin, 1995).

While many academics doubt, or reject, the logic of the New Public Management in these respects, the practice of at least some governments has demonstrated that improved public management, as governance, can be effected via decentralization schemes within the core executive–bureaucratic structures. It is not without some evidence of progress that government and parliamentary evaluations of reform efforts have generally supported such New Public Management reforms, even while they call for continued efforts to make further progress. For their part, precious few public managers responsible for the operations of government call for a return to prior practices of centralized management regimes. In these respects, the academic evaluation of the New Public Management is often out of step with the assessment of practitioners.

The ongoing debate about decentralization, however, is not only about the capacity of governance systems to secure good government. It is also an ideological debate about the role of the state in the socioeconomic order. From the perspective of the left, decentralization is viewed as part and parcel of a broader right-wing scheme to diminish the role of the state by making it less responsive to political direction and citizen demands via ministerial interventions in the management of operations. The fact that the New Public Management has also entailed a good deal of centralization of executive power in order to effect a diminished role for the state necessarily makes the perspective of the left on this score an awkward position. This is not to suggest that organizational structures and management systems are necessarily value free or neutral in their effects on public policy. Rather, it is to suggest that partisans on both the left and the right can use decentralized schemes to advance their respective causes, just as they can deploy centralized schemes to their different ideological ends. In short, the capacity of governments to steer the state is less a function of government organization than it is a function of the ideas about what the state should and can do coupled with the competence of political executives to secure the necessary political support to implement their ideas.

9 'Shackling the Leader?': Coherence, Capacity and the Hollow Crown

R. A. W. Rhodes

Patrick Weller and Herman Bakvis argue in the introductory chapter that governments struggle for coherence in both the aims and the outcomes of their policies. They strive to make the institutions of government work in harmony. They espouse a set of values which stress coordination, consistency and avoiding duplication and overlap. This statecentric view requires the government to control its own tools and to have consistent policies. But governments also want to have an impact on their society. This sociocentric view focuses on the influence of government on society and its ability to shape that society.

This concluding chapter draws together the threads on coherence, capacity and hollowing out of core executives. Unfortunately, my co-editors opined:

> it might be asked when comparative volumes on executives are going to contain some genuinely comparative conclusions, rather than setting out yet again a future research agenda.

There is no escape for me. They forbid suggestions for future research. I must revisit the earlier chapters to identify the most significant findings. Fortunately this task is easier than usual. Unlike most other edited, comparative books, the individual chapters are not country studies. My co-authors draw systematic comparisons across the five countries. I pull together their findings, focusing on: political parties and the processes of getting and building support; cabinets, collectivity and collegiality; policy advice; resource allocation; coordination; and managerialism and decentralization.

This selection of topics is a direct result of our decision to explore the effects of hollowing out on the core executive. At the risk of some repetition, the core executive includes:

> all those organisations and structures which primarily serve to pull together and integrate central government policies, or act as final arbiters within the executive of conflicts between different elements of the

government machine (Dunleavy and Rhodes, 1990: 4; Rhodes, 1995: 12).

We must examine, therefore, key institutions of coordination and conflict resolution — that is, party and cabinet (see also Aucoin, 1994b: 99) — and key processes which pull the parts together — that is, policy advice, resource allocation, coordination and management.

Coherence is under threat from, among many pressures, institutional differentiation and globalization. We used the notion of 'hollowing out' as an exploratory tool to analyse these pressures. Saward usefully specifies how hollowing out may erode the capacities and, therefore, the coherence of the state:

1. the core executive is losing or conceding capacities to societal actors;
2. the core executive is losing or conceding its capacity to control other state actors; and
3. the core executive is losing or conceding capacities to supra-state entities.

So, these conclusions also consider national and international trends towards or away from a 'hollow crown'. I adopt a statecentric perspective and focus on the alleged loss of core executive capacity to both other state actors and supra-state entities.

Such trends matter because they erode both capacity and coherence.[1] In other words, they change the nature and role of political leadership in and of the core executives of parliamentary democracies. So, this chapter discusses whether the leader's position in parliamentary systems has strengthened or weakened. Has hollowing out and its associated pressures changed the role of leaders? To explore whether the crown is hollow, I contrast the Westminster model of parliamentary democracy with its emphasis on, for example, cabinet government, parliamentary sovereignty and ministerial responsibility with the differentiated polity characterized by interdependence, a segmented executive, policy networks, governance and hollowing out.[2] Finally, I explore the implications of these trends for political accountability in parliamentary democracies.

To analyse the differentiated polity, I adopt an institutional approach which focuses on policy networks and governance (Rhodes, 1996: Chs 1–3). I develop three arguments:

1. that institutional differentiation and pluralization is a common challenge to all core executives;
2. that networks of organizations, not formal–legal institutions, are 'functionally equivalent' (Neustadt, 1969: 133) in all five parliamentary systems and, therefore, the appropriate unit of analysis; and

3. that traditional mechanisms of accountability in parliamentary democracy were never designed to cope with multi-organizational fragmented policy systems.

Institutional differentiation, or multiplying the organizational types through which government works, and institutional pluralization, or increasing numbers of the same type of organization, characterize advanced industrial democracies. They factor complex problems into manageable bits and reduce complexity by institutional differentiation and pluralization. Such trends make steering more difficult, so the mechanisms for integration multiply. All political leaders are shackled by institutional dependence. This chapter shows how institutional dependence can undermine core executive coherence and capacity.

Coherence and Capacity

To reduce repetition, I simply list the key findings without lengthy discussion. The supporting evidence and arguments are in the earlier chapters. My objective is to synthesize the findings of earlier chapters by providing a list of propositions for others to challenge.

Political Parties

Weller argues that three institutional variables have a significant impact on the capacity of executives to act: the existence of coalition or single-party governments; the unitary or federal nature of the constitution; and the basis of class support. This institutional impact takes the following forms:

•   Federal systems disperse authority and multiply veto points requiring the national government to negotiate policy with levels of government. They also fracture party unity, as the same party can govern at different levels with different interests, and mute the influence of party on policy.

•   The impact of party is pervasive. It ties ministers to government, casting them in the role of agents of their parties in departmental policy making (see also Laver and Shepsle, 1994a).

•   Policy communities act as a counterweight to party and departmental policy making and ministers are constrained by both.

•   In Westminster systems with an integrated government and parliament, and with ministers who must be members of parliament, policy belongs to government and is made by cabinet. In coalition governments, some policies must be negotiated between parties.

- Policy making in Westminster systems is more volatile and less coherent but leaders are answerable for the general performance of government. Coalition governments provide cautious government with more coherent policy agendas because they are negotiated between the parties. The parties constrain government over the detail of policy.

In short, Westminster systems make parties dependent on government whereas coalition governments make governments dependent on parties. For the latter, parties may act as an anchor, grounding the cabinet in its negotiated commitments to its constituent interests and discouraging sudden changes of direction. For the former, governments still have to maintain support but they are less committed to particular policies. They may be pulled in directions favoured by policy communities because there is no constant countervailing party influence. It is not possible to ignore parties. It is simply that policy views are less firmly established and party discipline gives cabinet greater freedom to act. When policy debates become fragmented, there is no party core to policy or coalition agreement to act as a counterweight to either policy communities or the processes of hollowing out.

Cabinets, Collectivity and Collegiality

Andeweg cogently disputes Laver and Shepsle's (1994b: 297–8 and 308) conclusion on the autonomy of cabinet ministers that they are constrained by the volume of collective decision making. Ministerial discretion is a product of their ability to shape collective decisions. Ministers do not have complete autonomy, but they do have a significant degree of relative autonomy and the parliamentary systems vary in their relative fragmentation of cabinet government. His assessment of collective and collegial government reaches four important conclusions:

1. Fragmented government is departmental government. Most conflicts are interdepartmental, not partisan, and ministers' reputations depend on their performance as heads of department (see also Dunleavy and Rhodes, 1990: 11–15; Heclo and Wildavsky, 1974: 369, 371; James, 1992: Ch. 2; King, 1994: 207).
2. There are six causes of relative departmental autonomy: organizational complexity, often in the form of strong policy networks; functional specialization and the technocratic recruitment of ministers, especially when coupled with long tenure; a self-contained portfolio; a politically non-controversial portfolio; a tradition of autonomy; and few internal or external pressures either to expand or reduce the budget (see also Bayliss, 1989: 11–13; King, 1994: 214–17).

3. Variations in collective government are not related to such distinctions as Westminster versus continental parliamentary systems, unitary versus federal, single-party versus coalition (see also Frognier, 1993: 70). Size or ministerial quality may also have an impact.
4. Multiple representation (of territorial, ethnic, linguistic and religious interests, rather than functional or departmental interests) leads to collective rather than segmented government. Paradoxically, it strengthens rather than weakens collective government because ministers wear more than one hat and have a direct incentive to take an interest in other ministers' portfolios. (see also Bakvis, 1991.)

Andeweg also raises interesting questions about the way in which we have defined and analysed the 'core executive'. He criticizes the focus on 'coordination' as 'the defining function of cabinet government', arguing that another function — such as 'the provision of democratic legitimation to government', or 'the creation of a channel for political accountability', or the 'authoritative allocation of values' — is equally valid. He also claims the term coordination is unclear: 'what is and what is not included in that term?' In other words, the functional approach does not dispel 'the fog around the edges of the concept of cabinet government'.

Dunleavy and Rhodes deliberately avoid defining 'cabinet government' and use the broader term of the 'core executive' to draw attention to the 'fog around the edges'. The objective was to avoid the perceived constitutional certainties of existing definitions of cabinet government which assume cabinet is the ultimate coordinator and ask who is coordinating whom to do what? The parallel with Bagehot's definition of the cabinet as a buckle is not accidental because the function of a buckle is to join. The aim was to stimulate a re-examination of institutional and procedural linkages. By focusing on the core executive, we ask which institutions coordinate and resolve conflicts, leaving institutional roles to empirical investigation but combining institutions and functions in the one definition.

The available evidence supports the claim that fragmentation, coordination and conflict resolution are key features not just of the British executive, but in all the parliamentary systems under study to varying degrees. For the UK, ironically, fragmentation has a basis in law! The legal power of the executive is fragmented among departments which are not subject to a higher legal authority. Equivalent powers are not vested in either cabinet or prime ministers. Many other commentators also note both the fragmentation at the heart of British government (see Burch and Holliday, 1995: Ch. 5; Campbell and Wilson, 1995: 246 and 258; James, 1992: 181–4) and the role of the cabinet in solving interdepartmental conflicts (Nousiainen and Blondel, 1993: 302).

Dunleavy and Rhodes (1990) offered no comment on the functions of executives in other parliamentary democracies, the root of Andeweg's concern. But our definition is not specific to Britain. For example, Campbell and Szablowski's (1979: 9 and Ch. 2) comparative study of executives includes 'the development and adaptation of the strategic plans of a government/administration'; 'the formulation of substantive policies'; and the development and integration of economic and fiscal policies as key coordination and control functions of the executive. Davis notes that cabinets were common modes of coordination in all our parliamentary democracies.

However, my objective is not to defend the notion of the core executive against all-comers but to point out that Andeweg misses an important criticism. The phrase 'core executive' only *redescribes* the heart of the machine, it does not *explain* how it works.

This criticism can be overcome easily. Smith (1995: 109–12) argues there is 'mutual dependence' in the core executive and uses Rhodes's (1981: 98) power-dependence model to identify the resources of, and explore the interdependent interactions between, ministers and prime minister. In brief, actors in the core executive depend on other actors to achieve their goals. So they must exchange resources, for example money, legislative authority or expertise. These exchanges take the form of games in which actors seek to realize their objectives and manoeuvre for advantage, deploying their resources to maximize their advantage while minimizing their dependence on other actors. So, policy networks are both sets of resource-dependent organizations in their own game and a resource for ministers in their bargaining game with the core executive (see also Bayliss 1989: 58). In the same vein, Burch and Holliday (1995: Ch. 5) employ policy networks to analyse the key management tasks focused on the cabinet system (for example, European Union policy, government legislation). They conclude 'these networks have almost uniformly become more coordinated, more regularised and more focused on the cabinet system' (1956: 106). In short, the core executive is a set of interlinked networks with bargaining and the exchange of resources the key to explaining behaviour. It is the network which polices the functional policy networks.

Perhaps more important, Andeweg shows the variable incidence of collective government in the five systems (see also Bayliss, 1989: 147; Davis, 1996). He also identifies the pressures sustaining relative ministerial autonomy. The incidence of fragmentation and segmentation in Figure 4.2 clearly shows the limits to collective government and provides indirect evidence of hollowing out. Andeweg does not discuss whether these pressures have intensified.

Institutional differentiation and pluralization factor complex problems and reduce complexity. Such trends make steering more difficult, so the mechanisms for integration multiply. The term 'core executive' captures this trend by shifting attention away from cabinet and prime minister to all integrative mechanisms and the emerging networks policing the policy networks. Indeed, the phrase 'hollowing out' seeks to capture recent trends in these processes of differentiation and integration as they affect the core executive.

Policy Advice

Bakvis's survey of internal and external sources of policy advice suggests that:

- The permanent bureaucracy remains the main, if not exclusive, source of policy advice.
- In the Westminster systems, core executives: drew on thinks tanks in shaping the policy agenda; had close links with management consultants; and had weak political staff. The continental systems placed a higher value on expertise in political recruitment and relied more on policy-making networks incorporating party institutes or foundations.

He also identifies important countervailing trends:

- Pluralizing advice which: either shocks bureaucracies into innovation and increases the autonomy of the core executive; or fills the vacuum, acting as a substitute for action by core executives increasingly constrained by global factors.
- Globalizing advice by employing international management consultants which: either undermines accountability to the domestic electorate and uses managerialism to impose political agendas; or gives core executives tools to implement their preferred policy agendas.

In other words, the institutional differentiation of policy advice and the globalizing of policy advice produce contradictory outcomes for the five parliamentary democracies — a finding which suggests a key conclusion:

> Irrespective of which dimension of core executives is under examination, it is clear national historical traditions and the structure of government, even more than party, provide the framework which constrains executive behaviour (see also Elgie, 1995: 195; Nousiainen and Blondel, 1993: 301).

Bakvis's analysis of policy advice clearly illustrates this finding. National traditions and institutions exercise great influence on the demand for, and the forms of, policy advice (Elgie, 1995: 198 reinforces the point).

Coordination

Coordination is a defining function of the core executive and Davis maps the proliferation of horizontal coordinating mechanisms in parliamentary systems, suggesting six conclusions:

1. In continental systems, coordination is an essential role of the state, embodied in the rule of law and shared values about the nature of public authority. In Westminster systems, coordination is not built into state structures but is a political imperative for the core executive which must consciously design and redesign procedures and structures.

2. In both continental and Westminster systems, the problem of specialized, segmented decision making through policy communities limits the capacity of core executives to impose coherence. The persistent attempts to reform the core is itself evidence of the pressure from institutional differentiation and pluralization

3. There are three distinct coordination tasks: projecting an image of political coherence through an agreed public policy agenda; achieving consistent objectives; and running an efficient and effective public sector. But shared tasks produce divergent practice, reflecting state traditions and historical experience.

4. Cabinets are the common instrument of policy coordination, drawing together political and institutional interests.

5. Administrative coordination is achieved through designing the structure of government; controlling the budget; and consistent personnel procedures.

6. The spread of market mechanisms in Westminster systems provides the most persuasive evidence of hollowing out but, even here, policy complexity and national and international interdependence generate pressures to develop coherent, coordinated responses.

Davis makes the ironic comment that governments believe they have a tangible and real capacity to impose priorities and make choices. They are unaware of any loss of capacity to coordinate and would be surprised at the claim. The problem with this claim is that it pays too little attention to the pressure of events bearing down on government. They have little time to reflect on the results of their policies, and so remain unaware of many limits to their actions. And policies need not only horizontal integration at the centre but also vertical integration between levels of government, further compounding the problem of imposing priorities and reducing government to fretting and complaining.

For practitioners, the 'sour laws of unintended consequences' (Hennessy, 1992: 453) are a passport to electoral failure. Legislative action and symbolic politics, not outcomes, are the stuff of politics and the route to re-election. Indeed, on reflection, the awareness of their shackles presses in on them. Enoch Powell commented:

> In politics of all callings, the test of success or failure is so unsure that one is tempted to wonder whether there is such a thing as true political success at all: failure, or frustration, or reversal, seems so much to be the essence of any political career (cited in Hennessy, 1996).

The analysis of capacity must ask 'capacity for what?'. There are at least three possible answers to this question. Policy effectiveness can be defined as process, for example the '3Es' of economy, efficiency and effectiveness. It can be defined as outcomes, for example impact, equity and accountability (Rhodes, 1988a: 386–407). It can be defined as survival measured by electoral success for which the illusion of action is all too often an accepted and acceptable substitute for policy coherence and effectiveness.

Davis argues that Germany is the exception to the search for more effective coordination. The continental state tradition may indeed ease horizontal linkages. But *politikverflechtung* in the federal system shows that Germany is not immune to the pressures found in the Westminster systems, although here problems focus not on horizontal integration at the centre but on vertical integration between and across levels and types of government. There is a long-running debate in Germany on suboptimal decision making in multi-organizational policy contexts (see, for example, Hanf and Scharpf, 1978). This debate switches Westminster concerns about core executive coordination to intergovernmental relations and shows that institutional differentiation and pluralization pose common problems.

Resource Allocation

Wanna identifies a common preoccupation with reducing government spending and a wide diversity of responses.

- Core executives have responded to global economic trends and fiscal stress by searching for 'more control over less' and making the public sector more responsive to core executive priorities.
- There is no uniform, international reform movement. The New Public Management (NPM) is not the common model. Core executives use a wide variety of arbitrary and idiosyncratic tools and the scope of changes differ.
- Westminster systems combined expenditure restraint with reformed resource allocation mechanisms and improved financial management. Continental systems focused on expenditure restraint.
- Cabinets are rarely major players in budgeting. The focus must shift to the core executive and the role of the finance ministry within it.

- Although some recent reforms seek to strengthen the capacity of the core executive to set political priorities, many changes were a response to external economic pressures and not intended to strengthen central capability.
- The rhetoric of 'fiscal responsibility' is all-pervasive but the success of expenditure restraint is patchy. Policy is constrained by: internal structural conflict between guardians and advocates (Wildavsky, 1975: 7), institutional fragmentation which diffuses control, increases opportunities for political input and fuels intergovernmental conflicts; and continuing external demand for spending coupled with the unpopularity of cuts.
- In Westminster systems, cohesive cabinets, party discipline and unified executives and legislatures counter institutional fragmentation. In continental systems, fragmentation is countered by institutional consolidation, led by the finance ministry, and focused on expenditure restraint, not budgetary reform.

And as before, it is possible to identify countervailing trends. Wanna identifies two such trends. First, governments respond to their loss of control to external pressures on the economy by increasing their internal control over both total public expenditure and financial management. Second, to compound complexity, as the core executive centralizes budgetary control, it also espouses the New Public Management reforms which give greater autonomy to subordinate agencies. 'Off-loading to the periphery' is a well-known tactic for shifting the blame for spending cuts from the centre to other agencies, and subordinate agencies in both Britain and the Netherlands were unwilling victims of 'greater autonomy'. Campbell (1994: 2) argues that 'automatization of budgeting' and 'bribing' departments with 'discretionary financial authority made meaningless by fiscal stringency' are the distinctive characteristics of the New Public Management. These changes in resource allocation illustrate the core executive's search for a new operating code which both minimises its external dependence and increases centralization to give it greater autonomy from internal interests and pressures.

Managerialism and Decentralisation

'Management' is the 'buzz' word of the moment and decentralization is one of its more fashionable tools; both are popular with our parliamentary systems. Aucoin suggests four conclusions about the current stress on managerial decentralization:

1. Except for Germany, the parliamentary systems decentralized authority to public service managers in response to the manifold unintended consequences of centralized coordination and to introduce greater economy, efficiency and effectiveness.
2. Decentralization had three causes: the core executive could no longer afford to buy compliance to central guidelines; it off-loaded responsibilities it could not finance; and it responded to client complaints about bureaucratization.
3. Decentralization took three forms: streamlining, or deregulation of standardized rules about finance and personnel; delegation, or giving authority to departments to manage their own resources; and decentralization down organizational hierarchies so managers can design service delivery systems which are responsive to citizens.
4. Decentralization fragments central executive authority and increases indirect public administration. The consequences of this hollowing out for the core executive depend on its capacity to steer without extensive intervention.

Finally, Aucoin cautions that the capacity of the state to steer does not depend on organizational design but on ideas about what the state should do and the ability of political leaders to mobilize support for those ideas.

Indisputably, decentralization can improve public management but much less attention has been placed on its effects on responsible government. It is important to distinguish between shadow and substance in decentralization. At the heart of agencification is the 'distance' postulate: that agencies are at arm's length from the core ministry and there is freedom to manage. But British experience suggests that politically salient agencies are subject to extensive operational interventions, for example the Prison Service, the Child Support Agency. As with the old nationalized industries, there is a 'twilight zone' where ministers intervene but have no responsibility when things go wrong. When the Home Secretary fired Derek Lewis as chief executive of the Prison Service, he accused the minister of coming up with a new definition of 'operational'; it meant 'difficult'. So, if it was difficult, it was the chief executive's problem or fault. The language of contracts is a foreign tongue in this twilight zone. It may be too soon to separate the shadow and substance of decentralisation — to conclude that decentralization and the New Public Management are hollowing out the core executive — but the reforms still have the potential to do so.

By abandoning the usual focus on individual countries and asking contributors to examine institutions and processes across the five parliamentary systems, it is possible to generalize about the work of, and trends in, core executives. The findings are not predictable. The more centralized nations do not necessarily appear the most coherent. Britain is a unitary, single-party state which appears more vulnerable to the unintended consequences of differentiation and pluralization than federal, coalitional Germany. An important, counter-intuitive conclusion suggests that centralizing institutions may be coherent only when they are built on negotiation. Centralization needs consent. Contrary to the widespread belief that coalitions fragment, they make government more predictable. Whether it is necessary to maintain a coalition of parties or regions, the need to negotiate a settlement, and respect the interests involved, leads to greater coherence and a perception of common good more readily than a free-floating government only marginally tethered to its interests.

However, our prime objective is to explore trends in core executives to find out whether there was any loss of coherence and capacity. The next step is to focus, therefore, on hollowing out. I will draw together the discussions of coherence and hollowing out under the heading of the shackles on political leadership.

Core Executives and Hollowing Out the State

It should be no surprise to learn there are limits to the core executive's capacity in the modern world, but do these limits add up to a hollowing out of the state? This section discusses hollowing out, beginning with a reassessment of Saward's critique and ending with a summary of our collective findings.

Saward offers two criticisms of Rhodes's formulation.[3] First, he argues the evidence does not support the internal hollowing out thesis for the UK. The centre wanted to get rid of some functions and, therefore, they are no loss. The clear separation of politics and administration means the centre can exercise more effective control. Privatization strengthens the regulatory capacity of the state. The capacity of the core executive has not been reduced by decentralizing to other state actors. Agencification gives ministers a new freedom to manoeuvre; they can concentrate on selected issues, and shield themselves from both operational and policy failures. Second, he extends the argument that Europeanization fuels hollowing out to cover globalization.

Internal Hollowing Out

There are several difficulties with Saward's analysis of internal hollowing out. First, the centre's motives for getting rid of a function are not the point at issue. A function willingly lost is still a function lost; the centre can no longer do something it used to do. It may have more control, but it may be more control over less. Both Rhodes and Saward speculate on whether the change is significant, but it is an empirical question and many of the shifts are too recent for a definitive assessment.

Second, Saward's analysis of internal hollowing out does not distinguish clearly enough between intentions and outcome. Intentions all too often disappear in a flurry of unintended consequences. Marsh and Rhodes (1992b) explore policy implementation in nine policy areas, including health, housing, social security and local government finance. In each case, they show there is a marked disparity between legislative intent and the policy as put into practice. They conclude the effect of the Thatcher government on policy was overestimated, and point to the range of constraints on the centre, including conflicting objectives, lack of resources and poor policy design. Most significantly, Marsh and Rhodes (1992a: 185–6) show that stubborn policy networks were a significant constraint on the centre. The changes were not 'breathtaking', especially given the government's stated policy objectives. So, both Rhodes's and Saward's assertions about hollowing out are better recast as questions, and the analysis must look for the unintended consequences of government actions. Has privatization increased the regulatory capacity of the state or is the outcome regulatory capture? Can the core executive steer regulatory bodies? Regulation may increase the capacity of the state but if the core executive cannot steer these bodies, is it evidence of hollowing out or increased core executive capacity? What is the relationship between department and agency? Is there a working separation of roles or random departmental and ministerial intervention? Rationalization involves redefining state boundaries so the core executive does less. It also involves refocusing control. But does this refocusing deliver the desired control, or has the core executive the same control over less or less control over less?

Third, Saward's evidence can be interpreted as a loss of control. The UK may not have decentralized to local and regional governments but it multiplied special-purpose bodies. Counting these bodies is fraught with political controversy, but Weir and Hall (1994) estimate there are 5521, accounting for £52 billion of public spending. Also, Saward's evidence on strengthening central capability can be interpreted as evidence of core executive weakness. Reform was necessary because current machinery did not deliver the right capacity. And note, Saward describes reforms, not their outcomes. It is possible to agree core executives have sought to improve their capacity and to infer it is evidence of weakness. There is a high probability we will see further rounds of reform as core executives continue to seek for control.

External Hollowing Out

Saward argues that globalization causes external hollowing out, not just Europeanization, and his point is valid. Held (1991: 151–7) suggests that four processes are limiting the autonomy of nation states: the internationalization of production and financial transactions; international organizations; international law; and hegemonic powers and power blocs (see also Jessop, 1992: 27; and Rhodes, 1996: Ch. 10). As a result, the nation state's capacities for governance have weakened but 'it remains a pivotal institution' (Hirst and Thompson, 1995: 409). It is essential to the process of 'suturing' power upwards to the international level and downwards to subnational agencies (p. 423). So, the argument about hollowing out and the effects of Europeanization must be extended to include international interdependencies.

Although overstating the differences is good knockabout stuff, there is much common ground between Rhodes and Saward. Both argue the modern state is characterized by internal and externally produced complexity and interdependence which causes an internal reshaping of the state, involving both fragmentation and rationalization. Saward accepts there has been significant external hollowing out but prefers to talk of an internal 'reshaping' of the state to 'underscore what remains of their distinctive capabilities' and 'to shore up their own internal power'. Rhodes (1994) attaches greater importance to internal changes, dramatised as 'hollowing out', and speculates on their adverse consequences for central capacity. Saward identifies the same changes and, also speculating, concludes they are a source of opportunity as well as constraint, arguing not only that core executives asserted more control over less but that this control was effective. Both accept that policy networks are significant constraints on the capacity of the core executive and, therefore, are central to understanding internal hollowing out. Both accept that globalisation is central to understanding external hollowing out. Exploring the process of hollowing out, not the end state of the hollow state, is one way of getting to grips with the effects of institutional differentiation and pluralization.

Our several chapters suggest the evidence on internal and external hollowing out does not point clearly in one direction; there are six countervailing trends within and among the five parliamentary democracies.

1. *Fragmentation v. control.* The conflict between institutional fragmentation and core executive steering, captured by the phrase 'more control over less'.
2. *Internal independence v. external dependence.* Core executives responded to the constraints of international interdependence by asserting their

independence from domestic pressures. Global pressures produce distinctive national responses.

3. *Centralization v. autonomy.* The search for internal independence saw both a centralization of power on the core executive as it sought to assert its control over priorities and greater autonomy for other state actors in managing and implementing policy.

4. *Intended v. unintended consequences.* Assertive leadership produced unintended consequences which became ever more visible as institutional differentiation and pluralization, coupled with indirect or 'hands-off' management, multiplied the disparities between policy aims and implementation.

5. *Symbols v. substance.* Confounded by the sour laws of unintended consequences, core executives balance policy effectiveness against electoral survival by playing symbolic politics which value the appearance of coherence as much, if not more than, the substance. Media pressures fuel the desire to appear coherent, cohesive and effective (see Bayliss, 1989; Foley, 1993).

6. *Constraints v. opportunities.* The constraints on core executives are also opportunities to reassert control.

The hollowing out thesis identifies key trends, focusing attention on the consequences of institutional differentiation and pluralization for core executives. Although the evidence suggests contradictory trends, although the contributors differ in their interpretation of that evidence, none disagree with the basic proposition that institutional differentiation and pluralization is common, creating multiple challenges to the capacity of core executives to steer.

This interpretation is distinctive. It does not focus on the power of a specific institution or on the personality of a particular office holder. It stresses the institutional context, conceptualized as networks of resource-dependent organizations. This approach does not preclude the 'classical' or formal-legal definition of institutions (see Rhodes, 1996: Ch. 4). It does stress the need for a broader definition which encompasses not only the rules, procedures, practices and formal organizations of government but also the networks of organizations in which governments are embedded (see Figure 9.1). It also suggests that formal distinctions such as between federal and unitary systems may be less important than variations in the degree of differ-entiation and pluralization. This theme holds out the tantalizing prospect that Australian federalism is undifferentiated compared with the differentiated but 'unitary' Netherlands. Conventional rankings of states by their degree of decentralization were always crude and unsatisfactory, but the differentiated polities thesis makes such rankings positively misleading.

The Consequences for Political Leadership

There is an enormous literature on leadership in general and political leadership in particular. I do not propose to add to this large literature (see, for example, Chapter 1 above; Barber, 1972; Burns, 1978; and for a good recent review of the literature, Elgie, 1995). I have a more specific task: to explore the effects on political leadership of the hollowing out of the core executive. Or, to repeat the question given in the Preface: what is the impact on political leadership in the core executive of: complexity and interdependence, caused by both external and internal forces; and internal fragmentation and rationalization?

Attention moves from the broad theme of hollowing out the state to the narrower topic of 'the hollow crown'. Political leaders wear the crown. To refer to the hollow crown is to ask how the processes associated with hollowing out the state affect leaders' capacity to steer.

Robert Elgie's (1995: Chs 1 and 8)) comparative study of political leadership in six liberal democracies develops an interactionist approach in which leadership is a function of the leaders' aims and styles and the leadership environment. This environment comprises the needs of society and the institutional structure. The needs of society refers to the historical legacy, societal attitudes and short-term popular pressures. Most important for the analysis in this book he stresses the key influence of institutional structures, in particular:

1. 'The structure of resources within the executive branch of central government' (p. 14);
2. 'The structure of resources between the executive branch of central government and other branches and levels of government' (p. 16); and
3. 'The structure of resources within and between political parties' (p. 19). (See also Bayliss, 1989: 149–51.)

He also concludes that 'what these leaders can and cannot do is primarily determined by the institutional structures of their countries' (p. 210). Our study provides plentiful confirmation of Elgie's general conclusion.

Why do institutional structures have such an effect? Elgie (1995: 204–6) puts forward two reasons: institutions define the resources, rules and constraints which set the boundaries to leaders' actions; and institutions shape political behaviour by creating roles leaders must play, shaping their political behaviour. But there are weaknesses in Elgie's analysis: for example, he omits policy networks, and does not explore the link between the leadership process and policy implementation and effectiveness. It is possible to deepen Elgie's analysis by elaborating on the ways in which institutions affect leaders, the range of shackles binding leaders, and the results for policy effectiveness.

Despite his support for the institutional approach, Elgie does not directly address the policy networks literature. Indeed, he quotes with approval Hall's (1986: 19) definition of institutions but fails to note that Hall extends his definition from 'the constitution and formal political practices' to 'less formal organisational networks'. The omission is unfortunate because power dependence in policy networks is a prime cause of executive segmentation (see Rhodes, 1981; Smith, 1995). The professional–bureaucratic complexes of policy networks constrain all our core executives. More recently, hollowing out the state gained great impetus from, for example, privatization and globalization. These trends add to, and alter, existing network constraints. So, institutional differentiation and pluralization create imperatives to use policy networks to counter vertical fragmentation among levels of government; and underpin the horizontal fragmentation among functions which the core executive seeks to police.

These institutions and their networks also act as sutures for globalization, linking local, national, regional and global forces. A simple story will illustrate the point. At the Royal Institute of Public Administration Australia's Annual Conference in 1995 I learnt about globalization and fruit flies. Fruit flies infest mangoes and the Japanese refuse to import such 'infected' fruit. Millions of dollars hinged on a solution to this trade barrier. Queensland's Department of Primary Industries, in partnership with the private sectors in Australia and Japan, developed a heat technology which exterminates fruit flies without damaging the fruit and Australia now sells mangoes to the Japanese at $12 each!

This story shows how the private sector needs government to bridge the gap between the domestic economy and the international economy. The government got the mango farmers into the Japanese market; only a government could negotiate the access; and it did so by employing classical diplomatic skills. Globalization may hollow out the state by eroding its capacity to manage the national economy but it also enhances the important role of suturing the domestic and the international economy. The strategic position of the nation state creates opportunities as well as constraints, and this need for mediation, regulation and diplomacy will grow.[4]

So, Figure 9.1 extends Elgie's analysis to cover policy networks, resource-dependence relations and globalization. It tries to specify more fully the constraints on leaders. It tries to tie together the discussions of coherence, capacity and hollowing out. It would be unduly repetitive to discuss every heading. Thus, the distinction between domestic and global environmental influences is obvious and I discussed the several specific variables earlier (see also Bayliss, 1989: 148–9; Elgie, 1995: 20–3; Rose, 1991a). I concentrate, therefore, on the less obvious entries.

The box on 'Institutional variables' includes 'organizational variables' drawn from the literature on organizational analysis. It found that such characteristics as size, specialization, technology and complexity influence the structure of, and behaviour in, business organizations (see, for example, Donaldson, 1985). Applying contingency theory to the public sector produced less clear results (see Hood and Dunsire, 1981), but such organizational effects remain potentially important.

In any power-dependence relation, the ability to influence other actors by deploying needed resources is only potential influence unless the resources are used effectively. The rules of the game and the strategic behaviour of the actors condition the effective use of resources. The strategies listed in Figure 9.1 are examples, not a definitive list (for more examples see Rhodes, 1986: 392–4 and citations). Strategic choice and patterns of dependence are intimately linked to style, resources and aims of the leader, so these boxes deliberately overlap. Also, the choice of strategy and the degree of interdependence mediates the impact of institutional variables on political leadership, so the arrows show them as intervening variables and do not join the boxes.

There are several typologies of leadership styles; it is a mini-industry in studying managers (see Handy, 1993: Ch. 4). Simply to stress that styles vary, I use Burns's (1978: 20) distinction between transactional and transformational leadership. The former sees leadership as a process of bargaining and exchange. The latter sees leaders providing a sense of vision by aiming for 'higher levels of motivation and morality'. This box also covers the personality and aims of leaders. My objective is not to argue that personality, style and aims are irrelevant but that any satisfactory account of effective leadership must explore the context of leadership behaviour, especially institutional constraints.

Figure 9.1 tries to show that leaders confront a daunting array of constraints which limit their capacity to deliver their policy objectives. Here, I must be careful. The figure must not give the impression that leaders can do little or nothing. I must stress two points. First, the essence of the argument is that leadership is as much a process of negotiation in parliamentary democracies as in the USA (Neustadt, 1976; Weller, 1985a). Second, many of the constraints can also be opportunities for action; for example, the fragility of international negotiations may be an effective lever in the domestic arena for achieving a related policy. So, how do leaders deliver on their promises? What are the consequences for policy effectiveness of this analysis of the shackles on leadership?

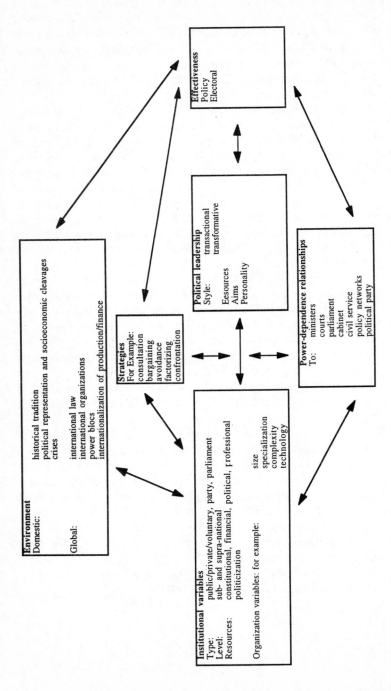

Figure 9.1 *The shackles on political leadership*

Steering the Hollow Crown

This chapter has argued that parliamentary democracies are characterized by a complexity and interdependence rooted in institutional differentiation and pluralization. Government was never supreme. For example, negotiation was always a defining element of Canadian executive federalism. But the constraints are more pressing, the imperative to negotiate more acute:

> No single actor, public or private, has all the knowledge and information required to solve complex dynamic diversified problems; no actor has sufficient overview to make the application of needed instruments effective, no single actor has sufficient action potential to dominate unilaterally in a particular governing model (Kooiman, 1993: 4).

Policies fail when the centre rejects cooperation for imposition; when it does not provide incentives to exchange. The 'implementation gap' so characteristic of the Thatcher years has its roots in the failure to manage networks effectively — in choosing imposition over negotiation and agreement.

Government can choose between 'governing structures'. To markets and hierarchies, we can add networks. None of these structures for authoritatively allocating resources and exercising control and coordination is intrinsically 'good' or 'bad'. The choice is not necessarily or inevitably a matter of ideological conviction but of practicality; that is, under what conditions does each governing structure work effectively. Bureaucracy remains the prime example of hierarchy or coordination by administrative order and, for all the recent changes, it is still a major way of delivering services. Privatization, contracting out and the purchaser–provider split are examples of government using markets or quasi-markets to deliver services. Price competition is the key to efficient and better quality services. Competition and markets are a fixed part of the governmental landscape. It is less widely recognized that government now works through networks characterized by trust and mutual adjustment, for example to provide welfare services. Governance has emerged as a key governing structure.

Governance refers to *self-organizing, interorganizational networks,* with the following characteristics:

1. Interdependence between organisations. Governance is broader than government, covering non-state actors. Changing the boundaries of the state meant the boundaries between public, private and voluntary sectors became shifting and opaque.
2. Continuing interactions between network members, caused by the need to exchange resources and negotiate shared purposes.

3. Game-like interactions, rooted in trust and regulated by rules of the game negotiated and agreed by network participants.
4. A significant degree of autonomy from the state. Networks are not accountable to the state; they are self-organising. Although the state does not occupy a privileged, sovereign position, it can indirectly and imperfectly steer networks (Rhodes, 1996: Ch. 3).

Governance as *self-organizing, interorganizational networks* poses important questions about the conditions under which the different governing structures work, that is, deliver equitable, accountable and effective services (see Rhodes, 1988a: 386–407).

Steering complex sets of organizations is difficult. In Britain, the government has adopted a strategy of 'more control over less'. It privatized the utilities. It contracted out services to the private sector. It introduced quasi-markets through purchaser–provider splits when services could not be privatized. It bypassed local authorities for special-purpose bodies. It removed operational management from central departments and vested it in separate agencies (see Rhodes, 1996: Chs 6–8). Central departments rarely delivered services themselves; they were non-executant. Government policy now fragmented service delivery systems. It compensated for its loss of hands-on controls by reinforcing its control over resources. Decentralizing service delivery has gone with centralising financial control. Such hands-off controls may not provide enough leverage for the centre to steer the networks. As networks multiply, so do doubts about the centre's capacity to steer. Kettl (1993: 206–7) argues that, since contracting out, government agencies found themselves 'sitting on top of complex public–private relationships whose dimensions they may only vaguely understand'. They had only 'loose leverage' but remained 'responsible for a system over which they had little real control'.

Other terms for 'loose leverage' include intergovernmental management (IGM) and indirect management. Such network management, the shift from direct to indirect controls, is a topic of current academic and political debate in both the Netherlands and Germany (see, for example, Marin and Mayntz, 1991). The UK government has not sought to develop the indirect management of networks.

Drawing on extensive evidence from Dutch policy making, Klijn *et al.* (1995) argue that networks do not respond to managers as controllers. Effective managers play a facilitative role, that is, do not seek to achieve their own objectives. They can follow two broad strategies: game management or identifying the conditions which will sustain joint action; and network structuring which involves changing the rules of the game. Alexander (1995: 276) identifies six strategies and five groups of tools for managing interorganizational coordination (IOC). The strategies are: cultural–persuasive (e.g. public relations); communicative (e.g. information exchange); functional (e.g. coalition formation); cooperative (e.g. resource exchange); control (e.g. monitoring and enforcement) and structural e.g. reorganisation). The five groups of tools are: structural (e.g. standard operating procedures); anticipatory linkages (e.g. joint planning, overlapping membership); operational linkages (e.g. staff secondments, consultation); programme management (e.g. regulations); and fiscal (e.g. grants and subsidies). He concludes:

> There is no universal algorithm that can present the IOC structure's critical attributes, identify the relevant factors in the IOC structure's setting, and describe their relationship in a way that offers a set of unequivocal design norms. There is so much complexity in the interorganizational systems . . . that it is unlikely that such a recipe will ever be found (Alexander 1995: 325).

None the less the challenge for central elites is to develop an operating code which steers through indirect management; 'meta-monitoring' or regulation by oversight, management of contracts and strategic surveillance (Grabosky, 1995: 543–4).

So, managing interorganizational networks is game-like, needs strategies rooted in trust, and employs an indirect style of management. Facilitating, mediating and bargaining are the keys to effective network management. If there is one phrase which captures the nature of network management, it is 'mutual adjustment'. Such skills are increasingly commonplace in continental parliamentary systems. They are virgin territory for Westminster systems still in the thrall of parliamentary sovereignty and 'strong leaders know best'.

The main consequence for political leadership of institutional differentiation and pluralization is aptly summarized by the phrase 'leading by indirection'. In other words, prime ministers must not confuse 'leadership with command' but adopt hands-off, negotiative strategies, reflecting the complex set of dependencies (institutional roles, resources and relationships) in which they are embedded (see also Weller, 1985a: 11–12). The hollowing out thesis and Figure 9.1 show the many dependencies which enmesh political leaders. This section shows how they can respond by adding governance to their choice of governing structures and network management to their tool kit.

Conclusions: Evaluating the Hollow Crown

I now turn to my final theme: traditional mechanisms of accountability in parliamentary democracy cannot cope with multi-organizational fragmented policy systems. Barker (1982: 17) talks of networks of mutual account-

ability and identifies downward accountability to clienteles, upward accountability to ministers and parliament and horizontal accountability to peer and
references groups. The conventional account of networks treats them as
private government, arguing that networks

> destroy political responsibility by shutting out the public; create
> privileged oligarchies; and are conservative in their impact because, for
> example, the rules of the game and access favour established interests.
> (Marsh and Rhodes, 1992b: 265).

Rhodes (1988a: 405) concludes that accountability can no longer be specific
to an institution but must fit the policy and its network. In short, the
mechanisms of parliamentary democracy need urgent adjustment to the
workings of differentiated polities.

Normative questions raise their head only briefly in this book.
Rhodes's theory of 'the good public administrator' sees him or her as a
counterweight to executive power. Saward's 'amoral', 'predatory theory of
rule' focuses on the capacity of core executives to impose their will and
celebrates their power. But the distinctive feature of parliamentary
democracies is supposed to be the accountability of executive power through
elected parliaments to citizens. Parliaments are conspicuous by their
absence throughout this book and especially in Rhodes and Saward.
Accountability in parliamentary democracies is never central to the
discussion of policy networks. Implicitly, describing and explaining the
activities of policy networks justifies them. But private government is bad
government; openness is a basic axiom of parliamentary democracy. The
conflicts between parliamentary democracy and the differentiated polity is
too important a topic to be an afterthought.

Judge (1993: 120–30) criticizes the literature on policy networks
because it does not locate them 'within the broader framework of
representative government' (p. 124). Parliament is not peripheral to the
policy process because it provides 'diffuse support': 'the legitimating
framework of the parliamentary system itself' (p. 126). It also has some
specific roles. It is an 'insurance policy' (p. 130) for both insiders and
outsiders; for example, interests excluded from the policy community can
air their concerns. Judge's point about parliament as the legitimating
framework shows that parliamentary democracy is not just a myth but
informs everyday political practice. However, his reluctance to admit that
policy communities are *relatively* closed' (Marsh and Rhodes, 1992b: 296,
emphasis added) and that parliament is marginalized leads him to
underestimate the erosion of accountability. Judge (1993: 124) concedes the
legislature makes a 'limited' contribution to law making and is 'peripheral'
to policy formulation and implementation.

The marginal role of the British parliament is not unique. In the Netherlands parties vote in blocks; parliamentary activism is still limited to scrutiny. Parties may defect but not individuals. In Germany the *Bundestag* has never been a powerful brake on the government. Weller (1985a: 179) concludes the British parliament looms larger in the life of its core executive than the Australian, Canadian and New Zealand parliaments in their systems. The conclusion that all prime ministers must give parliament *'some* attention' (Weller 1985, emphasis in original) attests to parliamentary weakness, not strength. So, key tenets of parliamentary democracy do not work as intended. Such a mismatch between theory and practice will erode the legitimating role of parliament.

There are other pressures. The fall of the Berlin Wall heralded the end of ideology and the triumph of markets and capitalism. We may have lost that ideological debate, but we have some new ones voiced by the new tribes: vocal minorities with a predilection for direct action over representation in 'normal politics'. The new tribes include the environmentalists, the anti-roads lobby, the anti-smoking campaign, the campaign against blood sports, the gun lobby and the claims of religious and racial minorities. There are many new ideologies. Governments will have to cope with them and this challenge raises the problem of how to sustain the legitimacy of government. Westminster systems in particular have fetishised economy, efficiency and management over the past ten years. Governments reduce politics to managerial and institutional fixes. We have marginalized the new tribes. They are outside 'normal politics', possibly from choice but definitely by exclusion.

There is, therefore, a democratic deficit in the multiform maze of the new governance. Hirst (1990: 2) comments that representative democracy delivers 'low levels of governmental accountability and public influence on decision making'. He notes that 'big government is now so big' that it defeats effective coordination by the centre and grows 'undirected' and by 'accretion' (pp. 31–2). So, both the new tribes and the democratic deficit mean we need to reinvent parliamentary democracy; to experiment with new forms.

There is no shortage of proposals for new forms of democracy. Unfortunately, these proposals illustrate the adage, 'for every complex problem there is a simple solution, and it is always wrong'. Accountability in the differentiated polity requires 'indeterminate domains, openness of communication and the evaluation of policy impact'; messy problems need messy solutions or, more formally, complexity is reduced through institutional differentiation (Luhmann, 1982).

Hirst (1990: 8) argues for a pluralist state 'in which distinct functionally and territorially specific domains of authority enjoy the autonomy necessary to perform their tasks'. Such 'pluralising of the state' reduces 'the scope of central state power'. The ways of so containing the central state vary. He favours both functional representation in the guise of corporatism (1990: 12–15) and 'associational democracy' based on 'voluntary self-governing associations' (Hirst, 1994). Both schemes take domains of functional authority as the basic building block and are, therefore, consistent with a network interpretation (see also Rhodes, 1996: Ch. 10).

There is an obvious conflict between the principles of accountability in a parliamentary democracy and functional representation. But the differentiated polity poses important challenges for parliamentary democracy. The study of networks, governance and hollowing out raises issues of equivalent importance to the study of bureaucracy and democratic accountability. It gives these issues a distinctive twist because, for example, the assumption of institutional hierarchy which underpins so many discussions of bureaucratic accountability no longer holds.

It would take us too far afield to discuss new forms of democracy in any detail (but see Held and Pollitt, 1986). However, this brief discussion suggests that parliamentary democracy in differentiated polities needs: explicit accountability; with multiple forms and in many forums; with freedom of information, access, open communication and flexible institutions willing to encourage experiments with multiple and new forms of accountability. Reinventing parliamentary democracy for a differentiated polity in the twenty-first century is a task scarcely begun, in either theory or practice.

Perhaps the heroic model of parliamentary leaders taking their countries out of the economic mire into a glorious twenty-first century needs to be replaced with a humdrum model based on a realistic appreciation of the constraints on their actions. They have little or no control over these constraints. They have limited opportunities to steer other state actors, let alone shape the societies they seek to govern. There are opportunities, however. They can initiate or respond, they can support or veto policies, and they can exercise direct or indirect influence. But the capacity for independent action remains constrained because 'Prime ministers *only* have the power to "persuade"' (Weller, 1985a: 11, emphasis in original). It is no surprise, therefore, that so many policies fail. It is perhaps more a wonder, given the shackles they wear, that leaders achieve anything at all.

Notes

1. Coherence refers to logically and consistently related policies. Capacity refers to the ability to produce that coherence and, as Saward notes, it is the primary notion, although their meanings shade into each other. I follow Weller and Bakvis and use the general notion of coherence. I distinguish

between coherence and capacity when arguing that the process of hollowing out erodes core executive capacity to act coherently.

2. The Westminster model and the differentiated polity are examples of an organizing perspective or 'a framework for analysis, a map of how things relate, a set of research questions' (Gamble, 1990: 405). For a more detailed discussion see Rhodes (1996: Ch. 1).

3. Saward also criticizes Rhodes's formulation because of its 'implicit' support of the 'neutral' civil service as counterweight to 'partisan' governments. It would take this chapter too far afield to discuss this topic in detail, but see my discussion of the case for bureaucracy in Rhodes (1994), Etzioni-Halevy (1983) and Wamsley *et al.* (1987).

4. Policy networks link the domestic and international arenas. On transnational policy networks see Haas (1992) and Rhodes (1996: Ch. 8).

Bibliography

Abelson, D. E. (1992), 'A New Channel of Influence: American Think Tanks and the News Media', *Queen's Quarterly* 99 (Winter): 849–72.

Aberbach, J. D., R. D. Putnam and B. A. Rockman (1981), *Bureaucrats and Politicians in Western Democracies*, Cambridge, Mass.: Harvard University Press.

Albo, G., D. Langille and L. Panitch (eds) (1993), *A Different Kind of State? Popular Power and Democratic Administration*, Toronto: Oxford University Press.

Alexander, E. R. (1995), *How Organizations Act Together*, Amsterdam: OPA/Gordon & Breach.

Althusser, L. (1971), *Lenin and Philosophy and Other Essays*, London: New Left Books.

Andeweg, R. B. (1985), 'The Netherlands: Cabinet Committees in a Coalition Cabinet', in *Unlocking the Cabinet: Cabinet Structures in Comparative Perspective*, T. Mackie and B. W. Hogwood (eds), London: Sage.

Andeweg, R. B. (1986), 'Centrifugal Forces and Collective Decision-Making: The Case of the Dutch Cabinet', *European Journal of Political Research* 16: 125–51.

Andeweg, R. B. (1988), 'The Netherlands: Coalition Cabinets in Changing Circumstances', in *Cabinets in Western Europe*, J. Blondel and F. Müller-Rommel (eds), London: Macmillan.

Andeweg, R. B. (1989a), 'Institutional Conservatism in the Netherlands: Proposals for and Resistance to Change', *West European Politics* 12(1): 42–59.

Andeweg, R. B. (1989b), 'The Politics of Less: A Description of Changes in Financial Decision-Making in the Netherlands', Paper to the workshop on The Politics of Finance: Financial Decision-Making in West-European Governments, April, Paris.

Andeweg, R. B. (1990), 'Tweeërlei Ministerraad: besluitvorming in Nederlandse kabinetten', in *Ministers en Ministerraad*, R. B. Andeweg (ed.), The Hague: SDU.

Andeweg, R. B. (1991), 'The Dutch Prime Minister: Not Just Chairman, Not Yet Chief', *West European Politics* 14(2): 116–32.

Andeweg, R. B. (1993), 'A Model of the Cabinet System: The Dimensions of Cabinet Decision-Making Processes', in *Governing Together: The Extent and Limits of Joint Decision-Making in Western European Cabinets*, J. Blondel and F. Müller-Rommel (eds), London: Macmillan.

Andeweg, R. B. and W. Bakema (1994), 'The Netherlands: Ministers and Cabinet Policy', in *Cabinet Ministers and Parliamentary Government*,

M. Laver and K. A. Shepsle (eds), Cambridge: Cambridge University Press.

Andeweg, R. B. and G. A. Irwin (1993), *Dutch Government and Politics*, London: Macmillan.

Aucoin, P. (1986), 'Organizational Change in the Canadian Machinery of Government: From Rational Management to Brokerage Politics', *Canadian Journal of Political Science* 19(1): 3–27.

Aucoin, P. (1990), 'Administrative Reform in Public Management: Paradigms, Principles, Paradoxes and Pendulums', *Governance* 3(2): 115–37.

Aucoin, P. (1991a), 'Cabinet Government in Canada: Corporate Management of a Confederal Executive', in *Executive Leadership in Anglo-American Systems*, C. Campbell and M. J. Wyszomirski (eds), Pittsburgh: University of Pittsburgh Press.

Aucoin, P. (1991b), 'The Politics and Management of Restraint Budgeting', in *The Budget Maximising Bureaucrat*, A. Blais and S. Dion (eds), Pittsburgh: University of Pittsburgh Press.

Aucoin, P. (1994a), 'Prime Ministerial Leadership: Position, Power and Politics', in *Leaders and Leadership in Canada*, M. Mancuso *et al.* (eds), Toronto: Oxford University Press.

Aucoin, P. (1994b), 'Prime Minister and Cabinet', in *Canadian Politics*, 2nd edn, J. P. Bickerton and A. G. Gagnon (eds), Peterborough: Broadview Press.

Aucoin, P. (1995), 'Politicians, Public Servants and Public Management: Getting Government Right', in *Governance in a Changing Environment*, B. Guy Peters and D. J. Savoie (eds), Montreal: McGill–Queen's University Press.

Aucoin, P. (1996), *The New Public Management: Canada in Comparative Perspective*, Montreal: Institute for Research on Public Policy.

Aucoin, P. and H. Bakvis (1988), *The Centralization–Decentralization Conundrum: Organization and Management in the Canadian Government*, Halifax: Institute for Research on Public Policy.

Aucoin, P. and H. Bakvis (1993), 'Consolidating Cabinet Portfolios: Australian Lessons for Canada', *Canadian Public Administration* 36(3): 392–420.

Aucoin, P. and D. Savoie (1994), 'Innovative Budgeting and the Management of Public Spending in Anglo-American Democracies', Paper to 'Ten Years of Change', Organisation of Government Research Committee, IPSA, Manchester.

Austen-Smith, D. and J. Banks (1990), 'Stable Portfolio Allocations', *American Political Science Review* 84: 891–906.

Australia (1992), *Task Force on Management Improvement: The Australian Public Service Reformed*, Canberra: Australian Government Publishing Service.

Australia (1995), *Keeping the Customer Satisfied: Inquiry into the Devolution of Running Cost Flexibilities*, Report from the House of Representatives Standing Committee on Banking, Finance and Public Administration, Canberra: Australian Government Publishing Service.

Bagehot, W. (1965), *The English Constitution* (introduced by R. H. S. Crossman), London: Fontana. (Reprint of 1867 edition.)

Bakema, W. (1991), 'The Ministerial Career', in *The Profession of Government Minister in Western Europe*, J. Blondel and J. L. Thiébault (eds), London: Macmillan.

Bakema, W. E. and I. P. Secker (1988), 'Ministerial Expertise and the Dutch Case', *European Journal of Political Research* 16: 153–70.

Bakvis, H. (1991), *Regional Ministers: Power and Influence in the Canadian Cabinet*, Toronto: University of Toronto Press.

Bakvis, H. (1994), 'Cabinet Ministers: Leaders or Followers?', in *Leaders and Leadership in Canada*, M. Mancuso *et al.* (eds), Toronto: Oxford University Press.

Bakvis, H. and D. MacDonald (1993), 'The Canadian Cabinet: Organization, Decision-Rules and Policy Impact', in *Governing Canada: Institutions and Public Policy*, M. M. Atkinson (ed.), Toronto: Harcourt Brace Jovanovich.

Barber, J. D. (1972), *The Presidential Character: Prediction and Performance in the White House*, Englewood Cliffs, N J: Prentice Hall.

Barker, A. (1982), 'Governmental Bodies and Networks of Mutual Accountability', in *Quangos in Britain*, A. Barker (ed.), London: Macmillan.

Baylis, Th. A. (1989), *Governing by Committee: Collegial Leadership in Advanced Societies*, Albany: State University of New York Press.

Bendor, J. B. (1980), *Redundancy in Public Transit*, Vol. IV, *Structure, Competition and Reliability in Planning and Operations*, Final Report prepared for the U S Department of Transportation, Washington DC, August.

Bendor, J. B. (1985), *Parallel Systems: Redundancy in Government*, Berkeley: University of California Press.

Benz, A. (1987), 'Decentralization in the Federal Republic of Germany — A Case of Pragmatic Adaptation', *International Review of Administrative Sciences* 53: 467–81.

Bestebreur, A. (1993), 'Uitgavenbeheersing bij het Rijk Anno 1993', Scripte-thesis, Juridische Faculteit, Erasmus Universiteit, Rotterdam.

Bird, R. M. (1993), 'Federal–Provincial Taxation in Turbulent Times', *Canadian Public Administration* 36: 479–96.

Blondel, J. (1982), *The Organisation of Governments*, London: Sage.

Blondel, J. (1985), *Government Ministers in the Contemporary World*, London: Sage.

Blondel, J. (1987), *Political Leadership*, London: Sage.

Blondel, J. (1988), *Decision-Making Processes, Conflicts and Cabinet Government*, European University Institute Working Papers 88/327.

Blondel, J. (ed.) (1991), *The Profession of Government Minister in Western Europe*, London: Macmillan.

Blondel, J. (1995), 'Towards a Systematic Analysis of Government–Party Relationships', *International Political Science Review* 16(2), April: 127–44.

Blondel, J. and F. Müller-Rommel (eds) (1988), *Cabinets in Western Europe*, London: Macmillan.

Blondel, J. and F. Müller-Rommel (eds) (1993), *Governing Together: The Extent and Limits of Joint Decision-Making in Western European Cabinets*, London: Macmillan.

Boston, J., J. Martin and P. Walsh (eds) (1991), *Reshaping the State: New Zealand's Bureaucratic Revolution*, Auckland: Oxford University Press.

Bouchard, L. (1994), 'Why We Are Sovereignists', *Canadian Parliamentary Review* 17.

Breunese, J. N. and L. J. Roborgh (eds) (1992), *Ministeries van Algemeen Bestuur*, Leiden: Spuyt.

Brinks, R. and T. Witteveen (1994), *Toegang tot de Rijksbegroting*, Den Haag: SDU.

Budge, I. and R. Hofferbert (1990), 'Mandates and Policy Outputs', *American Political Science Review* 84 (March): 111–31.

Burch, M. and I. Holliday (1995), *The British Cabinet System*, Hemel Hempstead: Prentice Hall/Harvester Wheatsheaf.

Burnham, P. (1994), 'The Organisational View of the State', *Politics* 14.

Burns, D., R. Hambleton and P. Hoggett (1994), *The Politics of Decentralization: Revitalising Local Democracy*, London: Macmillan.

Burns, J. M. (1978), *Leadership*, New York: Harper.

Butler, D. (1973), *The Canberra Model: Essays on Australian Government*, London: Macmillan.

Butler, Sir Robin (1994), 'The Evolution of the Civil Service — a Progress Report', *Public Administration* 71: 402.

Cabinet Handbook (1988), Canberra: Australian Government Publishing Service.

Caiden, G. E. (1991), *Administrative Reform Comes of Age*, Berlin: de Gruyter.

Caiden, N. (1992), 'Budgetary Processes', in *Encyclopedia of Government and Politics*, Vol. 2, M. Hawkesworth and M. Kogan (eds), London: Routledge.

Campanella, M. L. (1991), 'Proactive Policy-Making: The New Role of the State-Actor', *Government and Opposition* 26.

Campbell, C. (1983), *Governments under Stress: Political Executives and Key Bureaucrats in Washington*, Toronto: University of Toronto Press.

Campbell, C. (1985), 'Cabinet Committees in Canada: Pressures and Dysfunctions Stemming from the Representational Imperative', in *Unlocking the Cabinet: Cabinet Structures in Comparative Perspective*, T. Mackie and B. W. Hogwood (eds), London: Sage.

Campbell, C. (1988a), 'Review Article: The Political Roles of Senior Government Officials in Advanced Democracies', *British Journal of Political Science* 18 (April): 243–72.

Campbell, C. (1988b), 'The Search for Coordination and Control: When and How are Central Agencies the Answer', in *Organizing Governance: Governing Organizations*, C. Campbell and B. G. Peters (eds), Pittsburgh: University of Pittsburgh Press.

Campbell, C. (1994), 'Reconciling Central Guidance and Managerialism: Conflicts Between Coherence and Discretion, the Case of Whitehall', Paper to the XVth World Congress of the International Political Science Association, Berlin, 21–25 August.

Campbell, C. and J. Halligan (1993), *Political Leadership in an Age of Constraint*, Sydney: Allen & Unwin.

Campbell, C. and B. G. Peters (eds) (1988), *Organizing Governance: Governing Organizations*, Pittsburgh: University of Pittsburgh Press.

Campbell, C. and G. J. Szablowski (1979), *The Superbureaucrats: Structure and Behaviour in Central Agencies*, Toronto: Macmillan.

Campbell, C. and G. K. Wilson (1995), *The End of Whitehall: Death of a Paradigm?*, Oxford: Blackwell.

Campbell, C. and M. Wyszomirski (eds) (1991), *Executive Leadership in Anglo-American Systems*, Pittsburgh: University of Pittsburgh Press.

Canada (1995a), *Third Annual Report to the Prime Minister on the Public Service of Canada*, Ottawa: Supply and Services.

Canada (1995b), *The Expenditure Management System of the Government of Canada*, Ottawa: Supply and Services.

Canada, Office of the Auditor General (1983), *Report to the House of Commons for the Fiscal Year Ended 31 March 1983*, Ottawa: Supply and Services.

Canada, Office of the Auditor General (1993), *Report of the Auditor General to the House of Commons, 1993*, Ottawa: Supply and Services.

Cansino, C. (1995), 'Party Government in Latin America: Theoretical Guidelines for an Empirical Analysis', *International Political Science Review* 16(2): 169–82.

Carroll, B. W. (1990), 'Politics and Administration: A Trichotomy?', *Governance* 3(4): 345–66.

Chandler, W. M. and A. Siaroff (1991), 'Parties and Party Government in Advanced Democracies', in *Canadian Political Parties: Leaders, Candidates and Organization*, H. Bakvis (ed.), Toronto: Dundurn. (Vol. 13 of the Research Studies of the Royal Commission on Electoral Reform and Party Financing).

Chisholm, D. (1989), *Coordination Without Hierarchy: Informal Structures in Multiorganizational Systems*, Berkeley: University of California Press.

Clark, I. D. (1994), 'Restraint, Renewal and the Treasury Board Secretariat', *Canadian Public Administration* 37(2): 1–40.

Clerx, J. M., P. G. van Griensven and R. J. Stevens (eds) (1993), *De Macht van Ministers van Financien*, Nijmegen: SMO.

Cockett, R. (1995), *Thinking the Unthinkable: Think Tanks and the Economic Counter-Revolution, 1931–1983*, London: Harper-Collins.

Craswell, E. and G. Davis (1993), 'Does Amalgamation Improve Policy Coordination?', in *Reforming the Public Service: Lessons from Recent Experience*, P. Weller, J. Forster and G. Davis (eds), Melbourne: Macmillan.

Criscitiello, A. (1994), 'Majority Summits: Decision-Making Inside the Cabinet and Out: Italy, 1970–1990', *West European Politics* 16: 581–94.

Crook, S., I. Pakulski and M. Waters (1992), *Postmodernization*, London: Sage.

Crowe, B. L. (1993), 'Foreign Policy-Making: Reflections of a Practitioner', *Government and Opposition* 28.

Daalder, H. (1989), 'The Mould of Dutch Politics: Themes for Comparative Inquiry', *West European Politics* 12(1): 1–20.

Dahl, R. A. (1989), *Democracy and its Critics*, New Haven: Yale University Press.

Davis, G. (1994), 'Executive Government: Cabinet and the Prime Minister', in *Government, Politics, Power and Policy in Australia*, 5th edn, A. Parkin, J. Summers and D. Woodward (eds), Melbourne: Longman Cheshire.

Davis, G. (1996), *A Government of Routines: Executive Co-ordination in an Australian State*, Melbourne: Macmillan.

De Winter, L. (1991), 'Parliamentary and Party Pathways to the Cabinet', in *The Profession of Government Minister in Western Europe*, J. Blondel and J. L. Thiébault (eds), London: Macmillan.

Denham, A. and M. Garnett (1994), 'The Idea Brokers: A Reply to Simon James', *Public Administration* 72: 482–5.

Derlien, H.-U. (1988), 'Repercussions of Government Change on the Career Civil Service in West Germany', *Governance* 1 (January): 50–78.

Derlien, H.-U. (1992), 'Observations on the State of Comparative Administration Research in Europe — Rather Comparable than Comparative', *Governance* 5(3).

Derlien, H.-U. (1993), 'Two-Track Processes: Budgeting, Auditing, and Evaluation in the Federal Republic of Germany', in *Budgeting, Auditing and Evaluation*, A. Gray *et al.* (eds), New Brunswick (USA): Transaction Publishers.

Desveaux, J. A., E. A. Lindquist and G. Toner (1994), 'Organizing for Policy Innovation in Public Bureaucracy', *Canadian Journal of Political Science* 27 (September): 493–528.

Dill, A. E. P. and D. A. Rochefort (1989), 'Coordination, Continuity, and Centralized Control: A Policy Perspective on Service Strategies for the Chronic Mentally Ill', *Journal of Social Issues* 45(3): 145–59.

Dirks, N.B. (1987), *The Hollow Crown. Ethnohistory of an Indian Kingdom*, Cambridge: Cambridge University Press.

Dodd, L. (1984), 'The Study of Cabinet Durability', *Comparative Political Studies* 17(2).

Dogan, M. (ed.) (1989), *Pathway to Power: Selecting Rulers in Pluralist Democracies*, London: Westview Press.

Donaldson, L. (1985), *In Defence of Organisation Theory*, Cambridge: Cambridge University Press.

Donnelly, M. and E. Ritchie (1994), 'The College of Commissioners and their Cabinets', in *The European Commission*, G. Edwards and D. Spence (eds), Harlow: Longman.

Dowding, K. (1993), 'Government at the Centre', in *Developments in British Politics 4*, P. Dunleavy *et al.* (eds), London: Macmillan.

Downs, A. (1957), *An Economic Theory of Democracy*, New York: Harper.

Drewry, G. (1994), 'Revolution in Whitehall: The Next Steps and Beyond', in *The Changing Constitution*, J. Jowell and D. Oliver (eds), Oxford: Clarendon Press.

Drewry, G. and T. Butcher (1988), *The Civil Service Today*, Oxford: Blackwell.

Dror, Y. (1987), 'Conclusions', in *Advising the Rulers*, W. Plowden (ed.), Oxford: Blackwell.

Dunleavy, P. (1989), 'The Architecture of the British Central State, Part 1: Framework for Analysis', *Public Administration*, 67, Autumn: 249–75.

Dunleavy, P. (1990), 'Government at the Centre', in *Developments in British Politics 3*, P. Dunleavy, A. Gamble and G. Peele (eds), London: Macmillan.

Dunleavy, P. (1991), *Democracy, Bureaucracy and Public Choice*, London: Harvester Wheatsheaf.

Dunleavy, P. and R. A. W. Rhodes (1990), 'Core Executive Studies in Britain', *Public Administration* 68: 3–28.

Dyson, K. H. F. (1980), *The State Tradition in Western Europe*, New York: Oxford University Press.

Eckstein, H. (1960), *Pressure Group Politics*, London: Allen & Unwin.

Edelman, M. (1977), *Political Language*, New York: Academic Press.

Edelman, M. (1987), *Constructing the Political Spectacle*, Chicago: Chicago University Press.

Elgie, R. (1995), *Political Leadership in Liberal Democracies*, London: Macmillan.

Ellis, D. L. (1989), 'Collective Ministerial Responsibility and Collective Solidarity', in *Ministerial Responsibility*, G. Marshall (ed.), Oxford: Oxford University Press.

Esser, J. (1988), 'Symbolic Privatisation: The Politics of Privatisation in West Germany', *West European Politics* 11.

Etzioni-Halevy, E. (1983), *Bureaucracy and Democracy*, London: Routledge and Kegan Paul.

Foley, M. (1993), *The Rise of the British Presidency*, Manchester: Manchester University Press.

Forster, J. and J. Wanna (eds) (1990), *Budgetary Management and Control*, Melbourne: Macmillan.

Fox, C. J. and H. T. Miller (1995), *Post-modern Public Administration: Towards Discourse,* London: Sage.

Freeman, J. L. (1965), *The Political Process*, 2nd edn, New York: Random House.

Frognier, A.-P. (1993), 'The Single Party/Coalition Distinction and Cabinet Decision-Making', in *Governing Together*, J. Blondel and F. Müller-Rommel (eds), London: Macmillan.

Galligan, B. (1992), 'Australian Federalism: Rethinking and Restructuring', *Australian Journal of Political Science* 27.

Gamble, A. (1990), 'Theories of British Politics', *Political Studies* 38: 404–20.

Gavney, J. (1991), 'The Political Think Tanks in the UK and the Ministerial Cabinets in France', *West European Politics* 14 (January): 1–17.

Gellner, W. (1990), 'Political Think Tanks: Functions and Perspectives of a Strategic Elite', Paper presented to the Annual Meeting of the American Political Science Association, San Francisco.

Gladdish, K. (1983), 'Coalition Government and Policy Outputs in the Netherlands', in *Coalition Government in Western Europe*, V. Bogdanor (ed.), London: Heinemann Educational Books.

Gladdish, K. (1990), 'Parliamentary Activism and Legitimacy in the Netherlands', *West European Politics* 13(3): 102–19.

Gladdish, K. (1991), *Governing from the Centre: Politics and Policy-Making in the Netherlands*, De Kalb: Northern Illinois University Press.

Grabosky, P. N. (1995), 'Using Non-governmental Resources to Foster Regulatory Compliance', *Governance* 8: 527–50.

Gray, A. and B. Jenkins (1992), 'The Civil Service and the Financial Management Initiative', in *Handbook of Public Services Management*, C. Pollitt and S. Harrison (eds), Oxford: Blackwell.

Guttman, J. and J. Willner (1976), *The Shadow Government*, New York: Random House.

Haas, P. M. (1992), 'Epistemic Communities and International Policy Co-ordination', *International Organisation* 46: 1–35.

Habermas, J. (1974), *Legitimation Crisis*, Boston: Beacon Press.

Hague, R. and R. Harrap (1987), *Comparative Politics and Government: An Introduction*, London: Macmillan.

Hailsham, Lord (1987), 'Will Cabinet Government Survive?', Granada Guildhall Lecture.

Hall, P. A. (1986), *Governing the Economy: The Politics of State Intervention in Britain and France*, Cambridge: Polity Press Press.

Halligan, J. (1991), 'Career Public Service and Administrative Reform in Australia', *International Review of Administrative Sciences* 57(3): 345–60.

Halligan, J. (1995), 'Policy Advice and the Public Service', in *Governance in a Changing Environment*, B. G. Peters and D. J. Savoie (eds), Montreal: McGill–Queen's University Press.

Halligan, J. and J. Power (1991), *Political Management in the 1990s*, Melbourne: Oxford University Press.

Handy, C. (1993), *Understanding Organisations*, 4th edn, Harmondsworth: Penguin Books.

Hanf, K. and F. W. Scharpf (1978), *Interorganisational Policy Making*, London: Sage.

Hardman, D. J. (1982), 'Models of Government Accounting', *Accounting and Finance* 50 (May): 23–40.

Headey, B. (1974), *British Cabinet Ministers: The Roles of Politicians in Executive Office*, London: Allen & Unwin.

Headey, B. (1985), 'The Role Skills of Cabinet Ministers: A Crossnational View', *Political Studies* 22.

Heclo, H. (1978), 'Issue Networks and the Executive Establishment', in *The New American Political System*, A. King (ed.), Washington: American Enterprise Institute.

Heclo, H. and A. Wildavsky (1974), *The Private Government of Public Money*, London: Macmillan.

Heinz, J. P., E. O. Laumann, R. H. Salisbury and R. L. Nelson (1990), 'Inner Circles or Hollow Cores? Elite Networks in National Policy Systems', *Journal of Politics* 52(2): 356–90.

Held, D. (1987), *Models of Democracy*, Cambridge: Polity Press.

Held, D. (1991), 'Democracy, the Nation State and the Global System', *Economy and Society* 20: 138–72.

Held, D. and C. Pollitt (eds) (1986), *New Forms of Democracy*, London: Sage.

Hennessy, P. (1986), *Cabinet*, Oxford: Blackwell.

Hennessy, P. (1992), *Never Again*, London: Jonathan Cape.

Hennessy, P. (1996), '"Shadow and Substance": Premiership for the Twenty-First Century', Gresham College, Rhetoric Lectures, 1995–96. Lecture 6, 5 March.

Hirst, P. (1990), *Representative Democracy and Its Limits*, Cambridge: Polity Press.

Hirst, P. (1994), *Associative Democracy*, Cambridge: Polity Press.

Hirst, P. and G. Thompson (1995), 'Globalisation and the Future of the Nation State', *Economy and Society* 24: 408–42.

HMSO (1994), *The Government's Use of External Consultants*, London: Efficiency Unit, Cabinet Office.

Hockin, T. (1991), 'A View from the Cabinet in Canada', in *Executive Leadership in Anglo-American Systems,* C. Campbell and M. J. Wyszomirski (eds), Pittsburgh: University of Pittsburgh Press.

Hodgetts, J. E. (1973), *The Canadian Public Service*, Toronto: University of Toronto Press.

Hofferbert, R. and H.-D. Klingemann (1990), 'The Policy Impact of Party Programmes and Government Declarations in the Federal Republic of Germany', *European Journal of Political Research* 18(3): 277–304.

Hogwood, B. W. (1995), 'Whitehall Families: Core Departments and Agency Forms in Britain', *International Review of Administrative Sciences* 61(4): 511–30.

Hood, C. (1995), 'Contemporary Public Management: A New Global Paradigm?', *Public Policy and Administration* 10(2), Summer: 104–17.

Hood, C. and A. Dunsire (1981), *Bureaumetrics*, Farnborough, Hants: Gower.

Huntington, S. P. (1994), 'Transnational Organizations in World Politics', in *Perspectives on World Politic,* 2nd edn, R. Little and M. Smith (eds), London: Routledge.

Hupe, P. L. (1990), 'Implementing a Meta-policy: The Case of Decentralisation in the Netherlands', *Policy and Politics* 18 (July): 181–91.

Inglehart, R. and R. B. Andeweg (1993), 'Change in Dutch Political Culture: A Silent or a Silenced Revolution?', *West European Politics* 16(3): 345–61.

Jackson, R. J. and D. Jackson (1990), *Politics in Canada: Culture, Institutions, Behaviour and Public Policy*, 2nd edn, Scarborough: Prentice Hall.

Jackson, R. J. and D. Jackson (1994), *Politics in Canada: Culture, Institutions, Behaviour and Public Policy*, 3rd edn, Scarborough: Prentice Hall.

Jackson, R., D. Jackson and N. Baxter-Moore (eds) (1987), *Contemporary Canadian Politics*, Scarborough: Prentice Hall.

Jaensch, D. (1992), *The Politics of Australia*, Melbourne: Macmillan.

James, S. (1992), *British Cabinet Government*, London: Routledge.

James, S. (1993), 'The Idea Brokers: The Impact of Think Tanks on British Government', *Public Administration* 71 (Winter): 491–506.

James, S. (1995), 'Relations between Prime Minister and Cabinet: From Wilson to Thatcher', in *Prime Minister, Cabinet and Core Government*, R. A. W. Rhodes and P. D. Dunleavy (eds), London: Macmillan.

Jarman, A. and A. Kouzmin (1993), 'Public Sector Think Tanks in Interagency Policy-Making', *Canadian Public Administration* 36 (Winter): 499–529.

Jenkins, B. and A. Gray (1993), 'Reshaping the Management of Government: The Next Steps Initiative in the United Kingdom', in *Rethinking Government: Reform or Reinvention?*, F. Leslie Seidle (ed.), Montreal: Institute for Research on Public Policy.

Jennings, W. I. (1969), *Cabinet Government*, 3rd edn, Cambridge: Cambridge University Press.

Jessop, B. (1982), *The Capitalist State*, Oxford: Martin Robertson.

Jessop, B. (1992), *From the Keynesian Welfare to the Schumpeterian Welfare State*, Lancaster: University of Lancaster. (Lancaster Regionalism Group, Working Paper 45, September.)

Jessop, B. (1994), 'The Transition to Post-Fordism and the Schumpeterian Welfare State', in *Towards a Post-Fordist Welfare State?*, R. Burrows and B. Loader (eds), London: Routledge.

Johnson, A. F. (1981), 'A Minister as an Agent of Policy Change: The Case of Unemployment Insurance in the Seventies', *Canadian Public Administration* 24 (Winter): 612–33.

Johnson, N. (1983), *State and Government in the Federal Republic of Germany: The Executive at Work*, 2nd edn, Oxford: Pergamon Press.

Jones, G. (1975), 'The Development of the Cabinet', in *The Modernization of British Government*, W. Thornhill (ed.), London: Pitman.

Jordan, G. (1990), 'Sub-governments, Policy Communities and Networks', *Journal of Theoretical Politics* 2(3): 319–38.

Judge, D. (1993), *The Parliamentary State*, London: Sage.

Katz, R. S. (1986), 'Party Government: A Rationalistic Conception', in *The Future of Party Government*, R. Wildermann (ed.), Berlin: de Gruyter.

Katzenstein, P. J. (1987), *Policy and Politics in West Germany*, Philadelphia: Temple University Press.

Kaufman, F.-X., G. Majone and V. Ostrom (eds) (1986), *Guidance, Control and Evaluation in the Public Sector: The Bielfield Interdisciplinary Project*, Berlin: de Gruyter.

Keating, M. (1993), 'Mega-departments: The Theory, Objectives and Outcomes of the 1987 Reforms', in *Reforming the Public Service: Lessons from Recent Experience*, P. Weller, J. Forster and G. Davis (eds), Melbourne: Macmillan.

Keating, M. and M. Holmes (1990), 'Australia's Budgetary and Financial Management Reforms', *Governance* 3(2): 168–85.

Kelly, P. (1994), *The End of Certainty*, Sydney: Allen & Unwin

Kemp, P. (1990), 'Next Steps for the British Civil Service', *Governance* 3(2): 186–96.

Keohane, R. O. and J. S. Nye (1991), 'Transgovernmental Relations and International Organizations', in *Perspectives on World Politics*, 2nd edn, R. Little and M. Smith (eds), London: Routledge.

Kernaghan, K. and D. Siegel (1991), *Public Administration in Canada*, 2nd edn, Toronto: Nelson Canada.

Kettl, D. F. (1993), *Sharing Power: Public Governance and Private Markets*, Washington DC: The Brookings Institution.

Kickert, W. J. M. (1994), 'Administrative Reform in the British, Dutch and Danish Civil Service', Paper presented to the ECPR Joint Sessions, Madrid.

Kickert, W., E. H. Klijn and J. F. N. Koppenjan (1996), *Network Management in the Public Sector*, London: Sage.

Kickert, W. J. M. and F. O. M. Verhaat (1995), 'Autonomizing Executive Tasks in Dutch Central Government', *International Review of Administrative Sciences* 61(4): 531–48.

King, A. (1975), 'Executives', in *Handbook of Political Science*, Vol. 5, F. I. Greenstein and N. W. Polsby (eds), Reading, Mass.: Addison Wesley.

King, A. (1994), 'Ministerial Autonomy in Britain', in *Cabinet Ministers and Parliamentary Government*, M. Laver and K. A. Shepsle (eds), Cambridge: Cambridge University Press.

King, D. (1993), 'Government Beyond Whitehall', in *Developments in British Politics 4*, P. Dunleavy *et al.* (eds), London: Macmillan.

Klatt, H. (1989), 'Forty Years of German Federalism: Past Trends and New Developments', *Publius* 19 (Fall): 185–202.

Klijn, E. H., J. Koopenjan and K. Termeer (1995), 'Managing Networks in the Public Sector', *Public Administration* 73: 437–54.

Kok, W. (1994), *Kabinet-Kok: Keuzen voor de Toekomst*, Den Haag: SDU.

Kooiman, J. (1993), 'Social–Political Governance: Introduction', in *Modern Governance*, J. Kooiman (ed.), London: Sage.

Kooiman, J. and K. A. Eliassen (eds) (1987), *Managing Public Organizations*, London: Sage.

Krasner, S. D. (1984), 'Approaches to the State: Alternative Conceptions and Historical Dynamics', *Comparative Politics* (January).

Krasner, S. D. (1994), 'State Power and the Structure of International Trade', in *Perspectives on World Politics*, 2nd edn, R. Little and M. Smith (eds), London: Routledge.

Kvistad, G. O. (1988), 'Radicals and the State: The Political Demands on West German Civil Servants', *Comparative Political Studies* 21(1): 95–125.

Laver, M. and K. A. Shepsle (1990a), 'Coalitions and Cabinet Government', *American Political Science Review* 84: 873–90.

Laver, M. and K. A. Shepsle (1990b), 'Government Coalitions and Intraparty Politics', *British Journal of Political Science* 20: 489–506.

Laver, M. and K. A. Shepsle (eds) (1994a), *Cabinet Ministers and Parliamentary Government*, Cambridge: Cambridge University Press.

Laver, M. and K. A. Shepsle (1994b), 'Cabinet Government in Theoretical Perspective', in *Cabinet Ministers and Parliamentary Government*, M. Laver and K. A. Shepsle (eds), Cambridge: Cambridge University Press.

Lawson, N. (1993), *The View From No. 11: Memoirs of a Tory Radical*, London: Corgi.

Lehmbruch, G. (1989), 'Institutional Linkages and Policy Networks in the Federal System of West Germany', *Publius* 9 (Fall): 221–35.

Leonardy, U. (1994), 'The German Model', Paper prepared for the Australian Federalism: Future Directions Conference, Melbourne, July.

Lessmann, S. (1987), *Budgetary Politics and Elections: An Investigation of Public Expenditures in West Germany*, New York: de Gruyter.

Levi, M. (1981), 'The Predatory Theory of Rule', *Politics and Society* 10.

Lijphart, A. (1971), 'Verzuiling', in *Verkenningen in de Politiek*, A. Hoogerwerf (ed.), Alphen: Samsom.

Lijphart, A. (1984a), 'Measures of Cabinet Durability', *Comparative Political Studies* 17(2).

Lijphart, A. (1984b), *Democracies*, New Haven: Yale University Press.

Lindblom, C. E. (1977), *Politics and Markets*, New York: Basic Books.

Lindblom, C. E. (1990), *Inquiry and Change: The Troubled Attempt to Understand and Shape Society*, New Haven: Yale University Press.

Lindquist, E. (1989), Behind the Myth of Think Tanks: The Organization and Relevance of Canadian Policy Institutes, PhD thesis, University of California at Berkeley.

Lindquist, E. (1990), 'The Third Community, Policy Inquiry, and Social Scientists', in *Social Scientists and the State*, S. Brooks and A. Gagnon (eds), New York: Praeger.

Lindquist, E. (1993), 'Think Tanks or Clubs? Assessing the Influence and Roles of Canadian Policy Institutes', *Canadian Public Administration* 36 (Winter): 547–79.

Lindquist, E. and T. Sica (1995), *Canadian Governments and the Search for Alternative Program Delivery and Financing*, Toronto: KPMG Centre for Government Foundation and the Institute of Public Administration of Canada.

Lucy, R. (1993), *The Australian Form of Government*, 2nd edn, Melbourne: Macmillan.

Luhmann, N. (1982), *The Differentiation of Society*, New York: Columbia University Press.

McGrew, A. G. (1992), 'Conceptualizing Global Politics', in *Global Politics: Globalization and the Nation-State*, A. G. McGrew *et al.* (eds), Cambridge: Polity Press Press.

Mackie, T. and B. Hogwood (eds) (1985), *Unlocking the Cabinet: Cabinet Structures in Comparative Perspective*, London: Sage.

Mackintosh, J. P. (1977), *The British Cabinet*, 3rd edn, London: Stevens.

Madgwick, P. (1991), *British Government: The Central Executive Territory*, London: Philip Allan.

Majone, G. (1994), 'The Rise of the Regulatory State in Europe', *West European Politics* 17.

Mallory, J. R. (1967), 'The Minister's Office Staff: An Unreformed Part of the Public Service', *Canadian Public Administration* 10 (Spring): 27–41.

March, J. G. and J. P. Olsen (1983), 'Organizing Political Life: What Administrative Reorganization Tells Us About Government', *American Political Science Review* 77: 281–97.

March, J. G. and J. P. Olsen (1989), *Rediscovering Institutions*, New York: The Free Press.

Marin, B. and R. Mayntz (eds) (1991), *Policy Networks: Empirical Evidence and Theoretical Considerations*, Frankfurt am Main: Campus Verlag.

Marsh, D. and R. A. W. Rhodes (eds) (1992a), *Policy Networks in British Government*, Oxford: Clarendon Press.

Marsh. D. and R. A. W. Rhodes (1992b), *Implementing Thatcherite Policies*, Buckingham: Open University Press.

Marsh, I. (1992), 'Globalisation and Australian "Think Tanks"', *Canberra Bulletin of Public Administration* 68 (March): 28–50.

Mayntz, R. (1980), 'Executive Leadership in Germany: Dispersion of Power or "Kanzlerdemokratie?"', in *Presidents and Prime Ministers*, R. Rose and E. N Suleiman (eds), Washington DC: American Enterprise Institute for Public Policy Research.

Mayntz, R. (1984), 'German Federal Bureaucrats: A Functional Elite Between Politics and Administration', in *Bureaucrats and Policy-Making: A Comparative Overview*, E. N. Suleiman (ed.), New York: Holmes and Meier.

Mayntz, R. (1987), 'West Germany', in *Advising the Rulers*, W. Plowden (ed.), Oxford: Blackwell.

Mayntz, R. and F. W. Scharpf (eds) (1975), *Policy-Making in the German Federal Bureaucracy*, Amsterdam: Elsevier Scientific Publishing Co.

Mény, Y. (1993), *Government and Politics in Western Europe — Britain, France, Italy and Germany,* 2nd edn, Oxford: Oxford University Press.

Mény, Y. and A. Knapp (eds) (1993), *Government and Politics in Western Europe*, New York: Oxford University Press.

Metcalfe, L. and S. Richards (1987), *Improving Public Management*, London: Sage.

Miljoennota (1995), *Samenvatting*, Den Haag: Ministerie van Financien.

Milne, K. (1994), 'Shedding New Light on Labour', *New Statesman and Society* 7, No. 313 (29 July): 23, 25.

Mintzberg, H. (1979), *The Structuring of Organizations*, Englewood Cliffs, N J: Prentice Hall.

Mintzberg, H. (1988), 'Opening up the Definition of Strategy', in *The Strategy Process: Concepts, Contexts and Cases,* J. B. Quinn, H. Mintzberg and R. James (eds), Englewood Cliffs, N J: Prentice Hall.

Modeen, T. and A. Rosas (eds) (1988), *Indirect Public Administration in Fourteen Countries*, Abo: Abo Academy Press.

Morley, J. (1889), 'The Principles of Cabinet Government, Fragment from The Life of Walpole', reprinted in *Ministerial Responsibility*, G. Marshall (ed.), Oxford: Oxford University Press.

Müller, W. C and V. Wright (1994), 'Reshaping the State in Western Europe: The Limits to Retreat', *West European Politics* 17.

Müller-Rommel, F. (1988), 'Federal Republic of Germany: A System of Party Government', in *Cabinets in Western Europe*, J. Blondel and F. Muller-Rommel (eds), London: Macmillan.

Müller-Rommel, F. (1994), 'The Role of German Ministers in Cabinet Decision Making', in *Cabinet Ministers and Parliamentary Government*, M. Laver and K. A. Shepsle (eds), Cambridge: Cambridge University Press.

Murswieck, A. (1993), 'Policy Advice and Decision-making in the German Federal System', in *Advising West European Governments*, B. G. Peters and A. Barker (eds), Pittsburgh: University of Pittsburgh Press.

Neustadt, R.E. (1969), 'White House and Whitehall', in *The British Prime Minister*, A. King (ed.), London: Macmillan.

Neustadt, R. E. (1976), *Presidential Power*, 2nd edn, New York: Wiley.

Nordlinger, E. (1981), *On the Autonomy of the Democratic State*, Cambridge, Mass.: Harvard University Press.

North, D. (1986), A Neoclassical Theory of the State', in *Rational Choice*, J. Elster (ed.), Oxford: Blackwell.

Nousiainen, J. and J. Blondel (1993), 'Conclusion', in *Governing Together*, J. Blondel and F. Müller-Rommel (eds), London: Macmillan.

Nugent, N. (1992), *The Government and Politics of the European Community*, 2nd edn, London: Macmillan.

OECD (1987), *The Control and Management of Government Expenditure*, Paris: OECD.

OECD (1990), *Public Management Developments: Survey 1990*, Paris: OECD (Overview 9–17, Australia 19–25, Canada 31–36, Germany 55–58, Netherlands 74–77, United Kingdom 112–119).

OECD (1992), *Public Management: Country Profiles*, Paris: OECD.

OECD (1993), *Public Management Developments: Survey 1993*, Paris: OECD (Overview 9–19, Australia 20–29, Canada 44–50, Germany 76–82, Netherlands 119–126, United Kingdom 179–187).

OECD (1995), *Budgeting for Results: Perspectives on Public Expenditure Management*, Paris: OECD.

OECD/G (1993), *Economic Surveys: Germany*, Paris: OECD.

OECD/UK (1993), *Economic Surveys: UK*, Paris: OECD.

Oliver, S. (1993), 'Lobby Groups, Think Tanks, the Universities and Media', *Canberra Bulletin of Public Administration* 75 (December): 134–7.

Olson, M. (1982), *The Rise and Decline of Nations: Economic Growth, Stagflation and Social Rigidities*, New Haven: Yale University Press.

Padgett, S. (ed.) (1994), *Adenauer to Kohl: The Development of the German Chancellorship*, London: Hurst.

Page, E. (1990), 'British Political Science and Comparative Politics', *Political Studies* 38(3).

Page, E. (1995), 'Comparative Public Administration in Britain', *Public Administration* 73(1).

Painter, M. (1981), 'Central Agencies and the Coordination Principle', *Australian Journal of Public Administration* 40(4): 265–80.

Painter, M. (1987), *Steering the Modern State: Changes in Central Coordination in Three Australian State Governments*, Sydney: University of Sydney Press.

Parekh, B. (1994), 'Cultural Diversity and Liberal Democracy', in *Defining and Measuring Democracy*, D. Beetham (ed.), London: Sage.

Parkinson, C. N. (1957), *Parkinson's Law*, London: John Murray.

Parry, G. (1993), 'The Interweaving of Foreign and Domestic Policy-Making', *Government and Opposition* 28.

Peters, B. G. (1986), *American Public Policy*, 2nd edn, Basingstoke: Macmillan.

Peters, B. G. (1991), *European Politics Reconsidered*, New York: Holmes and Meier.

Peters, B. G. (1994), 'If Administrative Reform is the Answer, What is the Question?', Paper presented at 'Frontiers of Reform' Conference, Canberra, May.

Peters, B. G. and A. Barker (eds) (1993), *Advising West European Governments*, Pittsburgh: University of Pittsburgh Press.

Pfiffner, J. P. (1994), *The Modern Presidency*, New York: St Martin's.

Pierre, J. (1995), 'The Marketization of the State: Citizens, Consumers, and the Emergence of the Public Market', in *Governance in a Changing Environment*, B. G. Peters and D. J. Savoie (eds), Montreal and Kingston: Canadian Centre for Management Development and McGill-Queen's University Press.

Pierson, P. (1995), *Dismantling the Welfare State?*, Cambridge: Cambridge University Press.

Pimlott, B. (1993), *Harold Wilson*, London: Harper-Collins.

Pinder, J. (1992), 'The Future of the European Community', *Government and Opposition*, 27: 414–32.

Pinto-Duschinsky, M. (1991), 'The Party Foundations and Political Finance in Germany', in *Comparative Issues in Party and Election Finance*, F. L. Seidle (ed.), Toronto: Dundurn. (Vol. 4 of the Research Studies of the Royal Commission on Electoral Reform and Party Financing).

Plasse, M. (1994), *Ministerial Chiefs of Staff in the Federal Government in 1990*, Ottawa: Canadian Centre for Management Development.

Plowden, W. (ed.) (1987), *Advising the Rulers*, Oxford: Blackwell.

Plowden, W. (1991), 'Providing Countervailing Analysis and Advice in a Career-Dominated Bureaucratic System: The British Experience, 1916-1988', in *Executive Leadership in Anglo-American Systems*, C. Campbell and M. J. Wyszomirski (eds), Pittsburgh: University of Pittsburgh Press.

Pollitt, C. (1990), *Managerialism and the Public Services*, Oxford: Blackwell.

Poulantzas, N. (1980), *State, Power, Socialism*, London: Verso.

Pusey, M. (1991), *Economic Rationalism in Canberra: A Nation Building State Changes its Mind*, Melbourne: Cambridge University Press.

Redner, H. (1990), 'Beyond Marx–Weber: A Diversified and International Approach to the State', *Political Studies* 38.

Rhodes, R. A. W. (1981), *Control and Power in Central–Local Government Relationships,* Aldershot: Gower.

Rhodes, R. A. W. (1986), *The National World of Local Government,* London: Allen & Unwin.

Rhodes, R. A. W. (1988a), *Beyond Westminster and Whitehall,* London: Unwin Hyman.

Rhodes, R. A. W. (1988b), 'Interorganisational Networks and the "Problem" of Control in the Policy Process: A Critique of the "New Institutionalism"', *West European Politics* 11(2): 119–30.

Rhodes, R. A. W. (1991), 'Theory and Methods in British Public Administration', *Political Studies* 39(3).

Rhodes, R. A. W. (1994), 'The Hollowing Out of the State: The Changing Nature of the Public Service in Britain', *Political Quarterly* 65(2): 138–51.

Rhodes, R. A. W. (1995), 'From Prime Ministerial Power to Core Executive', in *Prime Minister, Cabinet and Core Executive,* R. A. W. Rhodes and P. Dunleavy (eds), London: Macmillan.

Rhodes, R. A. W. (1996), *Understanding Governance,* Buckingham: Open University Press.

Rhodes, R. A. W. and P. Dunleavy (eds) (1995), Prime Minister, Cabinet and Core Executive, London: Macmillan.

Rhodes, R. A. W. and D. Marsh (1992), 'New Directions in the Study of Policy Networks', *European Journal of Political Research* 21: 181–205

Ricci, D. M. (1993), *The Transformation of American Politics,* New Haven: Yale University Press.

Richardson, J. (1994), 'Doing Less By Doing More: British Government 1979–1993', *West European Politics* 17.

Rockman, B. A. (1989), 'Minding the State — Or a State of Mind?', in *The Elusive State,* J. A. Caporaso (ed.), London: Sage.

Rose, R. (1969), 'The Variability of Party Government', *Political Studies* 17(4).

Rose, R. (1974), *The Problem of Party Government,* London: Macmillan.

Rose, R. (1980a), 'British Government: The Job at the Top', in *Presidents and Prime Ministers,* R. Rose and E. N. Suleiman (eds), Washington DC: American Enterprise Institute.

Rose, R. (1980b), 'Government Against Sub-Governments: A European Perspective on Washington', in *Presidents and Prime Ministers,* R. Rose and E. N. Suleiman (eds), Washington DC: American Enterprise Institute.

Rose, R. (1984), *Understanding Big Government,* London: Sage.

Rose, R. (1987), 'Steering the Ship of State', *British Journal of Political Science* 17 (October): 409–53.

Rose, R. (1991a), 'Prime Ministers in Parliamentary Democracies', *West European Politics* 14: 9–24.

Rose, R. (1991b), 'Comparing Forms of Comparative Analysis', *Political Studies* 39(3).

Rose, R. and E. N. Suleiman (eds) (1980), *Presidents and Prime Ministers*, Washington DC: American Enterprise Institute.

Rosenau, J. N. (1989), 'The State in an Era of Cascading Politics: Wavering Concept, Widening Competence, Withering Colossus, or Weathering Change?', in *The Elusive State*, I. A. Caporaso (ed.), London: Sage.

Rosenau, J. N. (1992), 'Governance, Order and Change in World Politics', in *Governance without Government: Order and Change in World Politics*, J. N. Rosenau and E.-O. Czempiel (eds), Cambridge, Cambridge University Press.

Rueschemeyer, D., E. H. Stephens and J. D. Stephens (1992), *Capitalist Development and Democracy*, Cambridge: Polity Press.

Saalfeld, T. (1990), 'The West German Bundestag after 40 Years: The Role of Parliament in a "Party Democracy"', *West European Politics* 13(3): 68–89.

Sabatier, P. (1988), 'An Advocacy Coalition Framework of Policy Change and the Role of Policy-Orientated Learning Therein', *Policy Sciences* 21: 129–68.

Saint-Martin, D. (1996), 'Reforming State Bureaucracies: Accountants and the Politics of Managerialism', PhD dissertation, Carleton University, Ottawa.

Sartori, G. (1991), 'Rethinking Democracy: Bad Polity Press and Bad Politics', *International Social Science Journal* 129.

Savoie, D. J. (1990), *The Politics of Public Spending in Canada*, Toronto: University of Toronto Press.

Savoie, D. J. (ed.) (1993), *Taking Power: Managing Government Transitions*, Toronto: Institute of Public Administration/Canadian Centre for Management Development.

Savoie, D. J. (1994), *Thatcher Reagan Mulroney: In Search of a New Bureaucracy*, Toronto: University of Toronto Press.

Schick, A. (1986), 'Macro-budgetary Adaptations to Fiscal Stress in Industrialized Democracies', *Public Administration Review* 46.

Schick, A. (1988). 'Micro-budgetary Adaptations to Fiscal Stress in Industrialized Democracies', *Public Administration Review* 48(1): 523–33.

Schick, A. (1990), 'Budgeting for Results: Recent Developments in Five Industrialized Countries', *Public Administration Review* 50(1): 26–34.

Schmidt, M. (1983), 'Two Logics of Coalition Policy: The West German Case', in *Coalition Government in Western Europe,* V. Bogdanor (ed.), London: Heinemann.

Schmidt, M. (1985), 'Budgetary Policy: A Comparative Perspective on Policy Outputs and Outcomes', in *Policy and Politics in the Federal Republic of Germany,* K. von Beyme and M. Schmidt (eds), Aldershot: Gower.

Schmidt, M. G. (1992), 'Political Consequences of German Unification', *West European Politics* 15: 1-15.

Schumpeter, I. A. (1976), *Capitalism, Socialism and Democracy,* 5th edn, London: Allen & Unwin.

Seidle, L. (1995), *Rethinking the Delivery of Public Services to Citizens,* Montreal: Institute for Research on Public Policy.

Seymour-Ure, C. (1971), 'The "Disintegration" of the Cabinet and the Neglected Question of Cabinet Reform', *Parliamentary Affairs* 24(3): 196–207.

Shand, D. (1996), 'Are We Reinventing Government?', in *New Ideas, Better Government,* P. Weller and G. Davis (eds), Sydney: Allen & Unwin.

Sharkansky, I. (1970), *The Routines of Politics,* New York: Van Nostrand Reinhold.

Singer, O. (1993), 'Knowledge and Politics in Economic Policy-Making', in *Advising West European Governments,* B. G. Peters and A. Barker (eds), Pittsburgh: University of Pittsburgh Press.

Skocpol, T. (1985), 'Bringing the State Back In: Current Research', in *Bringing the State Back In,* P. B. Evans, D. Rueschemeyer and T. Skocpol (eds), Cambridge: Cambridge University Press.

Smith, G. (1991), 'The Resources of a German Chancellor', *West European Politics* 14(2): 48–61.

Smith, J. A. (1991), *The Idea Brokers: Think Tanks and the Rise of the New Policy Elite,* New York: The Free Press.

Smith, M. J. (1995), 'Interpreting the Rise and Fall of Margaret Thatcher: Power Dependence and the Core Executive', in *Prime Minister, Cabinet and Core Executive,* R. A. W. Rhodes and P. Dunleavy (eds), London, Macmillan.

Snellen, I. T. M. (ed.) (1985), *Limits of Government: Dutch Experiences,* Amsterdam: Uitgeverij.

Steiner, J. and R. H. Dorff (1980), *A Theory of Political Decision Modes,* Chapel Hill: University of North Carolina Press.

Stevens, M. (1991), *The Big Six: The Selling Out of America's Top Accounting Firms,* New York: Simon and Schuster.

Stewart, R. G. and I. Ward (1992), *Politics One,* Melbourne: Macmillan.

Stone, D. (1992), 'Old Guard Versus New Partisans: Think Tanks in Transition', *Canberra Bulletin of Public Administration* 68 (March): 51–61.

Strom, K. (1988), 'Contending Models of Cabinet Stability', *American Political Science Review* 82(3).

Sturm, R. (1985), 'Budgetary Politics in the Federal Republic of Germany', *West European Politics* 8(3): 56–63.

Sturm, R. (1994), 'The Chancellor and the Executive', in *Adenauer to Kohl: The Development of the German Chancellorship*, S. Padgett (ed.), London: Hurst.

Sutherland, S. (1991), 'The Consequences of Electoral Volatility: Inexperienced Ministers 1949–90', in *Representation, Integration and Political Parties in Canada*, H. Bakvis (ed.), Toronto: Dundurn.

Sutherland, S. L. (1993), 'The Public Service and Policy Development', in *Governing Canada: Institutions and Public Policy*, M. M. Atkinson (ed.), Toronto: Harcourt Brace Jovanovich Canada.

Swimmer, G. *et al.* (1994), 'Public Service 2000: Dead or Alive?', in *How Ottawa Spends 1994–95: Making Change*, S. D. Phillips (ed.), Ottawa: Carleton University Press.

Thain, C. and M. Wright (1992a), 'Planning and Controlling Public Expenditure in the UK, Part 1: The Treasury's Public Expenditure Survey', *Public Administration* 70 (Spring): 3–24.

Thain, C. and M. Wright (1992b), 'Planning and Controlling Public Expenditure in the UK, Part 2: The Effects and Effectiveness of the Survey', *Public Administration* 70 (Summer): 193–224.

Thain, C. and M. Wright (1995), *The Treasury and Whitehall: The Planning and Control of Public Expenditure, 1976–1993*, Oxford: Clarendon Press.

Theakston, K. (1987), *Junior Ministers in British Government*, Oxford: Blackwell.

Thomassen, J. and J. van Deth (1989), 'How New is Dutch Politics?', *West European Politics* 12(1): 61–77.

Timmermans, A. and W. E. Bakema (1990), 'Conflicten in Nederlandse Kabinetten', in *Ministers en Ministerraad*, R. B. Andeweg (ed.), The Hague: SDU.

Toonen, T. A. J. (1987), 'The Netherlands: A Decentralized Unitary State in a Welfare Society', *West European Politics* 10: 108–29.

Tupper, A. (1993), 'Think Tanks, Public Debt, and the Politics of Expertise in Canada', *Canadian Public Administration* 36 (Winter): 530–46.

Van Delden, A. Th. (1993), 'Externe adviesorganen van de centrale overheid', in *Politiek in Nederland*, 4th edn, R. B. Andeweg *et al.* (eds), Alphen aan den Rijn: Samsom.

Van Loon, R. and M. Whittington (1981), *The Canadian Political System: Environment, Structure and Process*, Toronto: McGraw-Hill Ryerson.

Vermeulen, A. (1988), 'Contract Management in the Netherlands', *International Review of Information Sciences* 52 (June): 201–17.

Vickers, J. and V. Wright (1988), 'The Politics of Industrial Privatisation in Western Europe: An Overview', in *West European Politics* 11.

Vis, J. (1983), 'Coalition Government in a Constitutional Monarchy: The Dutch Experience', in *Coalition Government in Western Europe*, V. Bogdanor (ed.), London: Heinemann.

Vogelsang, I. (1988), 'Deregulation and Privatization in Germany', *Journal of Public Policy* 8: 195–212.

Von Beyme, K. (1983), 'Coalition Government in Western Germany', in *Coalition Government in Western Europe*, V. Bogdanor (ed.), London: Heinemann.

Walker, P. G. (1970), *The Cabinet: Political Authority in Britain*, New York: Basic Books.

Walsh, C. (1992), 'Federal Reform and the Politics of Vertical Fiscal Imbalance', *Australian Journal of Political Science* 27, Special Issue: 19–38.

Walsh, P. (1995), *Confessions of a Finance Minister*, Sydney: Random House.

Walter, J. (1986), *The Ministers' Minders: Personal Advisers in National Government*, Melbourne: Oxford University Press.

Wamsley, G. *et al.* (1987), 'The Public Administration and the Governance Process: Refocusing the American Dialogue', in *A Centennial History of the Amercian Administrative State*, R. C. Chandler (ed.), London: Collier Macmillan.

Wanna, J., C. O'Faircheallaigh and P. Weller (1992) *Public Sector Management in Australia*, Melbourne: Macmillan.

Weaver, K. and B. Rockman (eds) (1993), *Do Institutions Matter?*, Washington DC: The Brookings Institution.

Weaver, R. K. (1989), 'The Changing World of Think Tanks', *PS: Political Science and Politics* 22 (September): 563–78.

Webb, A. (1991), 'Coordination: A Problem in Public Sector Management', *Policy and Politics* 19(4): 229–41.

Weber, M. (1978), *Economy and Society*, Berkeley: University of California Press. (Reprint of 1921 edition.)

Weir, S. and W. Hall (eds) (1994), *Ego-trip: Extra Governmental Organisations in the UK and their Accountability*, London: Democratic Audit and Charter 88.

Weller, P. (1983), 'The Vulnerability of Prime Ministers: A Comparative Analysis', *Parliamentary Affairs* 36 (1): 96–117.

Weller, P. (1985a), *First Among Equals: Prime Ministers in Westminster Systems*, Sydney: Allen & Unwin.

Weller, P. (1985b), 'Cabinet Committees in Australia and New Zealand', in *Unlocking the Cabinet: Cabinet Structures in Comparative Perspectiv*, T. Mackie and B. W. Hogwood (eds), London: Sage.

Weller, P. (1987), 'Australia', in *Advising the Rulers*, W. Plowden (ed.), Oxford: Blackwell.

Weller, P. (1989a) 'Politicisation and the Australian Public Service', *Australian Journal of Public Administration* 48 (December): 369–81.

Weller, P. (1989b), *Malcolm Fraser PM: A Study of Prime-Ministerial Power in Australia*, Melbourne: Penguin.

Weller, P. (1990), 'The Cabinet', in *Hawke and Australian Public Policy: Consensus and Restructuring*, C. Jennett and R. G. Stewart (eds), Melbourne: Macmillan.

Weller, P. (1991a) 'Support for Prime Ministers', in *Executive Leadership in Anglo-American Systems*, C. Campbell and M. Wyszomirski (eds) Pittsburgh: University of Pittsburgh Press.

Weller, P. (1991b), 'Prime Ministers, Political Leadership and Cabinet Government', *Australian Journal of Public Administration* 50: 131–44.

Weller, P. (1994), 'Party Rules and the Dismissal of Prime Ministers: Comparative Perspectives from Britain, Canada and Australia', *Parliamentary Affairs* 47(1): 133–43.

Weller, P., J. Forster and G. Davis (eds) (1993), *Reforming the Public Service: Lessons from Recent Experience*, Melbourne: Macmillan.

Wewer, G. (1990), 'Richtlinienkompetenz und Koalitionsregierung: wo wird die Politik definiert?', in *Regieren in der Bundesrepublik 1*, H. H. Hartwich and G. Wewer (eds), Opladen: Leske & Budrich.

Wijngaarden, L. J. (1990), 'Management Development in the Dutch Public Administration: A Review and New Trends', in *Flexible Personnel Management in the Public Service*, Paris: OECD.

Wildavsky, A. (1973), 'If Planning is Everything, Maybe it's Nothing', *Policy Sciences* 4: 127–53.

Wildavsky, A. (1975), *Budgeting: A Comparative Theory of Budgetary Processes*, Boston: Little, Brown.

Wildavsky, A. (1987), *Speaking Truth to Power: The Art and Craft of Policy Analysis*, revised edn, New Brunswick: Transaction.

Wilks, S. (1993), 'Economic Policy', in *Developments in British Politics 4*, P. Dunleavy *et al.* (eds), London: Macmillan.

Willetts, D. (1987), 'The Role of the Prime Minister's Policy Unit', *Public Administration* 65 (Winter): 443–54.

Williams, W. (1988), *Washington, Westminster and Whitehall*, Cambridge: Cambridge University Press.

Wilson, G. K. (1991), 'Prospects for the Public Service in Britain. Major to the Rescue?', *International Review of Administrative Sciences* 57(3): 327–44.

Wilson, H. (1976), *The Governance of Britain*, London: Weidenfeld and Nicolson.

Wilson, J. Q. (1989), *Bureaucracy: What Government Agencies Do and Why They Do It*, New York: Basic Books.

Wolinetz, S. B. (1989), 'Socio-economic Bargaining in the Netherlands: Redefining the Post-war Policy Coalition', *West European Politics* 12(1): 79–98.

Wolinetz, S. B. (1990a), 'A Quarter Century of Dutch Politics: A Changing Political System or le plus que change . . .?', *Acta Politica* 25(4): 403–31.

Wolinetz, S. B. (1990b), 'The Dutch Election of 1989: Return to the Centre-Left', *West European Politics* 13(2): 280–6.

Wolinetz, S. B. (1991), 'Party Foundations in the Netherlands', Working Paper prepared for the Royal Commission on Electoral Reform and Party Financing, Ottawa: Government of Canada.

Wollmann, H. (1989), 'Policy Analysis in West Germany's Federal Government: A Case of Unfinished Governmental and Administrative Modernization?', *Governance* 2(3): 233–66.

Wright, D. S. (1983), 'Managing the Intergovernmental Scene: The Changing Dramas of Federalism, Intergovernmental Relations and Intergovernmental Management', in *Handbook of Organisation Management* W. B. Eddy (ed.) Berlin: de Gruyter.

Wright, M. (1988), 'Policy Community, Policy Network and Comparative Industrial Policies', *Political Studies* 36: 593–612.

Zifcak, S. (1994), *New Managerialism: Administrative Reform in Whitehall and Canberra*, Buckingham: Open University Press.

Zolo, D. (1992), *Democracy and Complexity*, Cambridge: Polity Press.

Index